The Midland Railway in Nottingham

Volume III 1948 - 1999

From Steam
to Diesel

by C J Perkins & R Padgett

First published in 2002 by C J Perkins, 17 Rufford Road, Ruddington, Notts NG11 6FT and R Padgett, 1 Chapel Mews, Bramcote, Notts NG9 3HB.

Designed by Two Faces Design, 80 Watling Street, Towcester, Northants NN12 6BS.

Printed by Henry Ling Limited, at the Dorset Press, Dorchester, DT1 1HD

ISBN 0-9539878-2-5

Foreword

From: The Rt. Hon. Kenneth Clarke, QC, MP

I have been looking forward to Volume III of Jim Perkins and Roy Padgett's 'History of the Midland Railway', as I have very much enjoyed reading the first two volumes. They have gone to great lengths to ensure the accuracy of what they have written and have obviously done a great deal of research. They mix history with anecdote in a very entertaining way, and this produces an enjoyable read for people who are interested in railways in general, or in the Midland Railway in particular.

This volume brings the story up to the years, which I can remember well, when I was a young schoolboy train spotter in Nottingham, giving an odd feeling of enjoyable nostalgia to my reading. I am sure that many people of my age, and even a little younger, will enjoy having their memories re-aroused of the railways around Nottingham, when there was still a lot of Midland Railway atmosphere about the system. Many of the buildings and much of the equipment dated back to the Midland Railway and Midland Railway locomotives from other parts of the system also began to turn up in the last years of steam.

I commend this book for anybody with a serious or casual interest in the subject.

The Rt Hon Kenneth Clarke, QC, MP

Introduction to the Authors

Both authors served their apprenticeship at Nottingham Loco Shed then coded 16A later 16D.

They both come from railway backgrounds, one generation removed, having had grandfathers who were contemporaries at Nottingham ending their service as Main Line Drivers. These were

> James Marshall   (1873-1944) born in Fairfield, Buxton
> William Padgett (1869-1948) born in Nottingham

Both authors have railway connections going back another generation. In Jim Perkins' case one of his great grandfathers, Henry Bratby, had been a Goods Guard on the Midland Railway at Burton on Trent. His elder brother Donald Perkins (1934 -1982) was also on the footplate staff and was a Driver Instructor at the time of his death in October1982. Roy Padgett also had a great grandfather in railway service, Thomas Scotchbrook, who was a Driver on the Great Northern Railway at Pickworth in Lincolnshire.

The men who worked in the Engine Sheds were often referred to as 'Sheddies'. This was certainly the case for those who were lodging away from home or working in the main works. In the Nottingham area the Sheds varied in size from the single road example at Southwell to the grander Roundhouses that housed a central turntable with the roads radiating around, usually twenty four in number. Although called Roundhouses the majority were actually square although the originals had been round. Fortunately a few examples survive: the old London & Birmingham Railway's at the top of Camden Bank, London; and the North Midland Railway's at Derby. Some other notable Roundhouses were the Midland Counties Railway's at Leicester; the North Staffordshire Railway's at Stoke-on-Trent and the Hull & Barnsley's at Selby. The earliest design of the Midland Railway's square Roundhouses featured three gables to each side resulting in an almost cathedral-like vaulted roof, part glazed, part louvred. Although soot blackened, on a sunny day the sun would stream through the three Sheds at Nottingham, not only through the glass but also through the louvres giving the impression of the clerestory windows of a cathedral. Shafts of light would illuminate engines, the turntable and Shed floor. The 'Sheddies' who worked in these Sheds were of many trades: Boilerwashers; Boilersmiths; Box Men; Bar Setters; Drivers; Engine Cleaners; Fireman; Fitters; Fitters Mates; Joiners; Labourers; Painters; Steam Raisers; Tubers; Tube Sweepers; Stores Staff; Chargehands; Mechanical and Running Foremen; Foreman's Assistants, all going about their daily duties in an environment that could be very hot in the summer, cold in the winter, but always interesting. It is true to say that the Loco Sheds never slept and the work in them was an all year round operation.

Both authors went through the same training regime and working experience right up to and beyond their apprentice days. Both worked on those MR types still surviving in the late 1950s along with LMS/BR and some LNER classes. During the severe early winter of 1963 both were fortunate to be at Derby Works for their works training and did not have to endure those sustained freezing conditions in the running Shed. Almost half way through their apprenticeship, a gradual, but nevertheless total switch, was made to Diesel Locomotive maintenance, the main classes being the 0-6-0 English Electric

Shunters and Sulzer type 4s (class 45) along with the occasional Railcar. The glorious summer of 1964 saw both authors at Crewe taking part in one of the early diesel training courses available to fitting staff. These were held in the Offices on Crewe Station and one interesting diversion was the final workings of the Stanier Pacifics.

After coming out of their time in 1964, Nottingham was due for closure and they transferred to Derby Etches Park. This only lasted for two months, a move to the recently completed Toton Diesel Depot coming later in that year. Late in 1966 Jim Perkins transferred to Colwick, then part of the LMR, as a Rolling Stock Inspector, being responsible for the Diesels working out of that Depot. Whilst at Colwick the last gasps of steam were experienced with a forlorn line of ex-LMS Black 5s and 8Fs standing outside the Shed. At about this time, the now preserved LNER B1 No 61264 was the Shed heating provider and it is nice to see this engine in steam at the GCR.

Jim departed Colwick in 1967 going into the Merchant Navy and eventually, via various jobs, working overseas in both Africa and Arabia. He is now a Civil Servant. Roy stayed with BR and now works for EWS at Toton where he is part of the Maintenance Team. Roy's area of interest is that of maps, tables and photographs. Our early estimate of a possible 100 photos that might turn up has changed and the latest total is more than 650, an amazing number! The need to document and record the history of Nottingham Loco Sheds, especially 16A since 1950, was recognised by both the authors. They eventually got together in 1989 to produce a joint effort. Early on it was realized that to cover only the later days would not do justice to the subject. It was therefore decided to undertake the research required for a comprehensive story covering the years 1839 to 1968 and beyond, and an absorbing task it has proved to be.

It quickly became apparent, that we should have taken more interest whilst we were working in the Sheds when we were living it on daily basis. The first volume was published in 2001 and dealt with the story from 1839, and the formation of the Midland Counties Railway, up to the Midland Railways' re-organisation of 1907. Volume II published in 2002 continued the story from 1908 up to 1947 and Nationalisation. This final volume takes the story from 1948 through to 1999.

Opposite Page
Plan of the Locoshed and Middle Furlong Road area of the Meadows, Nottingham

Jim Perkins

Following Page and below
Class 4F taking water on the 3rd of February 1954. This photograph was taken from halfway up the Coaling Tower of 16A

John Hutchinson

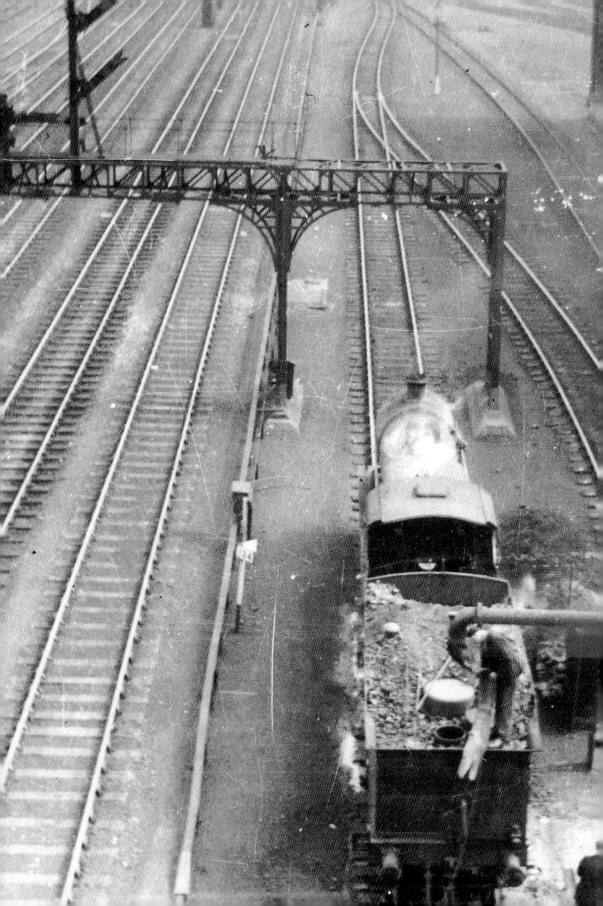

Contents

Page

Contents *continued*

Acknowledgments

The acknowledgments shown are for this Volume which deals with the 'History of the Midland Railway in Nottingham from 1948 to 1999'. A special thanks must be given to Sue Griffiths and Barbara Hornby of the Local History Press and to Drisc Wardle of Two Faces Design for setting out this volume. Also to those individuals and organisations who have contributed and whose photographs, even if not used, have been valuable for research and in creating an archive.

Name	Location	Contribution
Jack Backen	Nottingham	Information
Peter Bakewell	Powys	Photographs and documents
Chris Banks	Hinckley	Photographs
Les Batson	Nottingham	Photographs and Shed lists
Mr Alan Beck	Nottingham	Photographs
A G Bell		Photographs and Shed lists
Andrew Biwandi	West Sussex	Photographs and info on 8Fs
Jack Braithwaite	Cleethorpes	Photographs and information
Denys Brindley	Burton	Paintings
Frank Brunton	Lancs	Photographs and documents
Frank Brunton		Photographs and information
Chris Bush	Nottingham	Photographs
Richard Casserley	Berkhampstead	Photographs
Miss B Croydon	Nottingham	Photographs and literature (From Mr Percy Croydon estate)
Les Dodsley	Nottingham	Recollections
Frank Eite	Nottingham	Photographs and information
Bob Essery	Burton	Information proof reading and advice
Tony Etches	Clipstone, Mansfied	
F Gilford		Photograph
J Goss		Photographs
Martin Gregory	Burton	Information
Alen Grice	Kirkby	Personal memories and Information
Roger Griffiths		Photograph
Les Hanson	Northampton	LNW matters
Eric Hearn	Nottingham	Photographs
Mark Higginson	Ilkeston	Photographs and information
Sid Hill	Nottingham	Recollections
Roland Hoggard	Thurgarton	Recollections
David Hunt	Lincoln	Information
Jim Jackson	Newark	Photographs
Graham Kaye	Widnes	Shed List
John Keeling	Butterley	Photographs (MRC)
Ian Kenny LBIPP		Photographs
Laurence Knighton	Bakewell	Information
Keith Leah	Sheffield	Information on Driver Sam Leah
Jeff Marriott	Sandiacre	Photographs and personal

		memories
Bernard Matthews	Surrey	A special thanks for photographs and advice.
Mrs D Murdock	Nottingham	Photographs and literature (from the estate of Mr D Murdock)
Stan Needham	Nottingham	Photographs
Fred Pask	Nottingham	Personal memories and information
Jim Peden	Liverpool	Photographs
Norman Preedy	Gloucester	Photographs
J B Radford	Derby	Information
Mark Ratcliff	Burton	Information
Charlie Redfern	Nottingham	Personal memories and information
S A L Redshaw	Bottesford	Information
Bill Reed	Nottingham	Personal memories and photographs
Alan Robey		R C J No59
Ralph Savage and Neville Stead	Whitley Bay	Photographs
Eric Sawford		Photographs
Harold Smith	Nottingham	Personal memories
Michael Stanton	Nottingham	Photographs
Fred Straw	Nottingham	Personal memories
Barry Taylor	Nottingham	Photographs
Nigel Thompson	Nottingham	Information
Joe Vickers	Eastwood	Personal memories
Glynn Waite	Totley	Information and advice
Mick Watmough	Lincoln	Photographs and Information
Peter Watts	Nottingham	Photographs and diagrams
J Wayman	Nottingham	Photographs
P Webster	Stourbridge	Photographs and information
Ken Wilcox	Nottingham	Information
Bernard Willis	Nottingham	Information
J.P Wilson	Nottingham	Photgraphs and information

Organisations

British Library	Collingdale, London
Lloyds Foundry	Burton -on -Trent
Midland & Great Northern Circle	
Midland Railway Trust	Butterley
Midland Railway Society	
National Railway Museum	York
National Union of Railwaymen	
Railway & Canal Historical Society	
Railway Magazine	
RCTS	
Steam World Magazine	
Stephenson Locomotive Society	

And thanks to the late

T V R Barbour	Kent	Information
Joe Benson	Burton	Photographs and information
Dave Fell	Nottingham	Photographs
Sam Foster	Nottingham	Personal memories
Richard Hilton	Didcot	Information on narrow gauge Bagnall No I
Les Payne	Nottingham	Personal memories, information and photographs
Mrs Mary Reed	Nottingham	Personal memories and photographs
David Tee	Cumbria	Information on Midland Railway Locomotives
P. H Wells	Bourne	Photographs
Les Payne	Nottingham	Personal memories and photographs

Dedication

This book is especially dedicated to the memory of

Donald Peter Perkins
(1935-1982)

who started work as an Engine Cleaner at Nottingham Motive Power Depot in 1950 and died Oct 1982 aged 47.

And to the thousands of men and women of all occupations who over the years either worked in or passed through the Nottingham Midland Engine Sheds.

Chapter One
Nationalisation: The Early Years

In the 19th century, F S Williams, the Midland Railway chronicler and clergyman, had advocated government ownership in his pamphlet 'Ought the Government to Buy the Railways'. Yet, despite the government directing railway strategy in two World Wars, it was not until January 1st 1948 (Vesting Day) that all Britain's Mainline Railways came into public ownership. Nottingham retained its 16A Shed Code, becoming part of the London Midland Region. Thus the post war LMS Railway was to have a short-lived period of independence, only 28 months before Nationalisation. It was during this time that a few experimental liveries were tried out with red and dark blue /grey on Class 5X Jubilees of which there were still 14 running with the pre-war red livery. However black was eventually decided on for all engines, the only concession being limited lining out on passenger engines.

So, it was for the new regime to determine the colour and face of the Railway after Vesting Day. Plate 1 shows the local MP for East Nottingham, Mr James Harrison, addressing railway workers from the front of (1) LMS 8F No 8370 (48370) on that auspicious day when the possibility of a 'Railtrack' organisation was conceptually as distant as a black hole in space. The photograph was taken next to the No 1 Shed entrance line, the building to the right being No 2 Shed. With the MP on the engine are Mr J P Latham, Chief Clerk, Nottingham Loco and Mr S M Audinwood, District Locomotive Superintendent.

At this time a representative of the previous century still working at Nottingham was Kirtley 2-4-0 No 20002 (ex 158A) of 1866. The engine was withdrawn early in 1948 after 82 years service. This fine old engine, which had worked through three owners (Midland Railway, LMSR and now BR) had been the responsibility of eleven Locomotive Superintendents and Chief Mechanical Engineers from Matthew Kirtley to R A Riddles, and is now preserved at the Midland Railway Centre, Butterley. Although the railway had new owners, the same job had to be done with the same engines and the same bosses on a railway, which had still not recovered from the Second World War. Change was on its way however and the Locomotive exchanges in the summer of 1948 were to point towards the BR Standard Steam designs with the eventual abandonment of steam in favour of Dieselisation and Electrification. As an aside to our main story, it is an irony of technological change that the Rugby Testing Plant, an LMS/LNER inspired development that came to fruition in the early months of BR, had a very short life and came along at the very point of the steam locomotives technological obsolescence. That Britain did not have a modern testing facility until this time is a condemnation of the narrow attitudes to be found on nearly all of Britain's railways and most private locomotive builders, to their ultimate downfall. As a consequence, Britain lost most of the export markets to more progressive, mainly American, exemplary designs. Indeed, the LNER Class P2 2-8-2 'Cock O' the North' was taken to Vitry in France for testing! It was ALCO in the United States who announced, in late 1948, that it was to cease building steam locomotives and concentrate entirely on the production of Diesel Electric traction that pointed the way ahead. Even such a backward country as the old Imperial Russia had test plants and it was a Russian, N D Kondratiev, in 'Major Economic

Footnote 1 This engine was built at Horwich in the autumn of 1944 and withdrawn from Colwick (16B) in November 1966. It was in store there until April 1967 and then moved to Drapers of Hull for scrapping. It was one of the forlorn and condemned line of Black Fives and 8Fs that stood outside the Shed at the same time as one of the authors was working there and trying, with varying success, to keep the diesel fleet in business (J Perkins).

Plate 1
Vesting Day, January 1st 1948

W Padgett

Cycles 1925' who identified the cyclic nature of new technology. This analysis highlighted the fact that a technology is born during economic low points with its fruition coming when economies pick up. This was a situation of which a still creative Britain did not take advantage, having stuck with the old industries, with a few limited exceptions, and the millstone of war still apparent. Whilst the new order, based on similar designs to the LMS built Diesels 10000 and 10001, should have been the way ahead the money was not made available. So, thankfully for the enthusiasts, steam was to carry on for another 20 years.

However much we admired the steam locomotive, twenty years of BR managed steam operations were to draw to an end in August 1968. This rundown was due to perceived economic saving and the rapid returns to be made from the elimination of steam traction, ambitions which, in the light of events, were to prove unrealistic. These were part of the solution to the difficulties of finding labour to work in dirty conditions, declining traffic and the need to address the requirements of the Clean Air Act. However, Western Germany, allegedly the strongest economy in Europe, carried on for a further ten years with steam locomotives.

At the beginning of Nationalisation, Nottingham's allocation of front line motive power in the form of the elegant Class 5 X Jubilees was four, plus one on loan. These were 45554 'Ontario' (On Loan). 45568 'Western Australia', 45636 'Uganda', 45640 'Frobisher' and 45649 'Hawkins'. What a wonderful collection of names were conjured up in this class of engine with places in the old Empire followed by admirals and naval battles. Perhaps those most evocative of the spirit of steam were the ones named after ships of the line. After all, who could resist a class of locomotives which included 45714 'Revenge' and 45698 'Mars'. These names would have been recognised by those who had used the Midland Counties Railway in 1839. After all Traf- Al -Gar (an Arabic name) had taken place less than a life time before on October 21st 1805. There were exceptions within the naming regime with Rainhill Trials locomotives and provinces in

Ireland plus one outsider, 45665 'Lord Rutherford of Nelson' the scientist.

A record of a Shed visits carried out on the 15th August 1948 from the Chris Banks Collection which shows the variety of locomotives that were at Nottingham on that day can be seen at Annex A. The time of visit is given as 10.00am.

1949

This year saw the lowest numbered Black Five 44658, although not the first of its class, allocated, to Nottingham. This was one of the few Black Fives with electric lighting, equipment removed in 1952, the others being 44659/44755/44765-44767. In this year a tragedy occurred at Stanton Tunnel on the Melton Line when retired Driver Harry Burgess was killed by another Nottingham Black Five. He walked into the path of 44662 as it came out of the tunnel at the head of a special from St Pancras. The Driver was Fred Greensmith. In June this engine was also used on a Royal Train in connection with the Nottingham Quincentenary when Princess Elizabeth and the Duke of Edinburgh visited the city.

Plate 2
Black Five No 44662 with Gerald Hudson in the cab
G Hudson

Another tragedy was averted by good luck at Melton Station in 1952. Harold Smith relates how on a return working from Wellingborough with 8F No 48206 he approached Melton Station to see a woman standing in the four foot under the footbridge. She fell to the ground and the whole train passed over her, she then stood up and walked down the platform! Her only injury being a bump on the head from a coupling.

The locomotive scene around 16A at this time saw engines of the constituents of the LMS in both old and new liveries. The British Railways re-numbering style was originally that of a prefix letter M to the number and is shown on the 16A based Stanier 2-6-2T M178 (40178). This early nomenclature, which was a riveted-on extension to the number plate, eventually gave way to all former LMS engines being given either a 4 or 5

Plate 3
LMS 2-6-2T No 178 with its new and short-lived designation M178, 3th November 1949

M Whatmough Collection

prefix to their numbers or renumbered altogether with the 'BRITISH RAILWAYS' legend, on the engine or tender tanks. Until they could be properly repainted some engines ran with British Rail numbers. LMS and British Railways lettering. The Compound No 40929 is seen below on the left, painted and renumbered and the Johnson 0-6-0 half-cab tank engine No 41686 (Plate 5) can be seen in the interim condition. It took a few years to introduce the new British Railways legend and some engines, although allocated, were never re-numbered as the photographs taken by H C Casserley, dated 3rd June 1950, show. An interesting plate is Plate 6 which shows the Loco Coal Wagon standing between the Class 3F 0-6-0 No 3177 alongside the Water Tank and water softener plant. These distinctly marked wagons were restricted to the carrying of coal for Locomotive use only. Loco coal was a major item at the Shed with 10-15

Plate 4
Compound 40929 inside No 2 Roundhouse. Note the side rod trolley and Fitter's bench. This engine has a blue spot on the cab side denoting a talll chimney and was not to work over certain lines due to the restricted clearance

H C Casserley

wagonloads being used daily. During the cheaper priced summer months coal was stacked for use later. The price in the early 1950s was 18 shillings a ton and a feature of the south side of the Shed was the storing of the cheaper coal.

One of the ex-LT&S Tank engines No 2101 and the last surviving Johnson 2-4-0 No 20155 (once named 'Engineer South Wales' when based at Abergavenny) were both in store on the Field Side between the depleted coal stacks. (Plate 7) On the far right can be seen a Class 8F close to the Shed entrance on Middle Furlong Road. However this particular location was rarely used for engine storage, being mostly occupied with coal wagons. Some of the remaining ex-Lancashire & Yorkshire Railway 0-6-0 engines survived to be renumbered into the 5XXXX series. One of these was No 12135, which became 52135, an engine which one day ended up in No 2 Shed table hole!

Plate 7
Ex-L&Y 2-6-2T No 2101 and 20155, the sole surviving
Johnson 2-4-0 in store before W/D. The west end of the
No 2 Shed is seen on the left and the 8F on the right

H C Casserley

Plate 8
Ex-L&Y 0-6-0 52135 seen here between the repair shops.
This engine once moved on its own and ended up in the
tablehole in No 2 Shed

M Whatmough

The tale told was that the engine had moved forward on its own after steam had been raised from cold, the reason given that after the boiler had been washed out it had been over filled. The engine had also been left set in full forward gear. This is an unlikely story, as the regulator would also have had to be left open for the engine to move.

Accidents also happened to the footplate staff. An incident occurred at Stoke-on-Trent Station on Saturday 29th January which resulted in Driver Arthur Morris (staff list No 3211) losing a leg when he became caught under his engine. He was working a return football special from Liverpool when the incident happened. The water columns in the middle road at Stoke Station were of North Staffordshire Railway design and more awkward to use than those on the old Midland Railway lines. Driver Morris stepped back to get out of the way of the column arm and fell off the tender. An engine coming onto the adjacent line then ran over his leg.

Plate 11

Ivatt Mogul 46404 leaves Chilwell Ordnance Depot with a Whitwell train in October 1962

Bill Reed

Chapter Two
How the Shed Worked

The early 1950s were to become the Indian Summer for 16A with between 160 and 180 engines on Shed at weekends, 130 of which were Nottingham engines.

The allocation of particular classes of engines was according to type of work available and the number of turns of duty. There was work for 6 Jubilees on the London trains, 5MTs (Black Fives) for fitted freight trains and passenger work, Class 8Fs for coal traffic between the Leen Valley Collieries and Wellingborough and Class 4F for local freight and passengers and some Mansfield trains. There were Class 2P and 4P engines for passenger work and assisting expresses, Class 2 and Class 4MT for local passenger work, Class 3Fs for local trips and smaller classes for shunting. There were 2-6-4T engines for working the Tamworth Mail, the Derby to Lincoln and the Melton to Leicester services. The Shed also had an allocation of English Electric shunters to cover Nottingham and Beeston Yards. As commented upon by Ahrons, it was not only the Victorian engines that spent most of their working lives at one location. An example of later designs that fell into this category is that of the Class 5MT 2-6-0 No 42823 which was at 16A nearly all its life. It came to Nottingham new as 13123 in 1929 along with 42824 to 42827 (13124 to 13127). Appendix One shows the 16A allocation in the 1950s.

Signing On

At this point the signing on procedure at 16A should be mentioned. For footplate staff, signing on was completed in the 'Lobby'. The system of signing on for duty varied according to the grade and there was no clocking on at Nottingham. Staff, other than Supervisors, Clerical Staff, Drivers and Firemen, used a brass token on which was stamped the pay number. This token was collected when arriving on duty then handed in at the end of the shift. The system was sometimes amended to work in reverse order, but mostly stayed as the former. As mentioned previously, Drivers and Firemen signed on duty with a time card, on which was entered the time and turn of duty for the day and also their Mates' pay number. Cleaners passed for firing only signed on a time card when they performed firing duties and did not hand in a token. At the end of the turn of duty the Driver filled in a 'Daily Statement' of duties performed which showed his Fireman's pay number, the turn of duty, and diagram number. From this the office staff were able to enter any extras in pay on the same time cards and also obtain engine mileage and other statistics. Drivers and Firemen were allowed ten minutes when signing on duty to read notices to speed limits etc, especially over routes which they were about to work. At the end of a shift the Driver would also put in a 'Repair Card' or 'No Repair Card' later amended to a 'No Known Defects Card' to indicate the condition of the engine he had returned to the Shed. The first task for any crew when signing on was to read the latest Notices on the Notice Board. It was a requirement for drivers to check for any speed restrictions etc that were not shown in the previous week's publications. At Nottingham in later days some Firemen described the reading of notices as 'glimming the flimsies' - an American expression. This area also contained information on Enginemen's working and rosters; it also gave details of engineering works and their related speed restrictions. Job cards were also issued which were contained in a metal backed wallet in which a heavy-duty piece of paper or card was inserted which gave details of the particular working plus details of engine power classification and crew.

When all these preliminaries had been carried out the crew walked into No 1 Shed where, on the west wall, the Engine Arrangement Board gave the location of the engine in either Nos 1, 2 or 3 Sheds or on an outside road and the job it was allocated to. This board also indicated the whereabouts and status of engines on Shed for mileage examinations, waiting for and in works, plus repairs such as drop-pit work. It also included details of engines to be kept on local work as well as run down engines and those waiting for a works visit. Tenders awaiting wheel change were also shown, as were vacuum fitted jobs, which were shown in red chalk. The board was marked up for the whole week including BLS (Boiler Exams)

On finding the engine, the Driver would check around and then put on a set of dirty overalls (bib & brace) in order to carry out 'fatting up'. This was an expression that went back to the early days of grease lubricated engines, a procedure which entailed filling all oil boxes, except on prepared engines, and the cleaning of any windows. The Fireman would check the sandboxes and if they required filling would proceed to the Sand Hole which lay at the side of No 1 Shed on the through road from No 2 Shed to the drop-pit.

Plate 12
Seen from halfway up the coaling tower, 4F taking water. The ODM is on the right looking towards Wilford Road   *J Hutchinson*

This dry, very hot sand was moved about in 4-gallon sand containers. This was a heavy task as the sand had to be carried across the Shed to the engine and then lifted up to the framing before being poured in the sandbox making sure that the sand ran freely. If an engine had a full set of empty sandboxes it was a tedious and tiring job. Although good muscle building for heaving coal, it might not have seemed like it at the time! The Fireman then had to sweep the smoke box char from the framing below the smoke box so that it did not blow into their eyes when on the move. Before leaving the Shed the tender had to be tidied up to ensure that the coal was safe. It was also washed to keep dust down by using the 'slacking' or 'pep' pipe.

Whilst all this was going on a Fitters Mate, especially on a night shift, would be filling the Cylinder Lubricator and the Driver would top up the Axle Box Lubricator if required. On some of the older types such as 2F No 58175, MR 3Fs and the later WD Austerities and other classes, such as the ex-GCR Directors, a sight feed hydrostatic lubricator was topped up by either the Driver or Fireman. At this time the preparation men or steam raiser should have left the engine with a suitable fire and acceptable level of water in the boiler. The Fireman sorted out his tools from the stores, if they were any available! Frequently they were not, a situation due to shortages a consequence of the pooled tool arrangement, a topic dealt with in Volume II, with engines coming on Shed having to be relieved of their tools, or robbed. He also ensured that all the correct firing irons were in place and usable. In the course of time some of these long handled irons looked as though some demented giant had taken a liking to them and melted the ends to practice origami! The turntable was then organised to take account of the time off Shed and other engine movements. Lamps were set in their correct place for the type of train to be worked and the smoke box door checked for security.

On the subject of the quantity of coal in an engine's tender or bunker, engines were coaled coming on to Shed either by the coaling plant or by hand from the coal stage sited between Nos 1 and 2 Shed departure roads. (2)

This entailed a special trip to the coal stage for a refill. In very cold weather braziers were set up at strategic locations, such as water columns and Valves and Piston examinations. Such arrangements made the local coal supply even more parlous. On leaving the Shed the water column was visited in order to top up the tank. This was despite the engine having been topped up on entering the Shed and was a task made necessary due to topping up of the boiler whilst the engine had been standing, faulty tank gauges that required maintenance plus sieves cleaning, loose ventilators and scoop towers and leaking tanks. Tank filling was very difficult in icy weather when the tender top and handrails could be covered in ice and the leather bag as hard as iron. In really cold weather you could see how much water was in the tank by the frost line on the tank side, whilst a few feet away in the firebox and boiler was as much energy and heat you could want! After all these preliminaries the engine was recorded as 'Off Shed' after it had passed the points controlled by Mansfield Junction Signal Box. You might think that every engine likely to come on Shed would be known by all concerned but, as P N Townend relates in his tales about Kings Cross, a busy Loco Shed was capable of springing a few surprises on Running Foremen and Fitting Staff. This was when all concerned had to co-operate with the engine being coaled, watered, examined and oiled then sent on its way.

Coming Onto the Shed

This account of engines coming onto Nottingham Loco Shed summarises the amount of time, labour and organisation required, to maintain and service steam locomotives at the beginning of the second half of the 20th Century. If you compare this account with that of F S Williams in the 19th century, which was detailed in Volume 1, Chapter 2, the differences are apparent in both the language and understanding. What must be remembered however is that the later steam locomotive, although comparatively modern, had the same needs as in those far off Midland Railway days. Also, the facilities in which these engines were being disposed, repaired and prepared was exactly the same, except for No 3 Shed and the coaling plant, as was described by Williams in the 1870s.

At Nottingham the approach to the loco Shed for engines was via the junction at Wilford Road, which was controlled by a signal box of the same name. If we follow the procedure from entering the coaling plant road to the engine being made ready for its next turn of duty we will see what was required in the everyday and night operation of a BR Locomotive Depot.

In everyday speech a line was known as a road and this is perhaps an example of the earliest form of railway terminology surviving from before the term 'railways' became the accepted norm in Britain. There was a cabin situated near the coaling tower where engines coming on Shed were recorded by a man placed there. His purpose was to give the Running Foreman the up to date situation as to what locomotives were turning up. After entering onto the coaling plant road the footplate crew would leave their engine in the care of the disposal gang, who would fill the tender or side tanks with water from the numerous water columns. The engine was placed under the coaling plant. This towering structure of steel and concrete was built in 1935 replacing one of the two traditional manual coaling stages. In the type installed at Nottingham, coal wagon contents were tipped into steel lined hoppers which were then hoisted up and tipped into the bunker in the coaling tower. As the engine moved under the chutes underside, doors were opened via push button controls. (3)

As the mass of coal dropped into the tender with a great roar the volume was weighed and recorded automatically. The largest type of locomotive handled at 16A was the BR 9F, whose capacity of seven to nine tons needed a few bites at the bunker in order to obtain a tender-full. This was an exceptionally dusty and noisy operation. After coaling the next task was to move over the disposal pits where the smokebox, ash pan and firebox were cleaned. A few of the later LMS and all the BR types had a self-cleaning smokebox and were recognised by the small SC plate attached to the Shed plate. The action of this system was dependent on the baffle plate fitted inside the smokebox, a device that created a scouring action under influence of the exhaust blast. It was similar in action to the deflector plate designed by Samuel Hall in 1841 as described in Volume 1 which, in those far off days, had been tried on the Butterley built 'Ariel', later 'Bee'. The theory was that these SC fitted engines would only require to be emptied every ten days but, in reality, the screens were often removed to aid steaming and tended to pile up in a corner of the Shed the engines requiring, like the older ones, emptying every day. If the engine was needed for further duties, its fire would be maintained and only have the clinker cleaned out of the grate. The modern engines, fitted with rocking grates, enabled this job to be done quickly, an operation that could be carried out whilst the engine was in motion. On a bad steaming engine the tubes might also need to be cleaned in order to rid them of soot and char. Although most work in a firebox was in the Boilersmiths department, the Fitting Staff looked after rocker gates.

The largest grates were those in 9Fs which had 12 sections each with 12 fire bars. They were level at the back and sloped down at the front. When people talk about 'Cathedrals of Steam' they must be thinking about Class 9F Fireboxes! If the engine's next turn of duty was on the following day, its fire would be dropped into the ash pit and would be kept in light steam then moved onto a stabling point, an old equine term.

Footnote 3 There was another coal stage up until the installation of the coaling plant in the 1930s which served locomotive movements onto No 3 Shed and can be seen in Plate 51 of Vol II of this history.

This would be either inside one of the three sheds or on one of the many outside roads. Prior to its next duty, the Examining Fitter might carry out an examination and note any repairs required, including those reported by drivers. These would be attended to by the 'On Shed' Fitters. Goods engines were examined weekly unless they were on a 'fitted job' which was a train consisting of all or some vacuum braked stock, and passenger engines were examined daily. Some repairs were deferred until the next X-day examination and repair cycle came around. Other activities included the testing of brakes, vacuum, injectors, blower, whistle, sands and all pipe work was checked for leaks. After all this it was time to go to work!

Routes Worked and the Links System

There were 4 basic types of link at Nottingham;
1 The Express Passenger Link.
2 Local Passenger Link
3 Goods Link, which had 3 main destinations; Birmingham, Crewe and Wellingborough (2 links)
4 The 'Old Mans Link' which covered local trips and Colliery jobs with reasonable rostered hours. This was almost like having a day job compared to the 13-week duty cycle normally inflicted on footplate staff.

Routes signed by Nottingham men in the 1950s and 1960s

Bourne (M&GN)
South Lynn (M&GN)
Eaton Mines
Holwell Sidings - The engine for this job, usually a Class 4F, was specially prepared with brakes, brake blocks and sands being adjusted if required. This was due to the undulating nature of this line and, in recent years, the new Asfordby Deep Mine (closed 1997) was accessed from this area.
Wellingborough
St Pancras
Northampton via Market Harborough and Tilton-on the Hill
(L&NWR & GN Jt)
Toton Depot and Sidings
Edge Hill
Shirebrook - only a few men signed for Sunday excursion work over this line
Bristol
Birmingham New St and Washwood Heath Sidings.
Hams Hall Power Station - a few men
Soho and Kingsbury Oil Terminal via both Derby and Nuneaton.
Leicester to Burton via Coalville
Sheffield via Derby and Ambergate
Erewash Valley routes.
Westhouse Shed and Blackwell Sidings and Tibshelf Sidings.
Manchester Central and Midland Junction
Belle View and Cheadle Heath
Peterborough (Stanground Sidings)
Kettering via Corby

Rowsley
Ambergate via Codnor Park and Butterley
Lincoln St Marks and Central Stations and GN Shed.
Rolleston Junction to Southwell
Pye Bridge - a few men.

Chilwell Depot (MOD) and Sidings

Plate 11 shows a workmans' train leaving the on site station. This was the 4/48pm return working to Elmton and Creswell, which had originated from Langwith at 06.00(SX). This service closed on 14 June 1963 and was the last regular passenger train to run over the Lenton South curve.

Colwick Shed, Sidings and Estate

Mansfield and Worksop (now re-opened as part of the Robin Hood Line) the Sunday service to Mansfield closed on 16th September 1956. Four years earlier BR had renamed four of the stations on this line. These all acquired a suffix to distinguish them from the former LNER stations and became Basford Vernon (closed 4 Jan 1960), Bulwell Market, Hucknall Byron and Mansfield Town.

Fiskerton Junction - Southwell-Farnsfield-Blidworth Colliery

Mansfield South Junction - Rufford Colliery-Farnsfield - Southwell - Fiskerton Junction
King Coal

Although Bass was the Midland Railways largest customer, it has often been stated that coal was the lifeblood of the Midland Railway. Listed here are the collieries in the Nottinghamshire coal field whose traffic had been worked by the Midland Railway and its successors.

Annesley Colliery - production commenced 1860. It was then linked to Bentinck which was opened in 1894 and merged with Brookhill (open 1909, Pit Head closed 1964) in 1968 and was still working and known as Annesley-Bentinck (Midlands Mining) until it closed in September 1999
Bestwood Colliery - production started in 1871 and closed in 1967
Bilsthorpe Colliery - production commenced in 1928 and closed in 1997
Calverton Colliery - production commenced in 1948 and closed in April 1999
Cinderhill (Babbington) Colliery - production commenced in 1841 and closed in 1986. The branch to this colliery was closed on 13 July 1983.
Clifton Colliery - production commenced in 1868 and closed in 1968. In 1944 this was the first coal mine to be nationalised.
Gedling Colliery (ex Colwick job) - closed in 1991 but the waste tip was opened up in 1998 to extract previously discarded coals. This traffic has now finished.
Cotgrave Colliery - production commenced in 1964 and closed in 1994.
Hucknall Colliery - opened in 1851. Hucknall No 1 closed in 1958 and complete closure was in 1986 when Hucknall No 2 finished working.
New Hucknall - this was closed in 1982. In the year prior to New Hucknall closing there were still 220 coal mines in Britain.
Kirkby to Rufford Colliery - Kirkby opened in 1890 and closed in 1968 and Rufford opened in 1913 and closed in 1993.
Radford/Wollaton Colliery - production commenced in 1874 and closed in 1965.

The Nottinghamshire Coal Field has been decimated in the last 30 years and the following list shows those collieries that had operated since the Midland Railway began carrying this traffic. Although not all were worked by Nottingham men directly, they did influence the traffic patterns as Nottingham men could relieve a job initially worked by another Shed and loco coal came from some of these collieries.

Awsworth- opened in 1875 and closed in 1899
Barlborough - later Oxcroft No 3, opened in 1878 and closed in 1928
Blidworth - closed in 1989
Bulwell - opened in 1877 and closed in 1944
Clipstone - opened in 1922 and due to close in 2003
Cossall - production commenced in 1870 and closed in 1966
Coates Park - production commenced in 1850 and closed in 1963
Creswell - opened in 1896 and closed in 1991
Digby - opened in 1866 and closed in 1937
Glapwell - closed in 1974
Hartington - opened in 1860
Harworth - still open in 2002
High Moor
Ireland (Speedwell)- opened in 1874
Kirkby - closed in 1968
Kiveton Park
Langton - production commenced in 1842 and closed in1968
Langwith - opened in 1880 and closed in 1974
Linby - closed in 1988
Lodge - production commenced in 1878 and closed in 1959
Mansfield - closed in 1988
Moor Green - closed in 1985
New London - opened in 1876 and closed in 1937
New Selston - production commenced in 1892 and closed in 1956
Newcastle - opened in 1853 and closed in 1929
Newstead - closed in 1987
Oakwood Grange - production commenced in 1932 and closed in 1956
Ollerton - opened in 1924 and closed in 1994
Pinxton - opened in 1780, main production commenced in 1836 and closed in 1950
Pleasley - opened in 1877
Portland - opened in 1850 and closed in 1887
Pye Hill No 2 - closed in 1985
Ramscroft - opened in 1916 and closed in 1966
Selston - production commenced in 1874 and closed in 1968
Seymour - opened in 1860
Sherwood - opened in 1902 and closed in 1992
Shireoaks - opened in 1856 and closed in 1990
Silverhill - opened in 1875
Skegby - opened in 1873 and closed in 1990
Southgate - opened in 1878 and closed as Oxcroft No 5 in 1929
South Normanton - production commenced in 1893 and closed in 1950
Speedwell - opened in 1869 and closed in 1905
Steetley - opened in 1875 and closed in 1984
Sutton - closed in 1989

Teversal - opened in 1867 and closed in 1980
Thoresby - opened in 1925 and still in production 2002
Tibshelf - opened in 1870 and closed in 1939
Trowell Moor - opened in 1880 and closed in 1928
Warsop Main - opened in 1895 and closed in 1989
Watnall - production commenced in 1839 and closed in 1950
Welbeck - opened in 1914 and it is still in production in 2002. The German Well sinkers who started this shaft were interned for the duration of WWI.
Whitwell - opened in 1890 and closed in 1986

Adjacent to the Nottinghamshire area were the Yorkshire, Leicestershire and Warwickshire coalfields, which also influenced traffic patterns. There were also brickyards, iron works, such as the one at Bennerley, breweries, chemical plants and agricultural producers. (4)

By 2003 there will only be three Collieries remaining in the Nottinghamshire area, Harworth, Thoresby and Welbeck. all of which are in the north of the county.

As well as domestic coal and supplies to the gasworks, which every town had, some of the coal went to the following power stations:
Wilford Power Station - opened in 1932 and closed in 1989
Staythorpe Power Station - now the site of a gas fired power station
Castle Donnington Power Station - opened in 1952 and demolished in 1995
Willington Power Station - opened in 1956, closed in 1998 and demolished - only the Coaling Tower remains (2002).

At one time there were so many Power Stations in the area that it was known as Megawatt Valley!

Other routes worked were:
Derby via Chellaston
Derby via Sawley
Sankey Pottery via Basford Junction
Syston South Junction and Melton Mowbray and Queniborough Sidings.
Crewe via Basford Hall Crewe South Shed (5B) and the Station.

Odd routes signed by a few men for special workings:
Buxton via Ashbourne
Tibshelf and Mansfield Woodhouse.
Uttoxeter to Alton Towers
Wellingborough to Northampton
Cheadle
Birmingham via Wichnor Junction
Lichfield
Bescot via Wichnor Junction and Sutton Park
Tamworth Mails later diverted to Stafford via Lichfield
Annesley Shed via Nottingham Victoria (for changing locomotives)
Drakelow Power Station

Footnote 4 The above information compiled thanks to the following publications: Notts Mineral Local Plan Sept 1993, The Coal Industry in Nottingham 1986 , South Nottingham Coal Digest 1983/1984, Mr Jim Rainbird , ex Hucknall Colliery Deputy, Michael Pollard *'The Hardest Work under Heaven'*. Hutchinson, 1984 published by Nottinghamshire County Council, *'The Midland Railway in Nottinghamshire'* by Geoffrey Hurst

There were also the regular ballast trains. Bill Reed, who was the source of a number of photographs in this Volume, was once on one of these jobs with Ivatt Class 4 Mogul No 43040 at Queniborough, on the 28 August 1955, the Driver was Tommy Whitt. When first built, these engines were fitted with double chimneys, a device that was not successful on this class, and class member No 43033 of 16A can be seen in this condition in Plate 50.

Plate 13
Fireman Bill Reed stands next to Ivatt Mogul 43040
Bill Reed

Footplate staff could be members of one of two unions, the NUR or ASLEF. Nottingham was predominately an ASLEF depot although the NUR was strongly represented with the Local District Committee being served by members of both unions. In the late 60s, hotly contested elections resulted in two NUR men and one ASLEF man occupying these positions. At times of strife, when one or other of the unions had been on strike, things could be very difficult for footplate crews with mixed loyalties. A number of local footplate men were elected to serve the wider community with Drivers Sid Hill and Hugh Bryan becoming Mayor and Sheriff of Nottingham respectively. George 'Pip' Chambers became President of the NUR as well as chairman of Nottinghamshire County Council. It was Pip Chambers (who died in May 2002) who had the sad honour to drive the last train from Nottingham Victoria Station on the 6th March 1967.

Maintaining Nottingham's Allocation

If an engine had been earmarked for repairs or mileage exams the fitting staff would move into action. This whole procedure was based on the pre-war LMS regime known as the MP11. (Fig 1) and was arranged around the principle of examining non-moving parts on a regular period basis and moving parts on a mileage basis. Locomotives were stopped at regular intervals for X day exams where the opportunity was taken to attend to any deferred repairs and to undertake mileage examinations. Express engines, like Nottingham Class 2Ps, Compounds, Passenger Tanks, Black Fives and Jubilees had X days every seven days. Freight engines had longer periods between X days.

BRITISH RAILWAYS

EXAMINATIONS OF STEAM LOCOMOTIVES   Locomotive No.................................

MOTIVE POWER DEPOT...

Motive Power Classification............................

Pass., Tender,
Mixed Traffic,
Freight, Tank.

Item	PARTS TO BE EXAMINED (Delete items not applicable)	Period Basis	JANUARY		FEBRUARY		MARCH		APRIL		MAY		JUNE		JULY		AUGUST		SEPTEMBER		OCTOBER		NOVEMBER		DECEMBER		MILEAGE ACCOUNT	
			Date	Initials	Date	Initials	Date	Initials	Date	Initials	Date	Initials	Date	Initials	Date	Initials	Date	Initials	Date	Initials	Date	Initials	Date	Initials	Date	Initials	DATE (up to and including)	Miles since last Shop Repair (other than casual)
2	A.W.S. - L.T.S.	DAILY																										
3	A.W.S., B.R.	"																										
4	Centre Big End (ex S.R. M.N.)	"																										
8	Self Cleaning smoke box fittings	WASHOUT																										
10	T.I.A.-Apparatus	12-16 days																										
11	Electric lighting (Turbo-generator	" "																										
12	Boiler water gauge glasses, 200 p.s.i. and over (not W.R. & S.R.) ...	" "																										
13	Boiler water gauge glasses, over 200 p.s.i. in W.R. & S.R.	" "																										
14	Gauge frames and trial taps (independent handles)	3-5 weeks																										
15	" " " " (coupled cocks)	" "																										
16	Boiler water gauge glasses (Klinger)	" "																										
17	Automatic vacuum or auto-stream and vacuum brake:-																											
	(a) Vacuum pump	" "																										
	(b) Retaining valve	" "																										
	(c) Drip valves and relief valves	" "																										
	(d) Driver's brake valve, etc.	" "																										
18	Ejector efficiency test (except ex-G.W.R. types)	" "																										
19	" " (ex-G.W.R. types)	" "																										
20	Vacuum controlled gear	" "																										
21	Mechanically controlled regulator gear	" "																										
22	Carriage warming apparatus (during season)	" "																										
23	Tablet exchange apparatus	" "																										
24	A.W.S. gear (ex-G.W.R.) (1) Electrician	3-4 weeks																										
	(2) Fitter	" "																										
25	A.W.S. B.R. Type	3-5 weeks																										
26	Trip cocks	3-5 weeks																										
27	Main frame etc. (42XX class, Newport and Neath districts) ...	" "																										
28	Westinghouse air brake	" "																										
29	Steam reversing gear (1) ex-L.M.S.R. and ex-S.R. types	11-15 weeks																										
	(2) other types	3-5 weeks																										
30	Centre big end and oil sump filters ("Merchant Navy." etc.) ...	" "																										
31	Cylinder cocks and gear	" "																										
32	Sight-feed lubricators (ex-G.W.R. types)	" "																										
33	Manual blowdown valve or blow-off cock	" "																										
34	Continuous blowdown valve	" "																										
35	Timken roller bearings, (1) Cl. 6, 7 & 8	" "																										
	(2) all others	7-9 weeks																										
36	Continuous blowdown valve (except ex-G.W.R. types)	" "																										
37	Continuous blowdown valve (ex-G.W.R. types)	" "																										
38	T.I.A. apparatus	" "																										
40	Boiler water gauge glasses, under 200 p.s.i. (not Western Region) ...	" "																										
41	" " " " 200 p.s.i. and under in Western Region	" "																										
42	" " " " (Klinger)	" "																										
43	Injectors—Live steam	" "																										
44	Injectors—Independent check valve	" "																										
45	Injectors—Exhaust steam	" "																										
46	Tender tanks etc. (a)	" "																										
	" " " (b)	6 monthly																										
47	Feed pumps and fittings	7-9 weeks																										
48	Automatic vacuum or auto-stream and vacuum brake	" "																										
49	Hand brake	" "																										
50	Independent steam brake application valve	" "																										
51	Skefco roller bearings (axlebox)	" "																										
52	Electric-lighting (Turbo-generator)	11-15 weeks																										
53	Safety valve and steam pressure gauge	" "																										
54	Main stop valves to Manifold ("Merchant Navy", etc.)	" "																										
55	Top feed (where scale formation is heavy in Southern Region)	" "																										
56	Top feed	" "																										
57	Top feed (except ex-G.W.R. and where scale formation is heavy in the Southern Region)	6 monthly																										
58	Top feed (ex-G.W.R. types)	{ 12 monthly/ local instructions }																										
59	Injectors—Delivery pipes in boilers	6 monthly																										
60	A.W.S. B.R. type	5-6 monthly																										
61	Safety valve (ex-G.W.R. types)	{ 12 monthly at top feed examination }																										

Fig 1
Examination of Steam Locomotive

Authors Collection

Every alternate X day would involve a boiler washout but depended on the condition of the water in use. When hot, a complete examination would be made of the whole locomotive and tender, during which loose, missing and faulty items could be discovered. During the servicing, tender water sieves were cleaned out and the water scoop oiled and checked over for alignment if required and stiff scoop gear eased. The brake gear was also oiled or greased. The rocking grate and ashpan were tested on the more modern locomotives.

The reversers on ex-works engines could be very difficult for the old hand drivers and these sometime had to be attended to by Fitters. Tight water scoop mechanisms were also a problem but fit young Firemen wielding coal picks generally tackled these. Sometimes even this was not enough and they had to be examined by Fitting Staff.

The period exams P3 and P7 were of a minor nature but included some important servicing items and were undertaken at either 3 to 5 or 7 to 9 week intervals. Boiler gauge frames were checked, cocks repacked and gauge glasses changed while internal steam passages to the frames were rodded-out with a square edged tool, which, when rotated, cut away any lime scale. This was an important task as any build up of scale in these passages gave false boiler water level indication at the gauge glass. The continuous blow down valve was also serviced. Extras to the traditional exams came later in the 1950s when, after the Harrow crash in October 1952, AWS was gradually fitted to most passenger engines. This required battery testing/charging and the testing of the pick up shoe/receiver. The 7 to 9 week examination had, in addition to the 3 to 5 week items, renewal of the fusible plug in the firebox crown, cleaning the live steam and exhaust injector cones and examining the injector steam valve seats, with re-cutting if required. Inside the tank the cleaning of sieves and the repair of the tank float and gauge were undertaken by an Apprentice or Mate when required. The slime found inside tanks was very messy and the tanks seemed to be inhabited by small crustaceans, plus lumps of coal and other foreign bodies. The writer once found a beret to which was attached a Northamptonshire Regiment WWI Old Comrades badge that had made its way to one of the sieves on a Class 8F and this badge is now in the Regimental Museum.

Moving parts such as valves and pistons came under the mileage exam regime and were conducted at 10-12000, 20-24000, 30-36000 and 40-48000 miles depending on the class of engine. The mileage clerk recorded the mileage, as all engines, except for a few experimental ones and the very early patent taken out by Ramsbottom of the L&NWR in 1851, were not fitted with a means of recording distance travelled. Shunting was recorded as 5 mph.

The 40-48000 exam was the heaviest undertaken by 16A. This involved the removal of valves, pistons, most motion parts, draw gear, which required the engine/tender to be split, axle box underkeeps and the requirements of any other exams. In these cases the exam would take longer than a day and sometimes a full week. Much of the work meant re-metalling the crossheads and the piston/valve rings being renewed. On some ex-LMS and BR engines the brass piston support slippers were changed, but not all engines had this feature. Even the standards varied depending on the type of piston fitted. For instance, the Swindon built 9Fs with the solid piston did not have a slipper. On these engines the level in all twelve under keeps had to be checked and water drained off as necessary. The tenders, however, were no problem having roller bearing axleboxes, as did all the BR Standard engines.

Another feature of the BR Standards was the seemingly endless number of grease nipples, which were attended to by the Greaser/Fitters Mate; George Etches. Boilers were examined regularly, mostly after washouts, and were carried out by a Boilersmith or Boiler Inspector whose job entailed the examination of the interior. This was carried out by inserting a long rod, to which a blazing paraffin soaked rag was attached. For any operation that required a strong light, and where the normal oil lamp was insufficient, an Acetylene (Carbide) light provided the best light or a strong electric light could be used in conjunction with a small mirror.

The firebox was also checked out with a stay hammer, when side stays and crown stays were tested. Another firebox fixture that required attention was the brick arch, which later became almost concrete with the use of Fondu Cement. This high Alumina Cement, which was nearly black in colour, lasted a great deal longer than the usual Firebrick variety. The brick arch gang, under the direction of a Boilersmith, attended to this item and in some places it was known as 'Instant Stonehenge', such was its rapidity of hardening. A BR 9F had an arch containing nearly a ton of concrete, which had to be mixed and then bucketed-in through the fire hole door. It was the rubble from brick arches that was a feature of most steam sheds with bits of coal, old fire irons and other debris mixed up with it. Plate 14 shows the other end of an engine, in this case the open smoke box door of an Ivatt 2-6-0 Mogul, which has its blast pipe removed, probably for working on the super heater elements.

Plate 14
Ivatt Class 2MT with blastpipe removed

Reddish

The Fitting Shop adjacent to No 1 Shed was the store for the specially shaped arch bricks, and was a place where other items were kept. These ranged from super heater elements to springs. In earlier years locomotives were also stored here. After all this activity, and sometimes at the same time, a gang of Cleaners or Passed Cleaners carried out the locomotive cleaning. Alas, the standards of the 1950s and 60s could not be compared with those F S Williams would have encountered in the 19th century, when even Fitters could go under an engine and come out clean! After cleaning had been completed, and if all was well, the boiler was filled via a washout plug. After this the steam raiser went onto the footplate with two firelighters made of wood shavings, sticks and tallow and resembling a one pound bag of sugar. Onto this was placed a layer of coal. This coal was placed over the entire grate. More often a shovel full of live coals was taken from the sand hole or an adjacent engine in steam. To maintain the fire before it took hold a few pieces of wood were added, then coal from the tender or bunker. It would take a number of hours for pressure to rise, depending on the size of the engine and amount of water in the boiler.

On a Sunday night the Shed would be full of yellow smoke which rolled out of the chimneys and fell to the floor. When steam was raised the blower would be used to clear the tubes.

During World War Two the MP11 regime was amended, as the document dated 11th October 1941 in Fig 2 shows. This was found pasted on the back of an ERO 10 form dated 2nd October 1941 (LMS Internal Correspondence) It gives authority for Repairing of Engines, Foremen, F W Hale and F Thompson, to move engines in steam within the Shed yard. A restriction that was honoured more in the breach than otherwise in later BR days when even Apprentices helped to move engines.

Engine Allocations at a Locomotive Depot

The number of engines allocated to a depot to encompass the diagrammed work (Fig 3) was adequate provided everyone used them properly and was prepared to let Control (Plate 107) know the exact situation. The Power Controller had a view of the position throughout the Division but this relied on him being given the full facts and that everyone followed them. The idea was that engines must not be kept up a Running Foreman's sleeve, for just-in-case needs, such as engine failure, but that all available engines must be known about at Control. The messages to Control must also be accurate in regards to engines away from the depot and foreign engines, ie engines not allocated to that particular depot, on Shed and available to work.

Shed visit listings (Annex A - F) show a variety of foreign engines on Shed at the time of a visit. These could range from engines from local depots to out-of-course workings terminating at Nottingham or engines breaking down in traffic. Following the formation of British Railways the number of foreign engine workings increased and those from the ER (the branch line to Nottingham men) could be seen regularly. An example of foreign engines working in the Nottingham area in the early 50s was when ex-LNER 4-4-0 Class D16s were on test trains to check clearances between Derby and Lincoln. One of these was No 62590 from 32B (Ipswich) which was to be seen on Shed on 29th April 1951. Nottingham engines were also venturing further afield. An extra working to London with the train engine going onto Willesden Shed was the 'Nottingham Aquarist Group' special of 18th May 1952, the train having a special headboard.

Fig 3 shows the Nottingham passenger workings as of Programme 23 of 1951.

In the mid 1950s the former LNER/GCR locomotive Shed at Annesley became part of the LMR and within the Nottingham Concentration area. This meant that all the non-LMS types came to 16A for drop-pit work. Colwick had an hydraulic drop-pit and Annesley, an ex-GCR Shed, had a small wheel jack for changing brasses on Class 01s and 04s, 2-8-0s It was at this time that the last ex-Great Central Driver, Bill Todd, transferred to Nottingham. Although others said they were ex-GC they had actually started in LNER days.

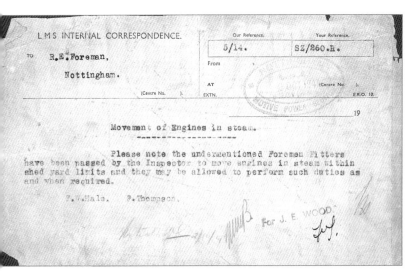

LMS INTERNAL CORRESPONDENCE.

TO   R.E. Foreman,

Nottingham.

Our Reference.   5/14.

Your Reference.   SZ/260.H.

Movement of Engines in steam.

Please note the undermentioned Foremen Fitters have been passed by the Inspector to move engines in steam within shed yard limits and they may be allowed to perform such duties as and when required.

T.V.Hale.   F.Thompson.

For J. E. WOOD

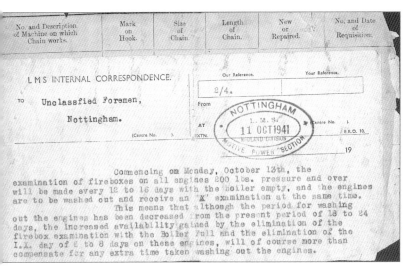

No. and Description of Machine on which Chain works.	Mark on Hook.	Size of Chain.	Length of Chain.	New or Repaired.	No. and Date of Requisition.

LMS INTERNAL CORRESPONDENCE.

TO   Unclassfied Foremen,

Nottingham.

Our Reference.   2/4.

From   NOTTINGHAM
L. M. 34
11 OCT 1941
MIDLAND DIVISION

Commencing on Monday, October 13th, the examination of fireboxes on all engines 200 lbs. pressure and over will be made every 12 to 16 days with the boiler empty, and the engines are to be washed out and receive an 'X' examination at the same time.
This means that although the period for washing out the engines has been decreased from the present period of 18 to 24 days, the increased availability gained by the elimination of the firebox examination with the Boiler Full and the elimination of the I.X. day of 6 to 8 days on these engines, will of course more than compensate for any extra time taken washing out the engines.

Fig 2
Authority form for the moving of engines during the War and reduction in the Firebox examination   *N Thompson*

A distinction that seems academic today eight decades after the amalgamation!

The Annesley BR types, mainly 2-10-0s and Britannias, and the ex-LMS classes, such as Royal Scots and Black Fives, came to Nottingham for valves and pistons and mileage exams. The BR 7P Pacifics and 9F 2-10-0 locomotives had to have all their superheater elements changed due to poor water at their home Shed and at Woodford Halse. Nottingham never had any of these classes allocated. Although taken on the Great Central line (ex-LNER) at Wilford, Plate 15 shows the external condition of the Annesley 9Fs in this 1960 view of single chimney No 92070 and an unidentified engine.
The amount of lime scale on the boiler and cylinders is typical of the condition of these engines and was caused by the poor quality water. Nottingham also carried out what were termed TRDs (Tubes Removed for Dirt) a procedure known as a BCO (Boiler Clean Out) at Derby and this was a method of de-scaling the internals of boilers. When a boiler was becoming scaled up and the tubes wearing thin and leaking they would have a tube examination. All the tubes that had wasted away and were very thin would be removed. New tubes would be cut to length, fitted to the boiler and then expanded until tight. On one occasion BR Class 5MT No 73010 had all its small tubes removed and the quantity of scale removed almost filled the pit. The former repair shop at the end of No 1 Shed was equipped with a tube saw and it was in this building that all the spare tubes were stored and sawn off to correct length.

Nottingham also carried out TRDs on engines from depots where there were staff shortages. On one occasion the Neasden (14D) 2-6-4T No 42222, which featured in the film 'Wash & Brush Up', was treated to a TRD at Nottingham. The need to carry out washouts and X day exams was considered to be extremely important and difficulties could be encountered when engines had been 'borrowed' by other depots due to local motive power problems and then moved well out of the division.

One example of this in the late 50s was that of Jubilee No 45620 'North Borneo' which disappeared for a week and was only recovered by 16A when the Mechanical Forman, Mr Percy Croydon, sent out a message via control that it was long overdue a boiler washout and exam. 'North Borneo' can be seen in Plate 16 with two very young enthusiasts as it stands outside No 3 Shed, sometime in the early 1950s.

The Red Book (ERO 53984/1), which gave full details of how to run a Shed, was a great help to Shed Foremen and Locomotive Superintendents. The following extracts show some of the guidelines and advice given in this publication.

'Engines to leave Shed on time, a most important point is to see that engines leave the Shed to time, but sufficient time must be allowed for them to be serviced properly on the Shed and a close watch must be kept on the arrival times on the Ash Pit. If an engine is consistently late on the Shed and so misses its subsequent booked work, the facts must be reported so that arrangements can be made to have the diagram altered to give an adequate margin. If this margin can be made right, late starts from the Shed will to a large extent, be avoided, but servicing of the engines must not be allowed to suffer in order to avoid late starts, or trouble on the road will result'.

Note again the use of the expression 'on the road'.

Of course, everything did not always run smoothly, especially when engines failed in traffic. When this occurred the District Operating Manager advised the Divisional Power Controller particulars of the failed engine, its home depot and details of replacement engines. As a Driver, Charlie Redfern, with Fireman George Chambers,

Fig 3
Midland Division Working (for other sheets please see following pages)
G Waite

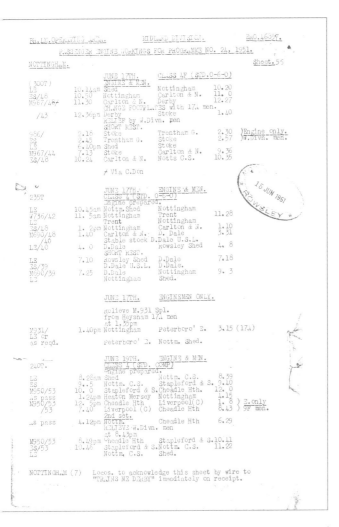

Fig 3 continued

relates the story of 3F No 43249, which failed Melton Junction on Wednesday 12th March 1952, having dropped a top left hand slide bar. This was on the 12.47 Coal Train to Wellingborough and No 43249 (a Nottingham engine) had to be swapped for 4F No 43958 off another train. Charlie also had the job of dragging No 43249 dead to Derby on 25th March 1952.

One aspect of engines failing in traffic was that of having an unbalanced engine on the Shed. Failures of this nature could occur at anytime but were mostly on fitted freights running at night. Any night-time failure could result in some rare foreigners on Shed for repairs or dragging off to their home Sheds or works. The authors can remember some of these occasions when, on arriving at work in the early morning, a Western Division, Scottish or Eastern Region engine had appeared on Shed one morning in late 1959 the 1B (Camden) based Jubilee No 45676 'Codrington' was found in one of the dead end roads outside No 2 Shed. It had failed in the night with a hot box.

Unbalanced engines on hand at Motive Power Depots. From ERO 53984/1 'Motive Power Organisation & Practice' of December 1946 (Known as the Red Book).

'Information, in regard to unbalanced engines on hand must be given by the Motive Power Depot to the District Operating Manager or Control Office. The District Operating Manager or Control Office must telephone to the Divisional Control Office particulars of foreign engines, which will become unbalanced immediately this is known, in order that disposal instructions can be obtained.'

The regulation of unbalanced engines was carried out in the Divisional Control Office by means of a coloured card system, each concentration depot and its garage depots plus each Division were allotted a distinctive coloured card. These were placed in racks specially constructed for the purpose and were numbered to represent particular engines. When the engine became unbalanced the card was place in a metal docket and positioned under the Shed at which it became unbalanced. In the top left hand corner of the metal docket there was a revolving disc, which was divided into four colours.

These were Red, White, Blue and Green and denoted

RED: Arranged to go to home depot. either as a pilot or light engine
WHITE: On hand spare or local.
BLUE: Arriving on an inward train.
GREEN: On hand - stopped for repairs. having failed in traffic.

The advising of foreign or out of balance engines was very detailed and had to be recorded on form ERO 20711 (Motive Power Position).

Motive Power Organisation and Practice

This section is an extract from the Motive Power Organisation and Practice and reproduces the foreword written by Harold Rudgard (Derby MPD) and includes the Index. The actual document is 100 pages long and as can be seen from the index it is extremely comprehensive. The last entry in the index is X Examination and Repair; this is dealt with in more detail in a separate chapter.

Foreword

Contents of this publication deal with
Motive Power Organisation and stores
Foremanship RE and WE
Discipline
Locomotive Inspectors and Firing Instructors
Standard practices, Modernisation, Casualty &
Examination Schemes, Repair and Shopping of
Locomotives
Operating and Organisation as it Affects Motive Power Supervisory Staff, Including Outdoor
Machinery Services
Diesel Locomotives and Railcars

Further information can be gathered from the Appendices, and, of course, reference is made in the margin to standard instructions which have a bearing on any particular aspect of our work. When these are read by the younger members of our supervisory staff who are in the line for promotion they will have the advantage of accumulative knowledge of years which will enable them to develop their minds in the most efficient way of getting valve from Drivers, Firemen, static staff, machines and coal. Another object is with a view to assisting those concerned to realise what is in the minds of the management with regard to the various aspects of the sections of this department in order to train them for greater

Fig 3 continued

Plate 15
Annesley 9F's No 92070 and another unidentified Class member passing Wilford Brickyard. Only the houses now remain of the scene

C Beck

responsibility and to ensure a common outlook towards their work by the supervisory personnel of the Motive Power Department.

Read, digest and learn

Signed Harold Rudgard

Index

Plate 16
A nice shot of two young spotters in the early 1950s with a view of Jubilee 45620 'North Borneo' outside No 3 Shed. Note that the exhaust injection is blanked off as shown in the right hand inset

C Beck

Boilerwasher
Boilersmith
Booster Pumps
Breakdown Trains
Breakdown Staff and Equipment
Breakdown Crane
Breakdown Crane Maintenance and Examination
Breakdown of Machinery and Plant
Brick-arches
Calling-up
Canteens
Cards, Examination
Cards, Job
Cards, Repair
Cards, Road
Cards, Stock
Cards, washout
Casualties, Engine and Tender
Chains, Lifting Tackle, etc., Examination of
Chargeman Cleaner
Chief Clerk
Cleaners
Cleanliness of Premises, etc
Clerical Staff
Clerical Stores
Clerical Work
Coal, inferior
Coal on tender backs
Coaling Plants
Coal stacking and lifting
Coal stacking and lifting appliances
Coal Supplies
Concentration Areas
Conducting
Control (power)
Costing of repairs
Detonators
Diesel Units
Discipline
Discipline Scheme
Disposal duties
Distribution of work to R.E. staff
District Locomotive Superintendent
District Operating Manager or Control
Drivers
Drivers, relief of
Drivers reports
Drivers travelling as passengers
Engine allocation
Engine re-allocation

Fireboxes defective
Firebricks
Fitters' benches
Fitters, Grade 3
Foreman Boilersmiths
Fractures
Fusible plugs
Guards, goods
Guards, relief of
Gudgeon pins, fitted with split collars
Handbook for steam locomotive engineman
Hostals
Income Tax
Injectors
Lights, maintenance of
Lights, naked
Local Department Committees
Locomotive Inspectors
M P 9 instructions for working water pick -up apparatus
M P 19 cleaning of machinery and shafting and fixing of main driving belts
M P 37 instructions to be followed when cleaning out ash-lifting plants
M P 38 boiler empty targets
M P 39 movement of engines in locomotive sheds, yards and sidings
M P 41 engines emitting smoke, blowing off steam and whistling
M P 46 drivers and Fireman passed for driving, knowledge of roads, signals, speed restrictions, gradients, etc.
Notices
Notices Permanent Book
Notices Permanent
Oil
Oiling of machinery
Outdoor machinery department, maintenance
Passed Cleaners
Passed Firemen
Passed Firemen Examination Certificate
Passed Firemen Technical Examination
Payment of wages, hours of
Priming
Push and pull trains, working of
Questions for daily notice by District Locomotive Superintendent
Questions for enginemen, etc
Relief of enginemen and guards
Reporting breakdown of machinery and plant
Reporting of irregularities
Returns daily analysis
Returns engines out of service on weekdays
Returns extra duty
Returns 5.00PM coal return
Returns midnight engine return

Returns waiting material
Rosters
Rule books
Safety first
Sand drying
Scrap
Shop committees
Shortage of water in boiler
Shortage of water in tender
Shortage of steam
Slipping
Smoking in premises
Speed of trains
Springs
Staff
Staff recruiting of
Staff reporting for duty after sickness
Statements casualty
Statements comparative
Statements Driver's daily duty
Statements engine mile and engine hour
Statements engines out of service for distance, Loco, Superintendent
Statements engines stopped R E to W E Foreman
Steam-heating irregularities
Stores
Supervision of staff
Telephones
Tenders for conveyance of sludge from water softening plants
Tools ashpit
Tools boilersmiths'
Tools boilerwashers'
Tools engine
Tools fitters'
Tools machine
Tools Tubers'
Training of improvers and Apprentices
Travelling cranes
Tubes, cleaning
Tubes defective
Turntables
Tyres
Uniform clothing, wearing of
Water pick-up apparatus
Water services and treatment plants
X Examination and repair

OFFICE OF THE SUPERINTENDENT OF MOTIVE POWER,
WATFORD, HQ
1st October, 1945

LOCOMOTIVE MAINTENANCE AND MECHANICAL EFFICIENCY
(Known as X Scheme Examination and Repair)
The examinations Nos. 1X to 2X are to be carried out on the engines quoted each time it is stopped for X examination and repair. The principle of this examination is that at the periods stated below, the locomotive shall be given a thorough and detailed examination and repair so that it will run to the next X repair day with the absolute minimum of intermediate repairs. The general procedure should be as follows:

General Examination
On arrival on the Shed of an engine which is due for X examination, the engine must be given a thorough general examination and steam test, and all steam leakages, part loose and other defects noted on the X repair card, ERO 53927. All repair cards which have been put in for the particular engine under examination since the previous X examination must be scrutinised by the Foreman Fitter or leading Fitter and any repetition extracted onto ERO 53927, for special attention. When the examinations shown in this circular are carried out at each X repair and all repairs or other items booked on their X repair card have been completed. The engine must be given a thorough inspection by the Foreman Fitter, leading Fitter or his representative, to ensure that all repairs have been carried out efficiently and that the engine is in good condition. X scheme examinations must be carried out at periods not exceeding those shown below.

When an engine is washed out an X scheme examination must always be done.

Passenger Engines	
Class 7. 4-6-2, 6p 5xp	6-8 days
All the passenger engines	12-16 days
Freight engines	
All freight tender engines	12-16 days
Freight tank engines used for passenger or freight trains	12-16 days
All other freight tank engines used for freight shunting work	24-32 days

Shopping of Engines

As well as receiving regular maintenance on Shed, all engines were sent to the main Works for major overhauls, which ranged from light to heavy depending on the condition of the frames and boilers etc. The examiner had to fill in an especially large form in triplicate which required details of wheels and tyres, any cracks in the frames, the amount of wear between axle boxes and the horn cheeks etc. The time required to complete this form was dependent on the class of engine being examined.

This sensible approach to examining engines before sending them to the works was suggested by George Hughes when he came from the Lancashire & Yorkshire Railway to Crewe in 1922 but was rejected by the then Crewe hierarchy as not Crewe policy! At this time the L&Y works at Horwich was years ahead of L&NW Railway practice.

For Nottingham, in the Midland Division, the shopping proposal periods in months were as follows which, although laid down, could be extended if the engine was capable of further working or not able to find a space in the Works:

Plate 17

In this specially posed shot for a photo journal article *'Nottingham by Night'*, Fitter Herbert
Cook (kneeling) and Fitters Mate Herbert Tinsley are seen working on the right hand
crosshead nut of a Black Five 4-6-0

H Tinsley

Passenger Tender types:

Class 7P	8
Class 6P	8
Class 5X	10
Class 5	14
Class 4	15
Class 3 (Non standard types)	18
Class 2	24
Class 1 (Non standard types)	30

Passenger Tanks
Class 4	19
Class 3	21
Class 2	21
Class 1 (Non standard types)	24

Freight Tender and Tank engines
Class 8	20
Class 7	8
Class 5	21
Class 4	21
Class 4 (2-6-0)	24
Class 3 (Non standard types)	26
Class 2 (Freight tanks)	24
Class 3	30
Class 2	30
Class 1 (Non standard types)	30
Class 0	36

Nottingham engines went to various Works. These were Bow, Derby, Crewe, Darlington and Horwich.

Horwich was the furthest main Works to which Nottingham engines were sent. Some engines, such as the 4MT 'Moguls' which had been built at Horwich, and a few Class 8Fs and 4Fs went there. The actual location of an engine works visit was determined by the available space in the Works at that time and not where they had been built. This was also the case when engines went for scrap within the BR Works system. In BR days an engine was considered to have had a Heavy General Repair when two of the following conditions applied:

> Fitting new cylinders
> New tyres on four or more wheels
> Fitting new axle or axles in either engine or tender
> Re-tubing
> Motion and brake work stripped and overhauled or turning up wheels and re-fitting boxes
> Boiler repaired in frame with not less than 50 stays renewed.

The 3ft gauge engines at Beeston Creosote Works were also the responsibility of 16A but saw little maintenance whilst at Beeston. In April 1955 the Creosote Works 'Batley' 0-4-0ST engine No 10 which was built in 1929 by Bagnalls (Works No 2233) was in Derby Works for scrapping. Its replacement, in early 1956, was the Bagnall 3ft-gauge Saddle Tank No 1 which BR purchased specially for use at Beeston. This engine had Bagnall valve gear. Some of its later history was related to the author by the late Richard Hilton, who obtained the engine after its disposal by BR, which was in fact the second time he had owned it.

Plate 18
Bagnall 0-4-0 ST at Beeston Creosote Works
Bill Reed

Richard Hilton's Story

'The locomotive was given to me in 1948 by the owner of a Granite Quarry at Nuneaton, who was a family friend. Because of my service abroad as a pilot in the RAF I could not provide it with a home and I sold it to a London firm before it went to BR at the time of Suez. [This would make it 1956]

After retiring from the RAF, I contacted BR at Derby and met several of the staff who had worked on the engine during its works visits. It was out of service when Beeston Creosote closed and was purchased from a store in Cambridgshire. It was then in store for some years before I moved it to my home near Didcot'.

No 1 has been sold since the death of Richard Hilton. A 3ft gauge Bagnall 0-4-0ST No 1889 of 1911, it had spent 45 years at Judkins Limited, Tuttle Hill Granite Quarries, Nuneaton until arriving at Beeston in 1956 via M E Engineering, Cricklewood.

The engine was sold to S A Burgess of Haddenham near Ely in October 1962 and re-sold for preservation to Richard Hilton in 1972. This engine was the last one to be overhauled in the Nottingham 1868 repair shop and the first since the 1920s.

Plate 19
Saddle Tank No 1

Bill Reed

Locoshed Office Working

Much has been written about both footplate and fitting staff experiences in the steam years, but far less has been put in print regarding the activities of the office staff. Without the office staff the Shed could not function properly and as these extracts show the tasks were varied and endless. They are from the memoirs and diaries (unpublished) of Frank Eite who started in the office at 16A on 27th December 1957, having applied for a clerical job from the footplate grades (see appendix five for extracts from his footplate memories). These office work details show the procedures carried out behind the scenes and the staff involved in the Nottingham locoshed office. (Plate 20)

Amongst the office staff before Nationalisation were Clerks Roy Edwards and a Mr Bartle who during the Second World War worked as Fitters Mates on Sundays. Mr Bartle was also a local choirmaster. One of the first jobs undertaken by the office staff on a Monday morning was the analysis of the footplate staff's time cards for the previous week. This entailed the examination of the signing on and off times for the Friday and the working out of the total hours and minutes worked. All of the office staff were involved in completing the previous week's time cards for WE (Working Engines) and RE (Repairing Engines) staff. After 100 footplate staff cards had been completed, they would be sent to Derby Centralised Paybill Office (CPO) on the 09.30am train and a member of the WE staff (Ted Gent) would be on duty for the sole purpose of making the trips to Nottingham Station on Monday mornings. Ted was also responsible for progress chasing materials required by the fitting staff in which capacity he travelled to Derby Works and brought back what he could. The heavier items came by rail van and were unloaded in No 1 Shed. Before the footplate staff cards were sent to Derby, another function was calculating the amount due to staff for excessive mileage worked on the previous Friday and Saturday.

The mileage clerk would gather all the Drivers' daily duty tickets for the two days and sort them into seniority order for each day. Then, either from local knowledge or by consulting the WTT (Working Timetable), he would prepare a list of Drivers and Firemen who were due extra money. There was a scale laid down nationally from which the total miles could be translated into £.s.d and entered on the time cards. Different rates applied to Fitters who were paid double time for Sunday work and time and a third after 6pm. (5) Drivers were paid time and a quarter after 10pm and time and three quarters on a Sunday. The completed pay bills, showing the net pay for every man at the depot, would arrive back at the Depot Office on Thursdays. The Pay Bill Clerk, Herbert Dale, would then go through the whole pay bill finding out how many £5, £1 and ten shilling notes were required and also how many coins of each denomination. These were ordered from the Booking Office at Nottingham Station. Mr Dale would then go through the pay bills again and mark where the first bundle of £5 notes would run out and do likewise with the first bundle of £1 and ten shilling notes, repeating the process for all bundles. This served as a check at regular intervals to ensure that extra notes were not accidentally put in wage packets. The pay was made up and then paid out from the pay office in the stores corner of No 1 Shed. In 1964/65 all the Victorian sloping desks from 1868 in the main office, on which this work was carried out, together with the high chairs were overhauled by a carpenter and two french polishers from Derby.

Footnote 5   Before the 24-hour clock was introduced am was identified by a dot between the hours and minutes (eg 6.00), while for pm there was a forward slash (eg 6/00)

The Mahogany desks tops were reversed to hide the scratches and damage of nearly one hundred years use and then polished to a high finish to look as good as new. This took many months to complete and, with the Depot closing in 1966, seemed in retrospect a waste of time and effort. Plate 20 shows a view of some of the office staff and desks. The Driver's daily duty tickets detailed the workings of

Plate 20
Left to right, Ted Brett, Ken Waltho and Dennis Lill seen here in the main office. This office had a glass ceiling. The Midland Railway sloping desks can be seen

W Newton

each engine on a daily basis, and involved two types of action concerning distance travelled by engines. The first of these was carried out by the RE Shop Office Clerk, Harry Don, who calculated the total mileage for every engine from whatever depot it had been used. This was subsequently passed to Derby eventually to be aggregated by the Statistics Office. From here the details were sent back to the depots where the engines were allocated and, on a monthly basis, entered on the boiler cards for assessing when the next boiler washout was due.

As well as the weekly operations, other aspects of Shed life, such as eyesight tests and annual leave rosters, were also managed. For the practical eyesight test the Drivers were taken to Attenborough Junction where they were asked to read the position of the semaphore signals at Meadow Lane Junction (Long Eaton) which was situated at about 1000 yards to the West of Attenborough Junction. The Locomotive Inspector would ask the Signalman at Attenborough to contact the Signalman at Meadow Lane Junction to operate the signals as and when required. This section of line was chosen because it was straight and because the signals were situated fairly high up with just the sky in the background. There were three directional signals; one on the left for the Goods Line in front of the present Power Signal Box, middle for straight on to Trent Station and the one on the right for the low level line to the old Long Eaton Station and the Erewash Valley Line. (6) Tests were also carried out at the Medical Office, Derby for colour blindness. A book with pages covered in various coloured dots was used for

Footnote 6 The boundary between Derbyshire and Nottinghamshire and Erewash, supposedly meaning 'river of heroes' in pre-Saxon times

this purpose. A doctor would ask the Driver to say what number was represented by the dots. If he were not colour blind then a number would appear amongst the dots. If he was found to be colour blind then he would see an entirely different number.

The management was not particularly sympathetic to Drivers who failed with eyesight other than accommodating them within Union agreements. We recall Sid 'Trader' Horn, a mild man, telling how he realised his eyesight had deteriorated slightly over the years and how he went for his eyesight test and was expecting the worst. On reporting for duty next he was met by the Foreman who handed him a letter saying 'I know what's in the letter Sid and I am sorry'. Sid was no longer a main line Driver. Sid went on to be the Shed Driver who along with his Mate Frank Breffitt, a diabetic, worked closely with the Fitting Staff moving and setting engines, shunting the drop and assisting in picking winners. When Sid was required, you walked round the Shed asking, 'Anyone seen Trader?'

The inner office was also used for the Shed management to conduct disciplinary hearings when a breach of the rules had occurred. When a new manager took over and such hearings were organised the office would be smartened up and the miscreants 'wheeled in'. On one occasion a particularly fussy and keen manager was to interview a Driver attired in overalls with an old overcoat, muffler and dirty cloth cap. On being confronted by this apparition the manager said 'Don't you take your hat off when you come in front of me?' to which the Driver replied 'I didn't know I was coming in for a bloody haircut!' It was apparent that a sense of humour was essential in order to survive at Nottingham or any other locoshed.

Firing Inspectors were not left unscathed when it came to the receiving side of humourous comments as this tale related by Bill Davies illustrates. A set of Cockney men from Kentish Town Loco came onto the Shed and were joined by a Firing Inspector complete with bowler hat. These were invented c1850 by Edward Coke and known as a boiler front by ex-LNWR men. When the Fireman was observed hurling massive lumps of coal in the firebox the Inspector remarked to the Fireman that 'All coal should be broken up into orange sized lumps' to which the Fireman replied 'Don't worry guvnor these are Jaffas!'

The same Inspector had the habit of asking questions to which he already knew the answers. On passing St Albans one day he asked Fireman Dennis Langley 'Isn't that the Mental Institution over there?' to which Dennis replied 'No they have closed it, given them all bowler hats and called them Firing Inspectors'. Nottingham footplate men also had an expression concerning London-based crews which was 'You can always tell a Cockney, but not much!'

If a Driver was taken off main line duties and put into a side or shunting link due to a disability, then his rate of pay would be reduced by 10 shilling (50p). Considering that a Driver's basic pay was about £12 per week, this was a significant drop. If he was taken off the footplate completely, owing to a disability and allocated a job on Shed duties his new rate of pay would be called a Mean Rate, which consisted of half his Driver's rate and half of his new job on Shed. Annual leave for footplate staff would be spread over a period of 26 weeks. starting from the first week in April to the last week in September with approximately 20 Drivers and Firemen allocated to each fortnight. To make the system fair each block of men would be moved six weeks forward each year.

The promotion system for footplate staff was Cleaner to Passed Cleaner to Fireman to Passed Fireman and then Driver. After a Cleaner became a Passed Cleaner and a Fireman became a Passed Fireman, every turn of duty that they worked in the higher grade was recorded and the total built up until the number reached 313. This was equal to one year of firing in the case of the Passed Cleaner or driving in the case of a Passed Fireman. After 313 turns had been worked, which could take 2 to 4 years to achieve, they then became a Registered Fireman or a Registered Driver. When, after a long apprenticeship, the status of Driver was eventually achieved a Driver signed for each route that he was confident he knew in detail. This road knowledge was learnt by what was known as 'road learning' and was religiously kept up to date, especially if a Driver had not travelled a particular route for a long time

MIC - Mutual Improvement Classes

These were set up as a means whereby any member of the footplate staff could increase his knowledge of Rules and Regulations, Firing or Driving Techniques on how locomotives worked. Lectures were given by Footplate Inspectors, Firing Instructors, Maintenance Foremen, Boiler Foremen and by anyone else who wanted to give a lecture, many were as good as the instructors. After the lectures debates would take place. The meetings were usually held on Sunday mornings and those who attended did so entirely voluntarily. No payment was made but the knowledge gained would come in useful when being questioned by the Inspector, possibly the same one who gave a lecture. Quizzes, for which paid time off was allowed, between Motive Power Depots would be held on a regular basis (see Frank Eite's diaries Appendix 5) and occasionally between Signalmen on just Rules and Regulations. Visits were made to various BR Works one of which was Crewe. Plate 21 shows the MIC group in front of newly built repaired Britannia No 70024 Vulcan and Plate 22 shows Class 9F No 92137 under construction in June 1957.

Once a year the MIC Instruction Train would visit and was usually stabled outside No 2 Shed dead. It consisted of two ex-London & North Western Railway six-wheeled bogie coaches with the entrance doors slightly inset, with long brass handles. The first coach had benches mounted just below the windows running almost the whole of its length. On these benches were mounted locomotive components: Exhaust and Live Steam Injectors; Vacuum Ejectors; Sand Valves; Brake Valves; CWA valves etc; all sectioned with the steam, water and vacuum passages colour coded and gleaming from the years and years of polishing. There were also models of various types of locomotive valve gear that could be hand operated complete with facilities for notching up showing the reduced port openings. At the end of the coach was an entire loco front fitted with operational AWS (Automatic Warning System) which was used for instructional purposes. The Instructor who travelled with the coaches was Charlie Watson, an ex-Newton Heath man, Lancashire & Yorkshire Railway through and through. He was not only a good instructor and had patience but actively encouraged debates. Drivers, and Firemen such as Bernard Willis the secretary of the MIC and Bill Clark, 'Piston Bill', another active member of the MIC would come early or stay late on more than one day in the week. The second coach was fitted out as a cinema, two films shown were 'Wash and Brush Up' which showed how a loco was cleaned and the boiler washed out. The second was 'A Study In Steel', this was of the building of one of the LMS Princess Royal class locomotives.

When the lights went on Albert 'Barny' Rudge had gone to sleep. On waking him Albert said 'If you didn't put the lights out I wouldn't have to sleep'. It was a very hot day. Albert was always moaning but was a kindly soul who was always there to help and religiously arranged a collection for people who had been off eight weeks, in the days when sick pay was only £2 per week.

LECTURES 1954

Date	Subject	Speaker
Jan. 17th.	From Fireman to Driver.	Mr. E. Barber
Feb. 7th.	Some Rules for Discussion	Mr. C. Brown
March 7th		Mr. Daft
April 11th.	Failures and Remedies	Mr. Haines
May 9th	British Railways Standard 5	Mr. Fowkes
Oct. 10th.	Round the Wheel	Mr. Barber

Fig 4
MIC Lectures 1954
F Eite

Plate 21
MIC visit to Crewe Works with Britannia Pacific 70024 'Vulcan' outside the paint shop
Bill Reed

Plate 22
Nw BR Class 9F No 92137, MIC visit June 1957

Bill Reed

Chapter Three
The Fifties

Tony Hewitt, who during this period worked at both Toton and Nottingham, documented the 16A locomotive scene in the 1950s. These extracts are from the years 1953 and 1954. Other information referring to 16A locomotive activities in and around Nottingham have been collated from various sources. Of special mention are those of Roy Batson, who has been a keen observer of the railway scene for many years having been to the Midland Station nearly every day since 1947!

On 1st and 11th January 1953 Hasland based 0-4-0Ts Nos 41528 and 41523 were on Shed. A class that had once worked around the smaller sidings in the area, they were no longer to be seen working out of 16A but were sometimes observed whilst in transit to and from their home depot and Derby Works. Ex-MR 0-6-0T No 41885 with round top boiler was also on the Shed on the 19th of the month. When Notts County played Rhyl in the 3rd round of the FA Cup in January the special train from Wales was pulled by Royal Scot No 46139 'The Welch Regiment' the train was turned on the Lenton Triangle and the engine stood outside No 3 Shed (Plate 23). In the post war modification of these engines No 46139 was the first one to be fitted with rocker grates and ashpans and was a victim of the experimental livery fetish when it was painted apple green. By the way, Rhyl beat Notts County 3-1.

In February the ex-Glasgow Polmadie (66A), based Jubilee No 45560 'Prince Edward Island' that had transferred to Nottingham earlier in the 50s was seen ex-works in the new BR passenger green. It had been transferred whilst still painted LMS black. Photographs of this period show No 45560 with the Scottish Region tablet catcher bracket still fitted to the Driver's side of the cab. The transfer of No 45560 was part of a move designed to ease maintenance in that all Scottish Jubilees were to have the later batch of sloping throatplate boilers. Eventually, due to new boilers being constructed, there were only five of these in service. The engines involved in the exchange programme were: SCR to LMR 45560/64/75/76/77/79/80/81/82/83/84, 45643/44/45 and 46. LMR to ScR 45621/40 (ex-Nottingham), 57/65/73/77/79/87/96/97, 45704/07/11/18/20/24.

The only remaining Jubilee painted black and allocated to Nottingham at this time was No 45650 'Blake'. Straight throat plate boilers were also fitted to the first 10 Class 8F 2-8-0s Nos 8000 to 8010.

The spring of this year saw 16A BR Standard No 73017 on loan to the SR Shed at Nine Elms as a replacement for the SR Region Bullied Pacifics which had been temporarily withdrawn due to failures with flawed crank axles. The most spectacular of these was the breaking of an axle on No 35020 'Bibby Line' at Crewkerne.

In May the ER had taken over Lincoln St Mark's duties replacing the MR types with their own ex-GCR 'Directors' most of which were to be seen on 16A at some time or other and were worked on by Shed duty Fitters for what were known as running repairs. These engines were Nos 62660 'Butler Henderson' (now at the National Railway

Plate 23

The Royal Scot Class No 46139 'The Welch Regiment', which came to Nottingham in January 1953, outside No 3 Shed. Also seen in the shot is a MR Class 2P and an 0-6-0 3F

T G Hepburn

Plate 24
Ex-GCR Director 4-4-0 No 62666 'Zeebrugge' out of service outside No 2 Shed

C Beck

Museum), 62663 'Prince Albert', 62666 'Zeebrugge', 62667 'Somme' and 62670 'Marne'

May also saw the Derby-based un-rebuilt Patriot Class 6P5F No 45509, 'The Derbyshire Yeomanry', on Shed. On 15th June, rarities passing the Shed were No 45661 'Vernon' on a St Pancras to Edinburgh and No 46108 'Seaforth Highlander' on St Pancras to Bradford trains. At this time 40504 worked the Inspection train and was noted on this duty on 12th August. The 23rd August saw a rare visit from Reidinger valve gear fitted 'Crab' No 42825, most of which at one time were based at Burton-on-Trent. On the drop-pit, MR 0-6-0T No 41712 was keeping company with ex LTSR Whitelegg 3P No 41943. This engine was still out of service on 28th September and had been joined by sister engine No 41947. Due to their peculiar design features both footplate men and fitting staff disliked these engines.

No 41925 was in store for some time alongside the short-lived oil storage tanks.

Other ex pre-grouping types to be seen were LNWR Super D No 49368, ex-MR 0-4-4T No 58085 and 0-6-0 No 58137. September visitors included WD 2-8-0 'Austerity' No 90118, which was described as being in a filthy condition! However this was the usual state of these engines being a class that were particularly unloved and uncleaned. Other ER based engines that visited were Gresley K2s (known as 'Ragtimers' due to their noisy connecting rods and motion) amongst which were Nos 61765 and 61767, both Lincoln engines.

The new Standard 5s Nos. 73000 and 73002 were also on Shed on the 10th October. Fowler, 0-8-0 No 49582 was seen on the 24th together with ex works Fairburn 2-6-4T No 42181.

When first built these Standard 73XXX Class Five engines were fitted with the GWR type regulator controlled atomiser for cylinder lubrication. This was provided with a gauge to tell the Driver 'No Oil' or 'Oil'. In service it was found to be unsatisfactory due to excessive ring wear. The reason for this was that Drivers could see the mechanical lubricator handle turning so did not leave the regulator open slightly to operate the atomiser valve. To overcome this problem the LMR type atomiser controlled from the cylinder cocks was substituted.

On 16th January 1954 both No 45611 'Hong Kong' and Burton based 1P No 58087 were to be seen sharing the drop pit along with ex-MR 0-4-4T No 58056. The following day Mr E Barber held the first of the Mutual Improvement Classes, the subject being 'From Fireman to Driver' the full list of lectures up until October can be seen in Fig 4. On 7th March No 62666 was on Shed as well as the push-pull fitted No 58085. The following week, ex-L&NWR No 49249 and two ex-20G engines Nos. 58075 and

Plate 26
Ex-MR 0-6-0 No 58133 entering No 1 Shed in September 1954

MRT

Plate 27
A group of men discuss engine movements inside No 3 Shed. A very atmosperic scene with class 2Ps and Black Fives looking on

T Hewitt

58056 were seen alongside stored No 58137. On the 21st the following ex-MR type passenger engines were on Shed: Nos. 40395, 40450, 40454, 40458, 40487, 40493 and 40504 (all 2Ps) Nos. 40900, 41082, 41144, 41181 and 41185 (Compounds), 0-6-0T No 47631 (Plate 31) and 0-4-4T No 58085.

Also to be seen were the snow plough fitted 8F No 48157 and the high sided tender fitted 4F No 44578 along with ex-LNER J39 0-6-0 No 64981 (known as Ukuleles).

In March the sole surviving Nottingham based 1F No 20185 (Plate 7) was on Shed along with Jubilees Nos. 45694 'Bellerophon', 45611 'Hong Kong', 45576 'Bombay' and 45648 'Wemyss'

On 1st April Caprotti Black Five No 44746 and the two BR standards Nos 73000/73002 were on Shed with Jubilees Nos 45554 'Ontario' 45611 'Hong Kong' and 45619 'Nigeria'. Note: These early Caprotti Black Fives had inside drive to the valve gear and were sluggish engines until running fast, whereas the final two Caprotti Black Fives Nos. 44686/87 had outside drive valve gear and were very strong engines

The ex-MR Class 2 Passenger engines were still being overhauled and on the 3rd March No 40553 was seen on Shed in ex-works condition, a magnificent sight. Other engines such as Nos 40088 and 41096 were to be seen in store alongside the Outdoor Machinery Department, perhaps waiting for a Works visit. Another ex-MR engine, No 58133 can

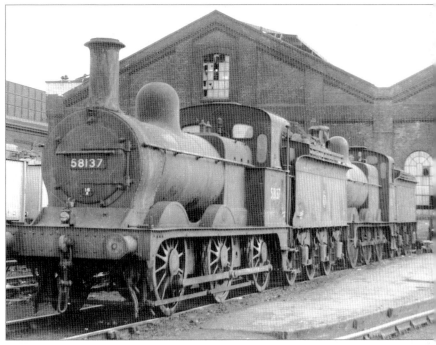

Plate 28
Ex-MR 0-6-6 Class 2F No 58137 and Class 3f 43369 outside No 2 Shed out of service

Tony Hill

be seen in Plate 26 where it is entering No 1 Shed in September 1954. The picture clearly shows the Cast Iron 'STOP' plate outside the entrance to the Shed. This scene is interesting for its detail. The Fireman has just removed the bucket and shovel for taking to the stores and his right arm can just be seen unscrewing the tender brake. The building jutting out to the left of No 58133 is No 2 Shed, the window being the outside of the Mechanical Foreman/Clerks Office and Fitters lobby. Built in 1877 this stood close to the location where the second exit/entrance road was situated when No 1 Shed had been built in 1868 (see Volume 1). A motorcycle shed was later erected in front of this window.

On May 9th ex-LNER K2 No 61743 was on the Shed for attention on the drop-pit. The same day the ex-MR engines Nos 58087 / 58137 and 43369 were in store. The 16th saw WD 2-8-0 No 90156 and a companion for the K2 on the wheel drop, ex-MR 4F No 43998 from 18D (Staveley). In late May and early June No 3 Shed was to fill up with visiting 5Xs (6P) Jubilees for the annual Raleigh Works Outing trains. These were a regular event at this time of the year with additional 6P power having to be borrowed for the jobs. These extra engines were needed to work up to 11 special trains which transported the nearly 8000 employees of Raleigh Industries. Arrangements for these extra engines were made through Derby Control and came from various depots.

Fowler Class 7F 0-8-0 No 49659

Plate 29

T Hewitt

For the 1954 visit to Blackpool there were eight trains and the engines allocated were 45569 'Tasmania', 20A Leeds Holbeck, 45576 'Bombay', 19B Millhouses, 45616 'Malta GC', 14B Kentish Town, 45636 'Uganda', 16A 45664 'Nelson', 19B 45667 'Jellicoe', 16A 45675 'Hardy', 20A 45699 'Galatea', and 22A Bristol Barrow Road. As a Nottingham engine at the end of 1946, 'Galatea' would have been returning to familiar territory. Fortunately it has survived into preservation, albeit now in a derelict state. It can be seen that only two Nottingham Jubilees were available for these specials, due to most of the 16A allocation being out on normal passenger duties. A feature of the trips that went to Blackpool was that of the Raleigh Directors seeing each train off to its destination and being there to greet them on arrival. This kind of planning could be accomplished in those days because of the numbers of routes that were available, with clever diagramming ensuring everything went to plan. Times have certainly changed and today this could not take place as most of the duplicate routes have closed along with Blackpool Central Station into which many happy holidaymakers were delivered. Before leaving the Shed all engines had to be examined with smokebox headboards fitted and all were well cleaned.

Although much time had already been spent at the Shed getting these engines ready, a Fitter and Mate had to be on duty at the station. The very atmospheric view of No 3 Shed in Plate 27 shows a group of men at the end of the turntable discussing these specials. The scene is full of detail with shafts of sunlight splitting the gloom of the Shed. A Driver, Dad Stevo, and his Fireman talk to an Inspector, whilst in the background a couple of Black Fives and a Class 2P quietly await their next turn of duty. The doorway on the far wall is the entrance to the Footplate Staff Messroom.

June 1954 also saw No 58137 out with the Inspection train and one year later was in store out of service (Plate 28) also the Compound No 41185 was seen with the 6 coach CTAC 'Scottish Tours Express'.

Nottingham engines were also used for specials outside the Division and on Thursday 5th February 1953 No 45560 'Prince Edward Island' was recorded at Edinburgh Princes Street station on one of the specials from Wales for the biennial Scotland v Wales rugby game. This engine was returning to familiar ground having been a Scottish engine before transferring to 16A in August 1952. The 20th June ex-GCR 4-4-0 No 62666 was on Shed and reportedly in a deplorable condition, as were many Trafford Park and Cricklewood engines at this time.

On the drop-pit was No 41078 (22B) and keeping it company outside No 2 Shed were Nos.43060 (35B), 42093 (21A) and 73049 (15C). At this time the last Nottingham based 2P with the LMS legend on its tender was No 40395, which was awaiting scrapping.

The 27th of June saw Longsight (9A) Black Five No 45113 on Shed with the MR Class 3F No 43369 continuing in store, although No 58133 was back in service. Other engines on Shed at this time were No 78020 (15B), round top boiler, No 41682, one of the Fowler 0-8-0 Austin 7s (Plate 29) and No 49451 (8A) (Plate 30) an ex-LNWR Super D 0-8-0 a class. Due to the restricted clearance on the footplate, these were known as Knuckle Crackers by Firemen. Sid Hill relates a story of when he was an Apprentice with Frank Mumby on the drop-pit when a Super D had to be tackled. The very thin flanged, 'e' profile, driving wheels had to be removed in order to deal with a

Plate 30
LMS rebuilt LNWR Super D 0-8-0-7F No 49451

C Beck

hot box and were particularly difficult to get into the wheel shop and on one occasion a set fell into the pit! Super D side rods were also very heavy and long. The trick was to use the drop-pit to lift the rods with packing. Later, in BR days, Riddles Standard Class 9Fs were flangeless on the driving wheels. Austerities also presented the same problems as Super 'D' engines in having thin-flanged driving wheels and heavy side rods (4 sections each side on a 9F).

In early July, Caprotti Black Five No 44756 was on Shed along with high sided tender fitted 4F No 44578 and a trio of BR Standard Fives Nos 73000/73002 and 73010. The drop pit was occupied by Class 2P No. 40504 and Compound No 41078 (22B). This three cylinder 4-4-0 must have failed in traffic, with 16A having the nearest repair facilities. These ex-MR type engines suffered from hot boxes, especially the trailing driving wheels. It was a long time before it was found that dirt was dropping onto the

Plate 31

LMS 0-6-0T 'Jocko' No 47631 in the Shed yard on the field side with Middle Furlong Road in the background

C Beck

journals when the wheels had been refitted after repairs to previous hot boxes or even works visits! As a consequence of this discovery the inside frames of these engines were always cleaned before the wheels were replaced.

A record of a visit to the Shed on 22nd August 1954 can be seen at Appendix B.

In May 1954 the late Tony Hill, a local enthusiast who photographed extensively in and around Nottingham, made a visit to the Southwell Branch, which was being worked by the ex-MR No 58085 with shunting being carried out by 'Jocko' 0-6-0T 47539 (Plate 33). On 8th of May an Eastern Region locomotive, Class B12 No 61554, was used to work the RCTS Nottingham to Horwich Works special and was in the charge of Driver Whitmoor.

Two views of Class 8F No 48305 can be seen in Plates 34 and 35 taken forty years apart. Although not a Nottingham engine, the earlier photograph shows Nottingham Fitter, Joe Vickers, sitting on the front of this engine outside No 1 Shed in the summer of 1954. Joe Vickers has retired and lives at Eastwood, Notts. 48305 was one of those engines that took part in the only major experiment with this class, which was the fitting of manual blow down valves to the boilers. Appendix 9 gives details of these engines. No 48305 has an interesting history with regard to boiler changes and the boiler it now

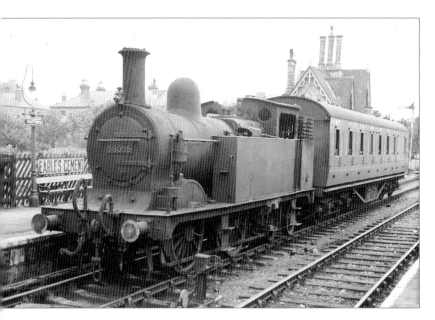

Plate 32
Push and Pull fitted ex-MR 0-4-4T No 58085 seen here at Southwell

G Kay

carries is ex-8644. The data on these items was kept on the Boiler /Tender record cards that were either side of a single document.

A manual blowdown valve was a device that allowed the boiler to be emptied into a special collecting pipe by the operation of a lever in the cab or at the side of the firebox. This device contrasts with a continuous blowdown valve fitted on the boiler, which was located in the cab. A CBV operated automatically when the engine was working and continually discharged a small amount of water and scum from the boiler onto the track.

In 1947, fifty LMS Class 8F locomotives were fitted with manual boiler blowdown valves in connection with water treatment experiments. These fifty engines were based at Toton and Wellingborough. 8305 was one of those chosen for the trials and by shear coincidence, when withdrawn from service in 1968, the engine survived with a similarly modified boiler. Whilst in service with the manual blow down all these engines had a large 'X' painted on the cab side below the engine number.

The boiler history of 8305

Number and Works Date		Boiler Built	Where fitted	Ex-Locomotive number
11566	Crewe	10/11/43	Crewe	New
X9593	Crewe	13/10/48	Vulcan Foundry	8037/8048
X11456	Derby	21/04/53	Gorton	8699/8635
X1178	Derby	21/10/58	Eastleigh	644/8645

No 48305 is now based at Cheddleton in Staffordshire.

A list of manual blowdown 8Fs
Nos 8024, 8037, 8050, 8075 and 8082
8112, 8117, 8178, 8180, 8181, 8182 and 8198
8204, 8221, 8222, 8264 and 8281

Plate 33
Ex-LMS 0-6-0T No 47539 at Southwell, note the high coal rails

Tony Hill

8304, 8305, 8334, 8338, 8359, 8360, 8361, 836, 83/63, 8364, 8365, 8371, 8374 and 8384
8492
8617, 8618, 8636, 8638, 8644, 8651, 8662, 867, 8672, 8678, 8681, 8684, 8685, 8692,
8694, 8695 and 8699.

1954 saw the repair of No 1 Shed roof and a continuing reduction in the ex-MR Class
2P engines, a class that had used the Shed for eighty years in both re-built and original
form. These were now reduced to eight. They were 40411, 40454, 40458, 40487, 40493,
40504, 40535 and 40553. In 1892 twenty 4-4-0s had worked out of Nottingham and by
1920/21 the number had risen to 32. By 1945 it had dropped to 13.

One unusual locomotive to be withdrawn was the 1924 built Bagnall narrow gauge
(3ft) 0-4-0ST No 10 which had been purchased from Messrs Twigg of Matlock in 1945.
They had previously bought it from the Admiralty. Whilst dealing with narrow gauge
matters, it was on 20th February 1955 that Charles Farr, who later became the
Foreman Boilersmith at Nottingham, went to Boston Lodge on the Festiniog Railway in
the company of J M Dunn in order to examine the boilers of all the locomotives. To
quote Dunn from his book *'Reflections on a Railway Career'*, they found 'a remarkable
state of affairs with No 1, 'Welsh Pony', 'Taliesin' and No10 'Merddin Emrys' all exactly as
they had been left over eight years previously'.

28th May 1955 was the start of a bad year for the railway industry, when 67,000 members of the footplate union the Associated Society of Locomotive Engineers & Firemen (ASLEF) went on strike. This action was created by the gradually erosion of Drivers' wages compared to other industries. This became known as the 'Differential Strike' and was to last until 14th June. This costly and damaging strike eventually led to a Driver's wage rising to £10-18s 6d per week.

On the 24th September the Class 5 X Jubilee 2 45659 'Drake' was transferred to 16A.

The Royal Visit

On 5th July 1955 Her Majesty the Queen visited Nottingham. The Royal Train was pulled by two Black Fives Nos 44943 and 45274, both of 20A Leeds Holbeck (Plate 36). The latter engine had been involved in the Sutton Coldfield accident in January and was ex-works at the time. The empty stock was worked by a Nottingham 8F No 48709 whose Driver was Les Neil. The

Plate 34
Joe Vickers seated on No 48305 at Nottingham in 1954. The entrance to No 2 Shed is in the background

Joe Vickers

train was working under a passenger headcode, which was correct for Royal Train empty stock. Les Neil was one of those footplate men who did not make it to retirement as he died in his early 50s. The management, footplate crews and their families took the opportunity to have their photograph taken in a posed shot outside the Shed offices near No 1 Shed (Plate 37). Both engines had been turned in order to face the correct direction for travelling to London St Pancras via Melton Mowbray. At St Pancras the crews were relieved and the engines went on to Kentish Town Shed. (6)

Driver Tom King of Bristol Barrow Road, who died in June 2002 aged 103, narrated a story about No 45274 to Roy Williams in Midland Record No 15. He had worked the 2.15 Bristol Temple Meads to York as far as Birmingham New Street. The engine had astonished him by its performance, being deceptively fast. On 17th January 1955 he actually arrived at New Street Station five minutes in front of his booked time. The following Monday he arrived at work to find that 45274 had been involved in an accident at Sutton Coldfield on the previous day, Sunday 23rd January.

Footnote 6 Information from Frank Brunton.

On that day, a conductor had taken the York to Bristol express at Burton-on-Trent as the train was to be diverted onto the L&NW line from Wichnor Junction to Lichfield due to engineering works at Tamworth. The de-railment took place on the section through the 300 yard tunnel leading to Sutton Coldfield Station, which was limited to 30mph. From details supplied by Tom King about the engine, the conductor might have been misled by the deceptive ride of the engine and taken the curve too fast. Unfortunately, both the conductor and the Gloucester Fireman died along with fifteen others. The engine was dragged to Aston Shed and then to Crewe Works in the early hours of the 27th January.

Nottingham was still the home of a few Compounds at this time, some of which were either allocated, like No 40900, or visitors such as No 40907 of 19B Millhouses, which had failed in traffic. Engines that had failed in traffic were sometimes stored on the dead ends before their fate was decided. No 40900 can also be seen (Plate 38) in a very dilapidated state with bent front framing and excessive limescale on the boiler and framing. At the back of No 40900 was the ex-MR 0-6-0 No 58137, which, from its white wheels, had probably been working the water softening plant/sludge dumping train to Attenborough. The significant event of November this year was the publication of the BTC Modernisation Plan. It was this £1,240 million plan that accelerated change on Britain's railways and it was the rush towards dieselisation, along with the unforeseen consequences of changing transport patterns that was to bring about the end of steam in under 13 years.

Plate 35
Joe Vickers on the same engine at the GCR Loughborough in 1995

Jim Perkins

1956 and 1957

The straight sided tender fitted Jubilee No 45612 of 14B (Kentish Town) (Plate 39) and the Leeds Holbeck (55A) based Caprotti Black Five No 44754 (Plate 40) were regular visitors at this time. Another infrequent visitor was the Stanier 2-6-0 Mogul No 42946 of Crewe South (5B). (Plate 41) A local engine at the time LMS Class 2P No 40685, can be seen in Plate 42 being coaled at the old coaling stage on 8th May 1956. This engine was soon to move on and was to be based at 24H Hellified from Jan 1957 until its withdrawal in July 1961.

In December of 1956, the District Motive Power Superintendent, Mr S Audinwood, advised those Firemen who were involved with the MIC, that a competition would be held at Derby 9th Jan 1957. (Fig 5)

Plate 36
Royal train engines Black Fives Nos 44943 and 45224

F Brunton

Plate 37
No 44943 and group of Shed staff and wives

F Brunton

Comments were made in the March 1957 Trains Illustrated (page 207) regarding the ageing Midland Region locomotive stock. It was pointed out that had the post-war LMS re-building policy of upgrading 5X (6P) Jubilees to 7P like Nos 45735 'Comet' and 45736 'Phoenix', Nottingham engines would have been able to run a faster

Plate 38

Ex-LMS Compound No 40900. Note the damaged framing and boiler scale

Tony Hill

service to London St Pancras. Although Jubilee No 45722 'Defence' had been tested on the Rugby Testing Station in the following year in both single and double chimney forms, any results gleaned did not make a difference to the rest of the fleet. Only 45596 'Bahamas' was to work on into eventual preservation with a double chimney. In 1957 the new schedules were equal to those of 1938 but with much heavier loads and inferior coal. This resulted in much piloting of Jubilees with ex-Midland Railway Class 2P and Compounds 4-4-0s plus Class Fives of both LMS and BR variety. At this time a couple of extra mileage Jubilee workings were as follows: Nottingham depart 6.40 to St Pancras then take 7.10 return 'Waverley' to Leeds, return to St Pancras and then to Nottingham. This diagramming went into a three-day cycle. The other working followed another route and went from Nottingham to St Pancras then on to Sheffield, then to Derby, working to home on the 1.32am Derby to Nottingham local. Most of Nottingham's passenger engines were out at the weekend and a Sunday visitor could be forgiven for thinking that 16A was mainly a freight depot as most engines on Shed were 4Fs and 8Fs.

As a result of the Jubilees not being rebuilt or fitted with double chimneys, and with the continuing need for double heading, it was in late 1959 and early 1960 that Class 7P power locomotives were transferred to Nottingham. These were: rebuilt Patriot Class 4-6-0 No 45532 'Illustrious'. In its original form, this engine was nominally a replacement for ex-LNWR 'Claughton' Class 4-6-0 No 6011,

Plate 39
Kentish Town (14B) Jubilee No 45612 'Jamaica' outside the ODM. Note the high sided narrow tender, a 3500 gallon Stanier type

B Morrison

Rebuilt Royal Scot Class 4-6-0:
No 46100 'Royal Scot' originally 46152 when it was built, it swapped numbers in 1933
No 46112 'Sherwood Forester'
No 46118 'Royal Welch Fusilier'
No 46140 'The Kings Royal Rifle Corps'
No 46157 'The Royal Artilleryman'

No 46140, was only at Nottingham for a few weeks as it was swapped for No 46112. The last of these engines No 46157 'The Royal Artilleryman' had been involved in the Bourne End accident of 3rd September 1945. When the Class 45s were seen at Nottingham they initially worked almost the same diagrams as the Black Fives, Jubilees and Scots.

18th March saw the D16 4-4-0 No 62571 working the Derby-Nottingham-Lincoln service, a class of Motive Power that was very rare in Nottingham. In this year the RCTS special went to York and was worked by this same engine in both directions with Driver G Kelsey and Fireman Ken Wilcox. Another rare visitor in September was named Black Five Class 5MT No 45154 'The Lanarkshire Yeomanry' (Plate 43)

The passenger loading book of 1956-57, the Brown Book, listed the loads for

Plate 40
Caprotti Black Five No 44754 in No 3 Shed, a Leeds Hobeck 55A engine
Tony Hewitt

Nottingham to St Pancras trains in XL timings. The timings were allowed for those trains with two of the heavier BR coaches in the formation. These trains could be piloted to keep to these XL timings, when a Class 2P or Compound was used.

5X (Jubilee) 300 tons, 5 (Black Five) 255 tons and Compound 220 tons.

When the BR Standard Class 4 75XXX came out they were used on some of these services. However if they ran at speeds over 70 mph the boiler tried to leave the frames due to poor balancing. As a result, the Local District Committee (LDC) succeeded in having these engines taken off these duties. (7) The Class 5 73XXX were also tried with similar results however these went back into the works for re-balancing and this cured the problem. The 75XXX class did not receive this treatment. If no pilot was available on these XL limit workings the Driver could book 'insufficient power' as the reason for any lost time. On one occasion, on 17th August 1959, a Saltley 2-6-0 'Crab' 42791 worked the 00.20 Nottingham to St Pancras and only dropped 15 minutes on the timing, which was a very good performance. Another Birmingham 'Crab' working was the Newark pick-up freight, the engine being utilised whilst waiting for a return working to Saltley. (8)

This class of engine was to be transferred away from Nottingham by early 1959, having

Footnote 7 The LDC system was started in 1922 /23 as a result of the appalling staff and management relationship revealed by the 1919 footplate staff strike.
Footnote 8 Information from Bill Reed and P Holmes.

Plate 41

One of a class that was an infrequent visitor to Nottingham, the Stanier 2-6-0 Mogul No 42946 seen on the 2nd August 1956

Tony Hewitt

Plate 42

LMS Class 2P No 40685 being coaled at the No 1 Shed coal stage

Tony Hewitt

been allocated to the depot since their introduction in 1926. However in 1961/1962 they returned with Nos 42756, 42763, 42769, 42784, 42799, 42826, 42839, 42855, 42872, 42896, 42997 and 42922 arriving. These engines had a very large taper cotter through their return arm cranks, items that could prove difficult if the return arm had moved on the square crank pin end and become necked ie out of line. This happened on 42763, which meant the wheels went out to Derby Works for a new crank pin to be fitted. Ron Bowler once made a taper reamer to clean one of these holes. He started by machining a blank from a piece of steel bar, turned a taper, machined the flutes and finished it by hardening and grinding. Considering the machine tools available it was an example of what could be achieved if you had the skill and knowledge. These 2-6-0s were strong machines, although working at only 180-psi boiler pressure, and were used on

Plate 43

A very rare visitor to 16A, Black Five No 45154 'The Lanarkshire Yeomanry' seen in September 1957 along with Jubilee 45560 'Prince Edward Island' and an LMS built Class 2P

D Murdock by courtesy of Mrs Murdock & coptright Middle Furlong Press

many seaside specials. The cab seats were large wooden mushrooms, very plain but reasonably comfortable. Along with the Class 4Fs 0-6-0s they were the last representatives of the old order in motive power terms and were slowly supplanted by the later LMS and BR types their work finally being taken over by the Type 2 diesels.

Shed visits in 1957 can be seen at Annex C.

Boundaries

Although the railways were Nationalised on 1st Jan 1948, the old regions and practices were still much in evidence until the middle of the 1950s. In 1957 a process was started called 'Elimination of Penetrating Lines'. Whereas lines had previously been LMS, ER, SR or WR they then became part of the regions in which they were located. Some former LMS lines such as those to Lincoln, Leeds, Sheffield, Glasgow, Carlisle, Yarmouth and Peterborough passed to Eastern Region control and those in Bristol to the Western Region. When the new arrangements came into operation Nottingham lost some destinations in other regions and in turn became responsible for Nottingham Victoria,

Colwick, Kirkby Bentick, Queens Walk, Nottingham and all the old GNR/GCR from Shirebrook to Leicester. The new boundary points for the LMR became Horns Bridge, Staythorpe, Aslockton, Barnt Green, Ketton and Shirebrook.

1958 and 1959

Railway operations were always subject to accidents and breakdowns. The minor occurrences in this series of reports starting on 29th March 1958 (9) where a coupling broke at low speed in Ambergate Station. This shows the type of correspondence that had to be entered into for any abnormal occurrence. The train appears to be a racecourse special from Lincoln, whose Racecourse has long gone, to Aintree for the build up to the Grand National meeting. This involved the now preserved No 44806 (16A) and No 44818, with Nottingham Driver Iowle (whose son was an Apprentice at 16A) and Derby Driver Radford. Correspondence on this rumbled on until 6th May.

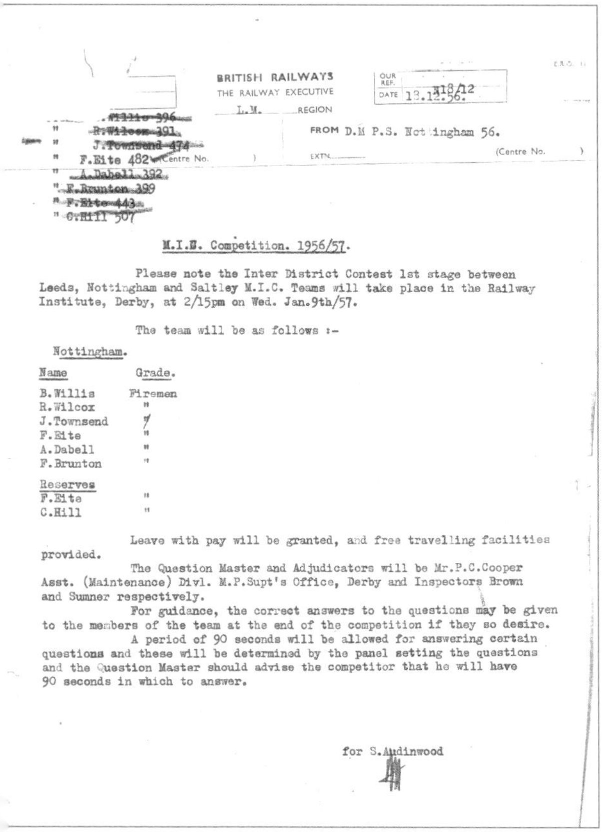

BRITISH RAILWAYS
THE RAILWAY EXECUTIVE
L.M. REGION

OUR REF. 318/12
DATE 13.12.56.

FROM D.M P.S. Nottingham 56.
EXTN. (Centre No.)

~~B. Willis 396~~
" ~~R. Wilcox 391~~
" ~~J. Townsend 474~~
" F.Eite 482 (Centre No.)
" ~~A. Dabell 392~~
" ~~F. Brunton 399~~
" ~~F. Eite 443~~
" ~~C. Hill 507~~

M.I.E. Competition. 1956/57.

Please note the Inter District Contest 1st stage between Leeds, Nottingham and Saltley M.I.C. Teams will take place in the Railway Institute, Derby, at 2/15pm on Wed. Jan.9th/57.

The team will be as follows :-

Nottingham.

Name	Grade.
B.Willis	Firemen
R.Wilcox	"
J.Townsend	"
F.Eite	"
A.Dabell	"
F.Brunton	"
Reserves	
F.Eite	"
C.Hill	"

Leave with pay will be granted, and free travelling facilities provided.

The Question Master and Adjudicators will be Mr.P.C.Cooper Asst. (Maintenance) Divl. M.P.Supt's Office, Derby and Inspectors Brown and Sumner respectively.

For guidance, the correct answers to the questions may be given to the members of the team at the end of the competition if they so desire.

A period of 90 seconds will be allowed for answering certain questions and these will be determined by the panel setting the questions and the Question Master should advise the competitor that he will have 90 seconds in which to answer.

for S.Audinwood

Fig 5
MIC competition

F Elite

At the other end of the locomotive scale a new narrow gauge 0-4-0 diesel engine ED10 was delivered to Beeston Creosote Works in May 1958 to work alongside saddle tank No 1. These engines were used to push narrow gauge bogie bolsters, known as trams, loaded with new sleepers around the creosote works where they were then immersed in hot creosote under pressure. The possibility of using diesels at this site was first mentioned in the Midland Railway minutes of 17 July 1919 (Vol II p 30). ED10 was built by Ruston & Hornsby (Type 48DS) No 411322 in 1958.

A photograph by George Heiron in 1958 shows two 16A men waiting for the road with Black Five No 44943 (Plate 44); Driver Sam 'Fiddler' Leah, so called beacuse he played the violin, whom we met in Volume II, and Ken 'Voodoo' Archer. Ken later left the footplate due to ill health and died whilst working as a number checker, a job that TOPS subsequently appears to have made redundant, in Nottingham Carriage Sidings Shunters Cabin.

The train shown was the return working lodge job ex 9.45pm Nottingham Yard to

Footnote 9 Authors' collection. See also Appendix 9

Birmingham, which was later extended to (Bristol) Westerleigh. This became one of the longest freight workings in the country. The return working was from Bristol-Birmingham-Derby-Sheffield-Leeds-Carlisle. Nottingham men were supposed to be relieved at Derby St Marys Goods but this usually happened at Derby Station. The unofficial arrangement was that the train came to a stand at No 1 platform with the relieving men walking up to the engine. At this time the Nottingham men were ready to rush off either to the 'Brunswick' or the 'Widows', opposite the station, and have a quick pint. On this lodge job the guards would not lodge at the appointed place in Bristol, the Redlands, and insisted on separate lodgings. Some of the guards were a bit choosy and nothing would suit them. This job only lasted six months until the diesels came in and was lost due to insufficient Nottingham men signing for the road. Saltley (21A) men were not happy to lose this job to Nottingham men in the first place and it caused much friction between the Union branches. The time off Shed at Bristol Barrow Road coincided with the 'Cornishman' passing up the bank and was apparently a real spectacle with the usual GWR 4-6-0 'Castle Class' at the head. 'Fiddler' Sam was one of five brothers who worked on the railway. Three of these were Drivers, one a Guard and one a Fitter. Sam was in the Express Link and his brothers Ray and Les were in the Freight Link. Norman was the Guard and Bill the Fitter. On the day of the photograph, his brother Ray, of 18B, took the train up the Erewash Valley Line, after relieving Sam. Earlier in his career Sam had achieved the fastest journey time with a Compound on a St Pancras-Nottingham Express. (10).

October 1958 saw Annesley engines No 61975 and O4/8 Nos 63579, 63752 and 63792 on the Shed for mileage repairs. One of the O4s (63792) was split from its tender in No 1 Shed and a large ring spanner had to be made to fit the nut on the draw bar at the tender end. It was flame cut from plate and had a rope attached for five or six men to pull on in order for the nut to be released. This kind of draw bar fitting was an ER and Bullied feature and was not as solid as the LMS two pin type, where the engine and tender were pushed together or pulled together with a large 'G' cramp and the pin dropped in. When the ER type of draw bar became worn and loose it gave a rough ride especially on unbalanced types like Austerities, and the nut could also come off. This happened to an early Britannia, a class that had the ER feature when first built, but these were later modified to the LMS pattern, as were all new builds.

A large number of Annesley O1s & O4s occasionally came onto 16A. Those known were Nos 63578, 63579, 63591, 63610, 63676, 63689, 63711, 63740, 63752, 63777, 63789, 63792, 63796, 63806, 63808, 63817, 63838, 63854, 63865, 63867, 63869, 63886 and 63901.

All were withdrawn between 28th October 1962 and 17th November 1962. A feature of the GCR 2-8-0s was the loose axlebox brass, which enabled a skilled Fitter to remove, re-metal and refit a worn, tight or run out brass in less than an hour! This was achieved by the use of a small wheel drop, a device peculiar to all ex-GCR Sheds, onto which an engine was run and the offending wheel set dropped down. By using the adjustable wedges to hold the box, the brass could be lifted out and worked on.

This novel approach seems to have been a boon to running Shed Fitters and Shed End Foremen who had to supply engines to work the intense coal traffic originating from the Nottinghamshire and Derbyshire coalfield, and then working to Colwick Yard, Woodford Halse and Whitemoor. A hot box failure on other classes meant a visit to

Footnote 10 Keith Leah, *'Bingley & Steam World'* March 1990.

the drop-pit, or shear legs in earlier days, an example of which lasted at Toton until the end of steam, and many hours work, depending on the severity of the journal damage. Even the mighty 9Fs occasionally suffered hot boxes on the Annesley to Woodford windcutters even though they had large bearings plus pumped lubrication.

As mentioned previously, when these needed attention the centre flangeless driving wheels were a particular problem to handle when removed and it was a bit of a balancing act to get them safely into the drop-pit workshop. K3 No 61975, a 'Jazzer', was the first locomotive many of us had seen that was fitted with a marine type middle big end and derived valve gear. This engine had come onto the drop-pit for attention to a driving wheel hotbox, which meant that the middle big end had to be dismantled. Midland/LMS engines had the strap type inside big end, where adjustment was taken up by a glutplate and wedge, but whichever type had to be dealt with they were heavy! Another notable item on LNER Class B1 engines were the hornstays which had 8 bolts compared to the normal 4 bolt LMS/BR horn stays. Also something that seemed strange was that the wartime built LNER locomotives such as B1s had used white metalled solid brass axle boxes, when materials were in short supply. The LMS type, based on GWR practice, were cast iron with white metalled brass inserts pressed in and seemed to be just as durable but lighter, cheaper and easier to handle. From 1944 the LMS started to fit hornguides thrust faces with manganese liners. This design change, based on London Underground experience, allowed engines to run between shopping periods without the wear that was normally found in these components.

Plate 44
Driver Sam Leah and Ken Archer with Black Five No 44943 at Bristol

G Hieron (K Leah)

Working in a Hot Place!

The centre rocking grate section on a 9F is probably the heaviest piece of cast iron on a British steam locomotive that was not bolted on. The grate itself comprised a number of smaller elements that were fitted onto bars that ran across the firebox from either side. A 2-6-4T would have elements that were approx. 12 feet wide.

Plate 45
Subject of casualty reports Saltley based Black Five No 44776

D East

Going into a 9F firebox with 20 lbs of steam on (no fire of course!) to release a jammed or melted rocker grate finger bar element, meant walking across this item. Releasing jammed rockers entailed dropping the fire, after which a sack was placed across the mouthpiece shield, then putting the blower on to pull cool air into the firebox. As an Apprentice you could nip in and out quickly. Provided you did not touch the sides of the firebox you were OK and, having spent about 20 seconds in there, it was time to get out! The BR engines had individual grate elements which could be slid off the rocker bars. This was a cheaper and more manageable design that the solid LMS type which covered the width of the firebox. The heat was the nearest thing to working in Saudi Arabia. There was no perspiration, it just evaporated! What would be said today with current Health and Safety concerns? If tubes were leaking, a Boilersmith would drop the fire then re-seal the tubes by hammering each one up as a temporary measure. You could hardly get your breath from the heat retained in the brick arch, especially if there was still steam in the boiler. Again you could put the blower on to draw air through the fire hole door. This, however, was counter-productive as it allowed cool air to hit the tube plate.

Plate 46
Cleaners working on a BR Standard Five in No 3 Shed

Tony Hewitt

A scene of cleaners working on another BR class, in this case a Standard Five in No 2 Shed, clearly shows the arches leading into No3 Shed (Plate 46). These arches were formed by extending the windows to ground level to allow staff to gain access to No 3 Shed, when that Shed had been built in 1893. In 1877, when No 2 Shed was built, access from No 1 Shed was by the previous extra entry and departure road shown in the 1868 plan of No 1 Shed, which was described in Volume 1.

1959
Casualty Reports

The following casualty reports show, as in the case of 44806 (Fig 6) described earlier, the information required when an engine failed in traffic.

Example 1
No 40552 (Leeds Holbeck) an ex-MR Class 2P, which failed with a hot tender axlebox whilst in the charge of Nottingham men who were assisting Black Five No 45076 of Newton Heath.

Example 2
No 41164 (Trafford Park) an ex-LMS Compound which had suffered a typical Compound failure of the High-Pressure (Middle Cylinder) valve spindle.
The correspondence went on for six months, eventually exonerating the Fitter.

Example 3
No 44776 (Saltley) engine (Plate 45) again in the charge of Nottingham men, which failed at Derby for lack of steam caused by leaking and burst superheater elements. At this time it was the commonly held opinion that the condition of both Saltley and Kentish Town engines left much to be desired due to shortage of maintenance staff. According to some Nottingham Running Foremen, in Saltley's case the 'STOPPED' list was longer than the engines available list!

'Robin Hood Express' (Plate 47)
On the 2nd February 1959 the inaugural run of the 'Robin Hood Express' took place, running in an earlier path to that which was to be established. This first 'Robin Hood' departed Nottingham at 0800. The following log of its run was recorded by Frank Eite.

Depart Nottingham	08.00
pass Widmerpool	08.10
Melton Jct	08.18
Oakham	08.29
Arrive Manton	08.32.30

The train stopped here to pick up local passengers, which included the Duke of Grafton.

Depart Manton	08.34.30
pass Corby	08.44.30
Kettering	08.53.30
Kettering Jct	08 55

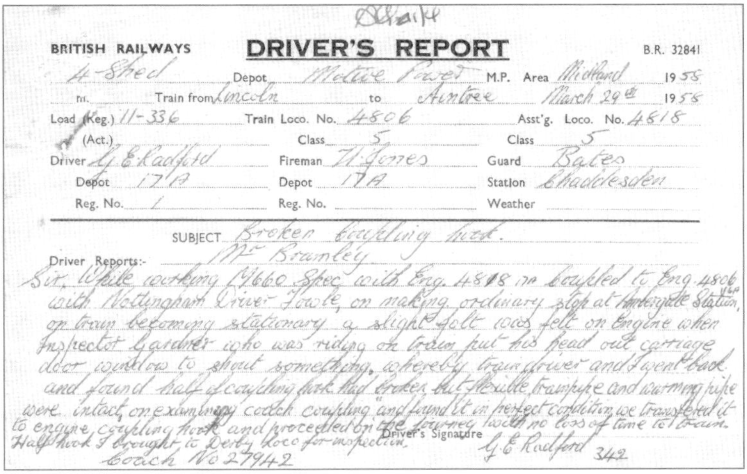

BRITISH RAILWAYS **DRIVER'S REPORT** B.R. 32841

4 Shed Depot Motive Power M.P. Area Midland 1958
Train from Lincoln to Aintree March 29th 1958
Load (Reg.) 11-336 Train Loco. No. 4806 Asst'g. Loco. No. 4818
(Act.) Class 5 Class 5
Driver G. E. Radford Fireman W. Jones Guard Bates
Depot 17A Depot 17A Station Chaddesden
Reg. No. 1 Reg. No. Weather

SUBJECT Broken coupling hook.

Driver Reports:- Mr Bramley

Sir, While working 1Y660 Spec with Eng. 4818 coupled to Eng. 4806 with Nottingham Driver Fowle, on making ordinary stop at Kentsgate Station, on train becoming stationary a slight jolt was felt on engine when Inspector Gardner who was riding on train put his head out carriage door window to shout something, whereby train driver and I went back and found half of coupling hook had broken but flexible trainpipe and warming pipe were intact, on examining coach coupling and found it in perfect condition we transferred it to engine coupling hook and proceeded on the journey with no loss of time to train. Half hook I brought to Derby Loco for inspection. Coach No 27942

Driver's Signature G. E. Radford 342

Fig 6

Casualty report No 44806 Further reports are reproduced in Appendix 9

Wellingboro	08 59
Sharnbrook	09 04.30
Bedford	09 12
Flitwick	09 21
Luton	09 29.30
St Albans	09 37.30
Hendon	09 51.30
Arrive St Pancras	10 .00.

The return working was the 16.45 out of London St Pancras.

30th November 1959 saw No 45532 and B1 No 61136 double headed on this train. It was a very rare occurrence for an ER engine to pilot to London. On 24 October 1959 one of the last LMS built 2Ps, No 40691. was allocated to Nottingham (the Class finished at No 40700). In June 1950 a rare class 2P visitor was the Dabeg Feed Water fitted engine No 40653 of 2C (Warwick). (Plate 49) The allocation of engines was dependent on the work available and if a particular job was lost to another Shed or the work disappeared, which was an increasing possibility, an engine of that particular power classification was transferred away or vice-versa if work was gained. Engines fitted with special equipment (Plate 51) were also occasional visitors and Class 9F No 92099, which eventually became a Tyne Dock engine (52H), can be seen with the coaling tower in the background. The youngest of the three Sheds had stood for over sixty years and if engines colliding with the Shed when they over ran the pit ends and time itself were not enough, the weather was trying to accelerate the process!

According to Bill Reed a strange weather phenomenon occurred in either August or September 1959, during a particularly severe storm. It was the passage of a bolt of lightning across the Shed site. This lightning strike hit the track at Mansfield Junction then moved down the rails into No 2 Shed. It then went across the turntable and out the

BRITISH RAILWAYS
TO: D.M.P.S., DERBY.
B.R. 87315

LOCOMOTIVE CASUALTY REPORT (MECHANICAL)
Locomotive Number....40552

Motive Power Running & Maintenance Depot...KENTISH TOWN...District...KENTISH TOWN...Date Initiated...10.12.58...

Locomotive No...40552...Class...2P...Allocated to...LEEDS...Date of Casualty...29.11.58...
Driver...NOTTINGHAM.(No.)............Fireman...............(No.)...........Stationed at...NOTTINGHAM.........
Working the 10.25...m Class...'A'...Train from...LONDON...to...MANCHESTER...
on...Satur...day, the...29th...day of...Nov...19 58.
Assisting / Locomotive No...45076...Class...5MT...Allocated to...NEWTON HEATH...
Assisted by \ Driver...Fosbrook...(No.)...Fireman...Simpson...(No.)...Stationed at...TRAFFORD PARK...
became a casualty at...............causing a delay at...........mins. Locomotive changed at.............
No. and Class of Locomotive working forward...............Load of train...............Regulation load .... for locomotive
NATURE OF CASUALTY
         R.T. Tender Axle Hot.
CAUSE OF CASUALTY (Full description)
         TRAFFORD PARK
                                    8 JAN 1959
PARTICULARS OF REPAIRS CARRIED OUT NECESSITATED BY CASUALTY
         TRAFFORD PARK.

BRITISH RAILWAYS   Cancelled 3.2.59   BR. 87315/1
LOCOMOTIVE CASUALTY REPORT (MECHANICAL)
                                    Initiated 23.1.59
...Nottingham...Depot...Nottingham...District...Engine No....44776...Class...5C...
Allocated to...Saltley...Depot. Driver...J.Naylor...(No...16A...) Fireman...Crowder...(No.16A)
working the...11.50...(class)...train from...Sheffield...to...Derby...
on...Wed...day, the...21 day of...Jan...19...Assisting/Assisted by Engine No..........Class.........
Allocated to...............Depot. Driver...............(No.......) Fireman...............(No.......)
became a casualty at...En route...causing a delay of...10...mins. Engine changed at...Derby...
No. and Class of engine working forward...Derby to State...Load of train...303T...Regulation load for engine...
NATURE OF CASUALTY   Driver states - On relieving Driver at Sheffield he told me engine did not steam and suspected elements. However on reaching Dore and Totley, I had to stop under signal protection to obtain steam. Fresh engine supplied at Derby.

CAUSE OF CASUALTY (Full description)
                                    5 FEB 1959
         1 Element burst at crown of ...
         ...joints leaking.
                                    0 0 0 0 0 0 0
                                    0 0 0 0 0 0 0
                                    0 0 0 0 0 0 0
                                    0 0 0 0 0 0 0
                                                   Leaking
                                                   Burst
PARTICULARS OF REPAIRS CARRIED OUT NECESSITATED BY CASUALTY
         Burst Elements renewed.
         Leaking joints refitted.

HISTORY OF ENGINE No...44776
Date of last Shop Repair......11.5.57...at...Crewe...Works
Estimated Mileage since Shop Repair...87,330
Date of last Routine Examination...21.1.59...at...Leeds...Depot
by......(No.......)...Grade......
Date of last Periodical (time or mileage) Examination...15.1.59...at...Saltley...Depot
Estimated mileage since Periodical Examination......Extent overdue......
Date defective part last examined...15.1.59...by...L.Herrs...(No......)...1905...Grade...Fitter
Last X Ray 15.1.59   P.T.O.

Fig 7
Casualty report 40552 and 44776.

Jim Perkins

other side, ending its brief existence next to the Sand Hole! Fortunately there were no engines or men on the track into the Shed or the turntable.

Royal Scots

Of all the Royal Scots transferred to 16A it was No 46157 'The Royal Artilleryman', something of an unlucky engine, that appeared always to have been in trouble. Perhaps the most serious event was the Bourne End accident on 30th September 1945. The engine was referred to by some as the 'Jinxed Gunner'. There were a couple of instances at Nottingham of this engine in trouble but without causing a disaster. One was when it nearly went into the table hole in No 3 Shed, the leading bogie wheel just remaining on the edge. An occasion that one of the authors remembers was in December 1959 when coming out of the Driver's mess room and waiting for No 46157 (Plate 55) to enter No 3 Shed he looked at engine and saw the Driver's side bogie spring resting on the L shaped safety plate. Both spring hangers had snapped, with only the safety plate holding the spring in place. The engine had just come off a London Express via the Edwalton Cut-off line. The possible consequences of the spring coming off on the Harringworth Viaduct and the check plate not holding it do not need too vivid an imagination.

This kind of notoriety also extended to diesels. The Great Train Robbery EE type 4 (Class 40) No D326 was in this category. After the Great Train Robbery it was used, coincidentally, as a training engine for Fitters attending the Artisans Training School at Crewe, to which both the authors were sent. Prior to the Great Train Robbery D326 had been involved in the Winsford Accident on Boxing Day 1962. It is said that Crewe men would not work the engine and, although diesels are supposed to be common user engines, it

Plate 47

The inaugural 'Robin Hood' Express on the 2nd Feb 1959. Fitter Charlie Turner is stepping down from the engine

C Redfern

was transferred to Birmingham where it was involved in yet another accident.

When they arrived on the Midland Lines the Class 7P Royal Scot engines were very rough, being run down and a long time out of shops. According to the Footplate men, they used to dance about and vibrate, especially the Fowler cab. However the re-built Patriot No 45532 (Plate 48) was a much better engine. Towards the end of its service life, No 46100 'Royal Scot' (Plate 59) only worked local slow speed trips due to its having a cracked frame. This did not prevent Fitter Granville Geeson, his Mate and an Apprentice (J Perkins) carrying out a valve and piston exam in No 3 Shed.

One difficulty was having to drill/heat the left-hand cross head then remove the bottom slide bar and turn the cross head over in order to get the cross head cotter out. After all this work 'Royal Scot' was then taken out of service.

Plate 48
Rebuilt Patriot 45532 'Illustrious' outside No 3 Shed on the 14th April 1961.
The tenders of stored class 2Ps and the Coaling Tower can be seen beyond

P H Groom

Plate 49
Class 2P No 40653 of Warwick (2C) at Nottingham on 3rd June 1950.
The Dabeg Feed water heater can clearly be seen

A G Elkes

Plate 50
Ivatt Mogul No 43033 fitted with a double chimney, seen here at
Nottingham in the early 1950s

Tony Hewitt

Plate 51
Seen at Nottingham, Westinghouse Pump Fitted Class 9F No 92099

RAS

Plate 52
Fowler class 4P 2-6-4T No 42331, a Leicester (Midland) 15C engine, stands outside
No 3 Shed close to the derelict ODM building

Dave East

In contrasting condition Plates 53 and 54 show later scenes on the Shed of Royal Scots
No 46111 'Royal Fusilier' of (16D) Annesley in early 1963 and No 46167
'The Hertfordshire Regiment' again of Annesley (by now 16B) without connecting rods
and nameplates removed ready for its last journey to the scrap yard in 1964.
Surprisingly there were twelve Royal Scots in total condemned from Annesley, Some
were examined after a main steam pipe failure on one engine (46111) which resulted in
three more becoming earlier victims to the torch.

The full list of Annesley Royal Scots was Nos 46101, 46111, 46112, 46126, 46143,
46153, 46156, 46158, 46163, 46165, 46167 and 46169. In contrast to the Royal Scots
the older Motive Power to be seen at Nottingham can be seen in Plates 56 and 57
which show ex-MR engines Nos. 44018 (Plate 56) and 41712 (Plate 57).

One local event that took place on 3rd December 1959 was the Nottingham Arts Ball
where ex-MR Class 3F No 43186 was auctioned for charity. This engine had been built
at Derby in 1887 as one of the '1698' Class and was withdrawn from 21B Bournville in
January 1959. It was bought at the auction by Mr E Pownall, Scrap Metal Merchant,
Manvers St, Nottingham. The sum bid was £1050, this being donated to the Ockenden
Trust. (Plate 58)

Plate 53

Royal Scot No 46111 'Royal Fusilier' inside No 3 Shed on July 7th 1963. Debris that can be seen include loco springs, a superheater element in the foreground and a Fitter's bench

G Coltas

Plate 54

Royal Scot No 46167 'The Hertfordshire Regiment', minus correcting rods and name plate, ready for its final journey

C Beck

Plate 55
Seen next to the breakdown crane in November 1959, the recently transferred
Royal Scot No 46157 'The Royal Artilleryman', looks in poor condition

B Matthews Collection

Plate 56
Ex-MR class 4F No 44018 seen here next to the coal stack area in November
1959

B Matthews Collection

Plate 59

An evocative view in No 3 Shed. Having just been turned off onto the pit roads were Nos 44806 16A and 46100 'Royal Scot' 16A, both now in preservation. It is raining outside as water can be seen steaming off the boiler cladding. The other engines are Black Five 44663 21A and 42636 (16A), one of the Stanier 2-6-4T engines. The buffer of another member of this class can also be seen

C Beck

Chapter Four
The Breakdown Train

All major depots and sites had breakdown crews who used a variety of equipment. Some had the luxury of modern steam cranes and some, such as Colwick, used specialised hydraulic lifting equipment. Others depots used hydraulic jacks and packing. This type of equipment also went with any crane in its tool and packing vans. These vans had a smell that was quite unique, a mixture of timber, oils and metal. Some of the wooden packing consisted of very substantial pieces of timber, which gradually began to break up due to the weights being placed on them. It was the oils being pressed and released again that gave these vans their wonderful aroma; it's a pity it was not bottled. The BD tool vans were well laid out to a company (LMS) standard with the sides being painted as shadow boards for the storage of tools. Some of the tools were very old and dated from the days of wooden coaches. In the Nottingham BD tool van there was an enormous Glasgow & SouthWestern Railway hand saw. When out on the line attending to a mishap, time could be taken up by having to position the crane: this could be a very complicated procedure.

This section deals with the two breakdown cranes and crews that were at Nottingham during this period, along with some of the incidents they attended. Super elevation was a danger, especially if the load moved and the wire ropes or slings and hooks had to be kept in good order or they could be lethal. The crane in use from 1931 to 1961 was a 4-axle type that had come from Kentish Town to Nottingham in 1931. The crane prior to this was hand operated! Built in 1899, the 15 ton steam crane MP31/RS 1037, had chains for both the jib and the block. It was broken up on site after its withdrawal. (Plate 60) The reason for its being scrapped was that whilst lifting a series of large concrete blocks that had been used as tank traps during the war, it suffered a cracked side casing. British Railways already had a crane replacement programme underway so it had to go. Cowans Sheldon of Carlisle built its replacement in 1960 (RS 1089). This was a 5 Axle model with a 30ton capacity. (Plate 61)

As well as six 30-ton cranes, at least two 75-ton cranes were also built at this time one of which was allocated to Wellingborough. Mechanical Foreman Percy Croydon, who was always called Mr Croydon by all at the Shed staff even the other Foremen, (Plate 62) was responsible for the crane and its crew, which could be called out at any time day or night in fair or foul weather. Mr Croyden had the reputation of being the best breakdown man in the region, if not the country. Whenever available he would be in charge of operations, especially with large and difficult breakdowns. Sometimes one of the Shift Foreman would be in charge of the crew. On one such occasion on a particularly dark night the Shift Foreman in charge was telling the Crane Driver to go up with the jib when one of the attending staff said 'Scuse me Foreman'. 'Not now' was the reply'. 'But Foreman'. 'NOT NOW, I KNOW WHAT I'M DOING', then suddenly there was a 'Ping, Ping, Ping' from overhead. The crane jib had caught telegraph cables and snapped three or four of them. Word soon got round the Shed and for quite a long time after the event the cry of 'Ping, Ping, Ping' could be heard, out of sight but within earshot of the poor unfortunate Shift Foreman.

Plate 60
The old crane at Kirkby-in-Ashfield Locoshed unloading an oil-fired Class
4F boiler
N Thompson

Plate 61
The new steam crane RS1089 at Nottingham
Jim Perkins

As Apprentices we listened to the tales of early winter 1947 when the crew went out for many days, eventually running out of food and fuel and being snowbound along with their customers!

The series of three photographs (Plates 63 to 65) show some of the Breakdown Gang with one of them, Bob Rowbottom, leaning out of the riding van in Plate 65. Another view shows the reason for the call out, a de-railed bogie bolster. When anything was off the rails the situation was, at 16A anyway, known by the footplate staff as being 'On England'. I was once asked to work overtime in order to repair the firegrate on the 30-ton crane. This was very unusual for an Apprentice and was agreed to as I was the only one small enough to get inside the firebox (Jim Perkins). The two Fitters Mates/Crane Drivers, brothers Colin and Eric Wheeler, carried out a few servicing tasks and the odd repair as they were part of the breakdown team. They both continued to work with the breakdown gang after Nottingham closed when they transferred to Toton. Once, when I lost my wages (I do not think they were stolen) Eric organised a whip round for me. This was typical of the generosity and help from fellow workmates. Breakdowns were always called 'Rabbits' at Nottingham, I supposed on the assumption that everybody came running, which they did! Although, one use of this term was for short distance travellers, the other theory was that the six shillings paid for turning out if the breakdown train left the Shed would pay for a rabbit for dinner. However, during World War Two, as the following tale related by Les Dodsley shows, it has yet another origin. The name stuck whatever its parentage!

A breakdown was nicknamed 'A Rabbit', a throwback from the wartime, when attending a breakdown gave the members of the gang a good chance to catch rabbits, thus supplementing the limited food supplies of those days. When attending a breakdown the members of the gang received a bonus, plus any overtime at a higher pay rate. One member of the breakdown gang, a Tuber named Tommy, was one of the keenest to glean the benefits of attending a 'Rabbit', especially when it was near the end of his shift and he was due to be very quickly onto overtime. The slightest murmur of a 'Rabbit' would find him standing at the desk outside the Foreman's office perusing a repair card. If the Foreman came into or out of the office Tommy would greet him with 'Good morning, Foreman' or something similar, just to let the Foreman know that he was there to hand if required. Just for a lark, his mates and other members of the maintenance staff would set him up. If Tommy was inside the smoke

Plate 62
Mr P Croydon, Mechanical Foreman, and a train Guard at Nottingham MPD

Miss B Croydon

box out of sight, men would walk by and shout 'Rabbit', or his Mate Cheggy (Len Chester) would carry on half of an imaginary conversation so that Tommy could hear. It used to go something like this: 'Fifty-seven off' - 'Loaded eh' - 'Fouling the main line at Trent' - 'That'll be a long job'. Within seconds Tommy would be out of the smoke box saying 'I won't be long, Leonard' and be off to the office like a streak of lightening, soon to realise that he had been conned, yet again.

Plate 63

Some of the breakdown gang pose between jobs. From left to right:
F Thompson, Foreman; A Hunt. Blacksmith; Len Booth, Blacksmith Striker;
S Wright, Chargehand; C Hooson, Fitter; and Bob Rowbottom, Fitter

G Hudson

The crane was always kept with a fire prepared for lighting up. This is no longer a problem with the modern diesel cranes which have power when required. On the closure of Nottingham, by then coded 16D, RS1089 was transferred to Toton, where it was converted to diesel power. It was eventually moved to Longsight. Some of the lifting, re-railing and clearing up tasks can be seen in Plates 62 to 71.

The old steam crane can be seen on a Sunday morning lifting job in the late spring of 1948, lifting an oil fired 4F boiler at Kirkby Locoshed. This was the last of the 4F oil fired boilers and was used as an experimental sand drier by surrounding it with steel plates and drying the sand between the plates and the boiler. It was an interim measure between the demolition of the old sand kiln and the setting up of a Kelbus sand drier at the same time the Shed end was rebuilt. (11) (Plate 60) Kirkby, as well as being the last major Midland Railway Shed to be built, was also to become the last Shed to be rebuilt under BR in 1961. It went from three to five roads plus a coal hopper and ash plant. The hopper had jacking points to counteract mining subsidence, but these were never needed. In the late 1940s it also had two ex-Class 3F boilers as part of the abortive oil fired locomotive experiment.

At Stanton Gate, modern motive power introduced some new lifting and recovery problems and was not immune from accidents. The Breakdown Gang had to turn out

Footnote 11 Info from Nigel Thompson & Alen Grice.

to the Stanton Gate accident in December 1963, when the Driver and Fireman of No D94, both Leicester men, were killed when their locomotive ran into a freight train that was moving across their path (Plate 71). The wagon that D94, 45114, collided with was a Tube wagon loaded with concrete track side ducting sections, the impact of which totally destroyed the front end of the engine. The next wagon behind this was a van loaded with bandages and Christmas Tree fairy lights destined for Boots. The engine crew had worked a steam loco to Sheffield and it was suggested that the cab heating on D94 caused them to drop to sleep. After the accident an order came out to check and remove any paper from cab roof vents. These cabs were very draughty and crews used to seal all the holes up with newspaper. The engine was taken to Derby Works where it lay unattended for months as the workshop staff would not work on it because it was still a mess.

Not all breakdown turnouts were hauled by Nottingham engines. Any available engine in steam was utilised and the Edge Hill (8A) Black Five No 45440 went on to the Lincoln line to attend to another incident. This engine was waiting for its next turn of duty, the Edge Hill Goods, and was pressed into service passing the Low Level Station whilst taking the breakdown train onto the Lincoln line (Plate 66)

An altogether bigger job was when Class 8F No 48193 (16B) went into Kirkby Locoshed turntable hole (Plate 69)

K1 No 62012 came off the rails at Lenton South Junction, having become foul of the trap points! The Nottingham breakdown gang was in attendance, plus a few onlookers (Plate 70).

Plate 64
The cause of all the trouble, 30 ton bogie bolster No M203389 loaded with rail panels

G Hudson

Plate 65
Bob Rowbottom leaning out of the riding van whilst on the way to a breakdown. The approaching Class 4F is No 43859

G Hudson

In 1950 the gang went to a particularly bad crash at Mansfield which resulted in ex-Midland Railway Class 2P No 40424 (2183 Class No 157 of 1896) having to be cut up on site by the breakdown gang. The bits arrived at Kirkby locoshed on lowflat wagons. This incident was a rare example of a boiler breaking its back, being damaged between the Belpaire Fire Box and Boiler barrel (Information from Alen Grice). The engine was officially withdrawn in April 1951. (Plate 70) One other instance of this occurring was in 1912 when an L&NW Rly Jumbo Class 2-4-0 broke its back in a crash at Ditton, Cheshire.

Plate 66
Black Five No 45440 of 8A (Edge Hill) seen passing the GN low level station on its way to a breakdown on the Lincoln line

Bill Reed

Plate 67
Jubilee No 45636 'Uganda' and the old steam crane. The assortment of vans is
really interesting

Bil Reed

Notts Rail Crash - Extracts from press cutting
*'The crews of both engines were taken to Mansfield General
Hospital yesterday after an empty passenger train travelling
from Nottingham to Mansfield collided head-on with a light
engine.*

*The collision occurred at Mansfield South Junction on the
Nottingham to Worksop (L M Region) line, half a mile out of
mansfield Town station, near Hermitage Lane.*

*The injured men are: Harold Higgins (33) Driver; Dennis Wood
(25) Fireman; Robert Savage (45) Driver; Eric Lacey (28)
Fireman, Wilfred Renshaw (34) Guard.*

*The two trains crashed in poor visibility and the passenger train
apparently pushed the light engine back for about 50 yards
before both came to a standstill.*

MANSFIELD RAIL CRASH

Plate 68

MansfieldClass 2P No 40423 and a very damaged front end!

N Thompson

Plate 70
Ex-LNER No 62012 off the road at the trap points close to Lenton South Junction

Bill Davies

Plate 71
Stanton Gate Crash, December 1963. The locomotive is D94

D East

Chapter Five
Special Workings

Throughout the existence of the railways there have been special workings and excursions. The first excursions from Nottingham were undertaken in Midland Counties Railway days, some of which are mentioned in Volume I. One of the most traumatic for the three footplate crews involved was the infant Nottingham & Grantham Railway Goose Fair Special, whose empty stock working came to grief near to Mansfield Junction in October 1850. After World War II there were many special workings by 16A locomotives and men, some of these are detailed in this chapter.

The engine for the Railway Correspondent and Travel Society (RCTS) special of 1954 was No 40935 (Plate 72). This engine was one of the LMS built series with the driving controls on the left-hand side. This special was running under reporting code M960. Sam Hewitt can be seen in Plate 73 outside the Shed offices with No 1 Shed in the background, in a posed shot with the CTC Scottish Tours headboard and lamps. The engines that were to work the Raleigh Cycle Company specials of 1956 were prepared in No 3 Shed. Some of which, as usual, had been brought in especially for this working which took place in May; the destination was Blackpool (Plate 74). The next year they were again Jubilee (Class 5X) powered, being cleaned and prepared in No 3 Shed, the main passenger engine Shed. (Plate 75) The following year a visit on 31st May was to the South Coast and one of the engines used was No 45650 'Blake' (Plate 76). The Raleigh Specials engines waited at Cricklewood MPD for the return working. Southern Region engines had taken the train on to Bournemouth. On Sunday 6th May 1956 the RCTS ran a rail tour to Swindon. The engine provided by 16A was the ex-MR Class 2P No 40454 (Plate 77). The advertisement for this day out can be seen in Fig 8. A summary was provided later in the month with emphasis being made on the degree of co-operation and preparation of the engine by Nottingham staff.

The engine had a load of six coaches, 200 tons gross, and had been transformed, being spotlessly clean. Both Mr Jack Thompson, the Assistant District Motive Power Superintendent, and Mr Chas Redfern, Running Shed Foreman, had not only had the engine cleaned but all copperwork had been exposed and polished with paint work touched up. This would have been done by the Shed painter, Tommy James. An equal amount of care had been lavished on the mechanical side. The Driver was George Kelsey and the Fireman Jack Green.

No 40454, a member of the 2203 Class, was built in 1894 as No 195. It was re-numbered 454 in 1907. Rebuilt in 1922, it was withdrawn in September 1960 and stored at Derby before being scrapped at Gorton Works. During the run, a poignant observation was that of the Lickey Banker No 58100 which was seen at Bromsgrove on its last day in service. This unique engine was moved to Derby Works the very next day for scrapping. From Gloucester another Class 2P No 40489 acted as pilot over the Cotswolds via Andoversford Junction over the Midland & South Western Junction line to Swindon.

Plate 72
The RCTS special of 1954 was hauled by Nottingham Compound 4-4-0 No 40935 and can be seen here on the ash pit after the return working

Tony Hill

Plate 73
Sam Hewitt in a posed shotoutside the Shed offices with the CTAC Scottish Tours Express Headboard

Tony Hewitt

The return route was via Oxford, Claydon, Wellingborough and Kettering via Grendon Underwood Junction thence over Harringworth Viaduct, re-entering Nottingham on the Edwalton line. The routes via Andoverford Junction or North of Edwalton are no longer used. You could expect any engine from Nottingham that worked a special to be clean and well prepared. What made the attention to No 40454 a little different was that it was working to Swindon the home of the alleged 'Gods Wonderful Railway' a former rival of the LMS and Midland Railways. On this engine, for some reason or other, the builder's plates were always painted red. Other members of this class allocated to 16A at this time were Nos. 40411, 40458, 40487, 40493, 40504, 40535 and 40553. On 2nd April No 40504 was piloting BR Standard No 73010 (55A) on the 6/33 St Pancras to Leicester, when the Standard Five failed with a hotbox.

The unusual combination of a 2P being piloted by a 9F was then experienced with No 92125 (15A) being attached.

There were many football specials and none more memorable than those that worked the Nottingham Forest supporters' specials when Forest played Luton Town in the FA Cup Final of 1959. One of these was No 45620 'North Borneo' (16A) which went onto Willesden MPD after working the train (Plate 78). Another excursion at this time was the City of Nottingham Holiday Express worked by Black Five No 45260, a Derby (17A) engine. Even the ex-Midland Railway 0-6-0 Class 4F engines were used for excursion trips and tours and the (17B) Burton based No 43953 went on an RCTS special in 1961.

Plate 74

One of the 1956 Raleigh Works outing specials seen in No 3 Shed

C Redfern

On the 13th October 1963 Driver Harold Smith worked another RCTS special to Horwich Works, which still stands in 2002, with Mogul (2-6-0) No 42896 (Plate 79) one of those that had been re-allocated to 16A after an absence of five years. This particular special had a complicated route, known as the circular route, and had four changes of crew. The working to Horwich was in charge of Driver Dennis Branson and Fireman Alan Hunt who were relieved at Crewe by men from Crewe South. The return trip, worked by Normanton men, was by another route across the Pennines with relief at Royston where Harold Smith and Fireman John Pollard took over. On the return journey a hotbox resulted from working the engine too hard due to a 10 Shilling tip being offered to the Driver if the train got to Nottingham on time. Also on the train was Inspector Weavings who, during his army service, was the Group Regimental Sergeant Major (Royal Engineers) for North-West Europe. (12).

Footnote 12 Information from Harold Smith

Plate 75
Raleigh Special of 1957 seen with a group of cleaners and other staff

Tony Hewitt

Plate 76
Jubilee No 45650 'Blake' at Cricklewood Shed on 31st May 1958

C Beck

Plate 77

Class 2P No 40454 at Nottingham Midland Station on Sunday 6th May
1956 ready to take the RCTS Special to Swindon

Bill Reed

THE EAST MIDLANDS BRANCH OF THE
RAILWAY CORRESPONDENCE AND TRAVEL SOCIETY
ARE RUNNING THEIR
THIRD ANNUAL
RAIL TOUR
"THE EAST MIDLANDER"
TO

SWINDON WORKS

On SUNDAY, 6th. MAY 1956

Fig 8
'The East Midlander' Special

Plate 78
Jubilee No 45620 'North Borneo' after bringing in a 1959 FA Cup Special

Transport Treasury

Plate 79
Mogul No 42896 leaves Nottingham Midland station on 13th October 1963

Bill Reed

Chapter Six
People, Places and Sport

In this chapter some of the outside activities undertaken by Shed staff can be seen. Some, like the MIC visits and BR sporting events, were railway related.

Let the captions tell the story (Plates 80 to 92)

Plate 80
Fitter Les Payne with a very young enthusiast

Les Payne

Plate 81
Outside the Diesel Fitters Workshop. From left to right:
John Bowers, Derek Towle, Stan Smith and John Wooley

Dave Fell & John Wooley

Plate 82
Notts Thursday League Team 1956
Back Row: (left to right) G Geeson,
P Palethorpe, R Parrott, T Smith,
J Boot
Front Row: R Geary, F Hardy,
T Brookbanks, R Middleton,
P Hayes

G Geeson

Plate 83
Storeman and former Driver Charlie Summers in the lamp section of the stores
T Hewitt

Plate 84
Les Payne, Danny Sheratt and English Electric rep, Phil Jones in the centre

Les Payne

Plate 85
Jeff Marriot and other apprentices at Derby Loco Works seen inside one of the
Fitting Shops

Jeff Marriot

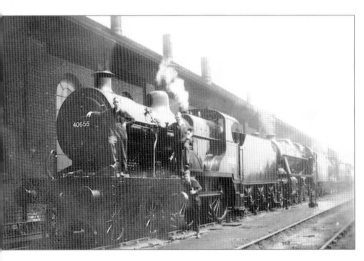

Plate 86
No 40655 seen here at Derby with Jeff Marriot and
other Apprentices

Jeff Marriot

Plate 87
Former Driver, Joe Simpson, seen here in the brass fitting section of the stores. Above him are sandpipes and piston rings

T Hewitt

Plate 88
Ready for the game

G Hudson

Fig 9

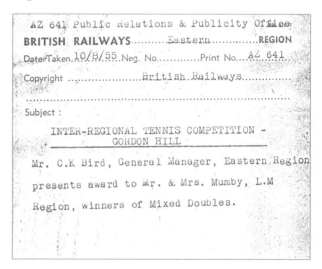

AZ 641 Public Relations & Publicity Office,
BRITISH RAILWAYS..........Eastern.............**REGION**
Date Taken.10/8/55.Neg. No...........Print No...AZ 641.
Copyright ....British.Railways............

....

Subject :

INTER-REGIONAL TENNIS COMPETITION -
GORDON HILL

Mr. C.K Bird, General Manager, Eastern Region

presents award to Mr. & Mrs. Mumby, L.M

Region, winners of Mixed Doubles.

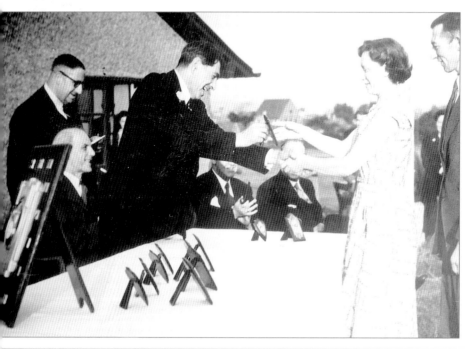

Plate 89
Receiving the
prize in the
Inter-Regional
Tennis
Competition

R Mumby

Plate 90
Bowling at lunchtime
F Eite

Plate 91
Sheriif of Nottingham,
Mr and Mrs H Bryan   *Bill Reed*

Plate 92
A view of the stores with a mouth-watering collection of fittings and fixtures
T Hewitt

Chapter Seven
Engines and Men

Occasionally someone would bring a camera to work with them and, thanks to these locoshed staff, we have photographs showing fitting and footplate staff in a variety of situations where they can be seen along with some of the engines on which they were working.

Let the Captions tell the story (Plates 93 to 106).

Plate 93
The old order. In the cab of a steam locomotive
with Driver Reg Gasgoine in the cab of a Black Five
Bill Reed

Plate 94
Jim Perkins - much slimmer, on an RCTS visit to Eastleigh and
ex-LSWR 2-4-0WT No 30585 now preserved as part of the National
Collection. 30587 also survives

Jim Perkins

Plate 95
Apprentice Dave Coverley on BR Britannia No 70019 'Lightning'

Dave Fell

Plate 96
In No 3 Shed cleaning Jubilee No 45636 'Uganda'

T Hewitt

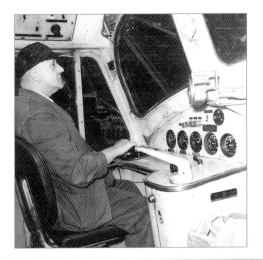

Plate 97
The new order - Driver Jack Rudford in the cab of a new Peak Type 4

Bill Reed

Plate 98
The Fatting Up gang. Driver Bob Nicholas and Fireman who both worked alternate days and nights

T Hewitt

Plate 99
No 46158 'The Loyal Regiment' with, from left to right, Dave Claveley and Derek Towle (Apprentices), Dennis Burdit and George Peach the Shed machinist and Turner

Dave Fell

Plate 100

Royal Scot Class No 46158 'The Loyal Regiment' with Shed Driver Syd 'Trader' Horne and his Fireman Frank Brefitt with Fitter Dennis Burdit on the left

Dave Fell

Plate 101

Driver Don Perkins at Derby on the footplate of Great Northern Atlantic No 251

Don Perkins

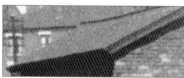

Plate 102
Bill Roe and T Hewitt pose on ex-MR Class 2P No 40557. This view is close to the Cattle Dock.
The only part of this scene remaining is the British Waterways Warehouse

T Hewitt

Plate 103
Driver J Worthington in a wonderful shot seen oiling Britannia Class 70041 'Sir John Moore'

J Worthington

Plate 104
Fitter Granville Geeson and Fitters Mate Nobby Clarke in the cab of Britannia 70019 'Lightning'

The late Dave Fell

Plate 105
Driver George Pickering on Horse Dock Shunt

F Eite

Plate 106
Fireman F Eite on the footplate on the Horse Dock Shunt

F Eite

*C*hapter *Eight*
Apprentice Days

The following anecdotes are typical of what could happen to new apprentices and everyone had to suffer this type of leg pulling at some time or another.

When he first joined the LMS, as an Apprentice Steam Fitter, Les Dodsley was subjected to all manner of undignified leg pulling by the Fitters and Fitters Mates, as are, no doubt, all new apprentices to all trades. The main gag was to send the poor unfortunate minor on a wild goose chase for some nonexistent item such as 'sky hooks', a box of half inch holes, a curved straightedge or a bucket of vacuum. One particular one which he fell for, was when the Fitter and Mate were discussing the need for a weight to help with a job they were engaged with. They weren't quite sure whether they needed a long or short one. After much perusing of the angle of access to the item they wanted to balance the weight with, the Fitter decided, 'Better make it a long one'. He turned to Les and said 'Go to the blacksmith and tell him that you want a long weight'. He dutifully obeyed and told the blacksmith 'Can I have a long weight', 'OK' he said, 'Wait here', and left him standing for about twenty minutes after which he returned and said, 'Have you had a long enough wait yet'. Les was furious and declared that he was never going to caught like that again, a decision that was going to backfire on him with much embarrassment on his part. The occasion was when the Fitter could not get a large nut to turn on a rather rusty bolt. 'Go to the tool stores and ask the store man for a pair of large 'Footprints'. Les duly told him in no uncertain terms to 'go away', or words to that effect. The result was that he grabbed his ear between his thumb and first finger and forced him over to the tool stores. He was then shown a special self-tightening spanner with a handle almost a yard long. This, spanner was made by a company whose logo was a footprint cast into the handle, and these particular tools were termed 'Footprints'. And as Les said 'You just can't win can you?'

The apprentice Days of Jim Perkins

My apprenticeship started on 8th September 1958, being signed on by Wilf Sidebottom, an old time Clerk, who sat on what appeared to be a Dickensian, but practical, high stool at one of those sloping desks mentioned earlier. I was allotted the check number 1115 (a good Compound number) for the next six years and at the time my retirement date of 4th September 2008 seemed a long way off. Not so now, Tempus Fugit! My first Fitter being Brian Cunnington and Mate Sos Parnham. The first job, after delving into his large steel tool locker, was changing the intermediate vacuum hoses on 2P No 40504 (Plate 108). This engine, unusually for a passenger engine, being in No 1 Shed. The engine which had come new to Nottingham as 150 class No 2422 in October 1899, was in steam and waiting to go out as pilot on a Nottingham-London express, with, as I remember, everything happening in a rush to avoid time being booked to Fitters for late off Shed. To make it even more exciting for the first hour on the first day No 40504 was blowing off, bringing down all manner of soot and grime from the 1868 built Shed.

Plate 107
A view of the Nottingham Control Office

Bill Reed

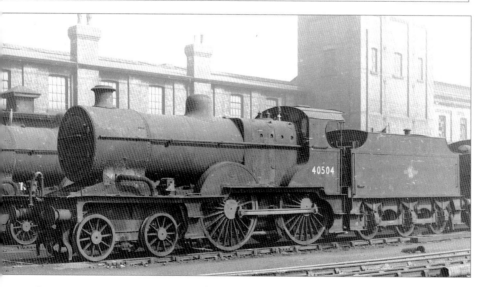

Plate 108
Jim Perkin's first experience of Shed life was with this engine Class 2P
No 40504

P H Groom

I happened to obtain the smoke box number plate of this engine in the 1970s. It was a traumatic introduction to Shed life and the start of a six-year apprenticeship.
I remember thinking 'Will I ever get used to this?' The rest of the week followed the same pattern but without the soot and with a variety of jobs being done.

These kind of running repairs were carried out by a pair of men on each shift, except on days. The early shift was 6.00 to 2.00 when an apprentice would join them 7.30 to 2.00 with the last couple of hours on the afternoon shift 02.00 to 10.00. This type of work was known as being 'On Shed' or 'Runners' and could be busy or slack according to what the Examining Fitter, known as 'The Lamp' and usually the province of an older hand Fitter, or what a Drivers Repair Cards dictated. Vacuum leaks were one problem that the on Shed Fitter looked at and were checked out by using an oil lamp that resembled a teapot. This lamp, variously known as a Duck or Smokey Joe lamp, was filled with paraffin and gave off an oily smoke which was drawn into wherever a leak occurred in the vacuum pipe. Another use for this lamp was in depositing a very thin layer of smoke on a surface to check that it was flat. One of the most important jobs undertaken by an Apprentice at the start of work and at other times of day, was the carrying out of the most important rule. This was Rule 1, make the tea! Although to footplate men Rule 55, letting the signalman know you were stopped at one of his signals, was almost as important. At this time Examining Fitters used a miner's type

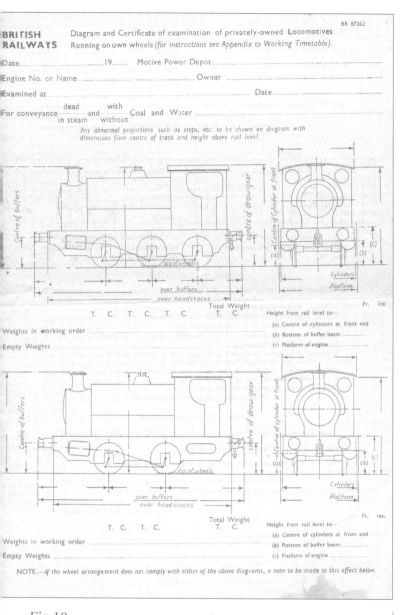

BR 87262

BRITISH RAILWAYS Diagram and Certificate of examination of privately-owned **Locomotives** Running on own wheels *(for instructions see Appendix to Working Timetable).*

Date......................................19........ Motive Power Depot...

Engine No. or Name.. Owner ....

Examined at.. Date...

For conveyance ─── dead ─ and ─ with ─── Coal and Water ....
in steam without

Any abnormal projections such as steps, etc. to be shown on diagram with dimensions from centre of track and height above rail level.

Weights in working order ....

Empty Weights ....

Total Weight — T. C. T. C. T. C. T. C.

Height from rail level to—
(a) Centre of cylinders at front end
(b) Bottom of buffer beam
(c) Platform of engine

Ft. ins.

Weights in working order ....

Empty Weights ....

Total Weight — T. C. T. C. T. C.

Height from rail level to—
(a) Centre of cylinders at front end
(b) Bottom of buffer beam
(c) Platform of engine

Ft. ins.

NOTE.—*If the wheel arrangement does not comply with either of the above diagrams, a note to be made to this effect below.*

Fig 10
BR 87262 the reverse of this sheet is shown in Appendix 10

Jim Perkins (courtesy A Grice)

helmet with an electric light to examine the darker corners of a steam locomotive. The men on 'The Lamp' at this time were Harold Wadsley, Norman Hudson and Paul Dickens. It was Paul who once related how he had worked on the Ljungstrom Turbine locomotive at Nottingham Station in the late 1920s. (Plate 33 page 56 Volume II)

The faults drivers booked on their repair cards usually involved sands, glands and leaks, with some having a fetish about certain faults and would book the same thing every time. At this time most engines had steam sanders (initiated on the Midland Railway by Frank Holt a cousin of the John Ramsbottom of the L&NWR) which could cause other problems if all were not working. Class 2P No 40502, was once reported having a bent side-rod, the cause was traced to one sand not working properly. With only three of those 7 feet diameter driving wheels gripping, the other one would still have momentum, causing the side rod to stress. According to Sid Hill a Nottingham Fitter, not to be confused with Sid Hill the Driver and one time Mayor of Nottingham, ex-works 2Ps were also prone to early draw gear spring slacking.

So, in order to tighten them up rapidly in service, the cotters were left out by Shed staff to be refitted when the springs had settled down. On the subject of springs, the screwed spring pillars fitted to MR/LMS types were a real drag when adjustments or spring changes were required. The later solid cotter type, like those on some Black Fives and all BR Standards, were much easier to adjust but you still had to jack up the engine whatever type it was with varying thickness of cotter being available. On the more modern engines they were jacked up, old cotter removed, then the next size put in to adjust the spring or the spring was changed, then you released the jack. Articulated brake blocks were also easier to work with, being much smaller than the single block and sometimes could be reversed to extend their usefulness. With two per hanger these were fitted to some of the later LMS and nearly all BR types. The heaviest blocks that you came across, however, were the ones fitted to the English Electric 0-6-0 Diesel shunters (Diesel Jockos), which came in Desperate Dan size, although some later shunters had the articulated blocks. There were larger blocks and if you look at some of the old Lancashire & Yorkshire tenders they appear to have huge, heavy brake blocks. However this was deceptive as they were made of wood. On one occasion whilst on Shed duties we examined a 14B (Kentish Town) Black Five whose condition was deplorable. This engine stood in No 3 Shed on the through road into No 1 Shed and was booked for groaning in the valves, that is lack of oil. Apart from this problem the engine had a loose live steam injector, which was almost falling off, and totally worn out brake blocks. They were so bad that the metal was peeling around the blocks and worn almost down to the brake block hanger. A cracked left-leading tender axlebox completed the picture.

An optimistic 14B Running Foreman had sent it to 16A on an express! His faith was justified as it did get to Nottingham but it was more by luck than judgement. With the maintenance situation being particularly parlous at this time it was perhaps thought that 16A would repair the engine. But Nottingham would have none of it and sent it back, light engine, as unfit to work a train.

Plate 110
Class 4 2-6-4T No 42598 and No 42636 in store at Nottingham, July 1962 with No 3 Shed in the background

Jim Perkins

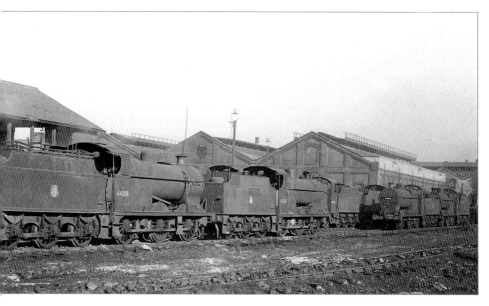

Plate 111
Ex-MR Class 4F Nos 44018 and 44021 with ex-LMS Class 4F Nos 44555 and 44204 stand condemned at Nottingham November 1959

B Matthews Collection

This was probably the worst engine that I had seen at this time actually able to move under its own steam. It was in fact in a worse condition than engines that we had standing out of service. Its condition was due to the inability of Kentish Town to recruit sufficient staff. That steam locomotives could still do a job when in such deplorable condition speaks highly of their robust design.

You never knew what to expect when the Chargehand Fitter came along with his little pile of Drivers' Repair Cards, and after deciphering the contents, the messages were acted on by either the Fitter the Mate or Apprentice. The 'On Shed' job or 'Runners' was a bit of a roving commission and after sorting out the cards you might have to visit the Enginemen's messroom to either find a Driver or his Mate. One of the permanent features of this messroom was what seemed like a perpetual game of cards. Another was the large black kettle, which was always on the boil to render service to those carrying out Rule 1. As well as Rule 55, already mentioned, the other one was not passing signals at red. Being unable to adhere to any of these rules was fraught with difficulties but to transgress Rule 1 had dire consequences.

Some drivers were quite humorous and I can remember a few funny Repair Cards. One was for a 4F and read 'Everything that can blow does blow and that which does not blow has fallen off'. One, for a particularly rough 'Royal Scot', stated 'Loud knocking noises in the cab, someone trying to get in!' But perhaps the funniest was for the then Annesley based No 70004 'William Shakespeare' which was standing between Nos 1 and 2 Sheds next to the sand hole. The repair card stated 'Whistle to be jacked up and new engine fitted underneath' a sad comment on an engine that had once hauled the 'Golden Arrow'. How the mighty had fallen.

When new, engines of this class had suffered loose axles. After the failure of this same engine at Headcorn on the Southern region the Britannia duties on the former Great Eastern route, where most of them were working at this time, had to be taken over by Bullied West Country and Battle of Britain Pacifics a class that had themselves suffered even worse crank axle failures. BR seemed to suffer axle problems with these two classes over a short time scale in the early 1950s.

9Fs

The Annesley Class 9F locomotives came to Nottingham at this time for valves and piston mileage exams, which meant dismantling all the motion and valve gear. On BR Standard engines an hydraulic crosshead breaking tool could be used rather than the gibs and wedges used on LMS engines. On a 2-10-0 engine there are four sections of side rods each side plus the connecting rods. After removal, the rods had to be split at the gradient pins then moved around to the stores for sending to Crewe Works, along with the valve gear. They were moved on a special side rod barrow - a narrow wheeled affair with chains on which the rods were suspended. At Crewe the brasses were pressed out then re-metalled, this was followed by boring out to size and fitting new felt oil pads. When the side rods were put back the Fitter first assembled them on the floor. He then obtained the services of four or five extra men. The rods were then offered up as a whole assembly. Even with the best machining and turning the fact that there were so many journals, five each side, to align made it inevitable that some white metal was shaved off the bush, especially when the rods were tapped on with a number of 14lb hammers and balks of timber. When it came to removing the valves it was better if the engine was warm. This was due to the great difficulties in removing the piston valves when cold. Some of the methods used to remove very tight Annesley 9F piston valves included: setting fire to the valve chest; soaking the valves in paraffin via the blast pipe; hitting the valve spindle with a heavy slide hammer; using an engine on the turntable to pull the valve out, the valve spindle having a thread in the end in which an eyebolt was fitted.

A tank engine or diesel shunter performed this latter option if available and could only be carried out if the engine was stabled facing the turntable and it had to be scotched securely, preferably, with an empty road opposite. Once, on a particularly difficult 9F (92011), all of these options were tried on the left hand, Driver's side, piston valve and only the services of Syd 'Trader' Horne, the Shed Shunt Driver at the regulator of an 8F, succeeding in extracting the large black tooth! At the time it was wondered if the liner would also move. 'Trader' Horne along with his two consecutive Firemen, Frank Brefitt, who died young, and Herbert Hopkinson, were almost members of the Fitting Staff. They provided all engine-moving facilities for the setting of engines and shunted the drop-pit. Resorting to the Shed shunt Driver was sometimes the only recourse to remove valves jammed up with carbon from overheated cylinder oil. The reason why this happened seems to be that the oil broke down under continual speed and sustained steaming on the Annesley to Woodford Halse 'Wind Cutters'. This must have been the most intensively worked service in the country and to say the 9Fs were run into the ground would be an understatement.

Only their robust design and their sheer size allowed them to survive on this route. After burning the carbon off the valves (you could not scrape it off) the rings were removed and were found to be so thin that they were more like Wilkinson razor blades than valve rings. Once, on a visit to the National Railway Museum, this point, regarding the melted valve spindle bushes on No 92220 'Evening Star' was raised in conversation with the staff. This engine had apparently suffered the same problems as the Annesley engines after sustained main line running. The excess carbon could be made worse by the setting of the mechanical lubricator feed at full throw creating over oiling. Another item that could give problems on a 9F was replacing the crosshead cotter. These could be really difficulty to drive home and had to be cleaned to a bright finish. On No 92078 this had been done but it was so tight going in that a small amount of rust that remained made it difficult to drive in with the standard 14-pound hammer. One 'cock-up' was fitting an exhaust injector steam pipe joint without a hole in it. After the injector had been refitted it would not pick up on exhaust steam: head scratching all round and then the penny dropped, words were spoken by the Fitter!

The Annesley 9Fs sent to Nottingham for valves and pistons were:

Nos. 92010-92014, 92030-92033, 92043, 92052*, 92057*, 92067-92076, 92083*, 92087 (This was the first Swindon built example) 92088-92096, 92117* and 92129*.

When built some of these engines had the BRIC (*) tenders, which held 9 tons of coal and 4,725 gallons of water; others had the BRIF which held 7 tons of coal and 5,625 gallons of water. All the Annesley engines were coupled to BRIF tenders.

Annesley Britannias at this time were:

70004 'William Shakespeare'
70014 'Iron Duke'
70015 'Apollo'
70043 'Lord Kitchener'
70048 'The Territorial Army 1908-1958'
70049 'Solway Firth'

Some humorous Drivers' Repair Cards relating to Annesley engines were:

'Floorboards leaking air' this meant they were dancing about due to another rough riding engine.

'Engine will not steam, rice pudding pulling difficult'

Many of the repair jobs were handed out around the Fitters' fire in No 2 Shed, which in the winter was stoked up to warm the cylinder oil as well as the staff and their toast. It was the responsibility of a Fitters Mate to put this oil in the cylinder lubricators. The Driver or Fireman who was taking the loco out had to fill the axlebox lubricator as part of the 'fatting up' routine, a term that was a throw back to the days of grease lubrication. The coal for this stove was obtained from any convenient coalmine such as a loco tender.

Sometimes the Fitters' fire was so hot it was almost translucent. Anybody in its vicinity had to stand at least 6 feet away! When the fire was this hot it made toasting bread difficult while the glue like cylinder oil became like water and you could pour it with ease.

A Fitters Mate, George Etches, carried out the greasing of those modern engines that were fitted with grease nipples on regular days, his kit being an electric Tecalemit pressure unit which also benefited from standing near the fire in the winter. On a really cold day Bob Rowbottom Senior once poured a bottle of oil on the fire in order to move the Apprentices and Mates. His Mate was one of them. The resulting effects would have put a Royal Navy destroyer laying a smoke screen to shame. Bob was ex-London & North Western from Stockport and never had a good word for the 0-8-0 Super D engines, which in his opinion was designed by a madman.

The dirtiest job on a steam locomotive was smokebox work and usually meant changing superheater elements, and for ordinary sized people there was enough room. The two Bobs were once given a smokebox job, this was work that was usually done on a rotation basis so that the dirty work was shared between the fitting staff. Big Bob at 20 plus stone and little Bob at nearly 30 stone, which was a bit of a contradiction, were too much even for a 9F smokebox! What was even more unacceptable for Bob was that this occurred on a Friday, the clean overall day! Jeff Marriott once described being grabbed in a pincer movement by these two characters and said it was like being smothered in two giant pillows.

Other jobs were not so funny, like the request to look for a head after an engine had struck a man at Lenton South. Control did not know which engine. Fortunately for us the engine went through to Kentish Town. This incident I remember very well as it took place on one of those foggy winter afternoons with the clanking of invisible engines and fog swirling into the Shed entrance. I was given a Black Five to look under and with some trepidation I descended into the pit in No 3 Shed. What with the smoke and fog, plus the cracking of pipes and dripping water, the imagination could have run riot. Another incident was when a Fitter went under an engine and saw two eyes steering at him. An owl had been drawn under the engine and settled on the Weighbar Shaft! On another occasion a Stanier Class 4, 2-6-4 Tank engine had struck a cow on a crossing and the hot sticky mess had to be cleaned off with a steam lance. You would not believe how much brown stuff there is in a brown cow! On a more bizarre note, an engine ran into Nottingham Station once with someone's head on the boiler front fall plate, giving waiting passengers a bad start to the day!

One of our Fitters Mates was Len 'Cheggy' Chester who could work out the most complicated odds when betting on horses but did not seem to be particularly interested in the job. When asked by Mr Croydon about the definition of a vacuum he replied '**** all rushing up a pipe!' an answer that was as unexpected as it was almost the truth. Len was a gentle soul who led a bachelor's life and was later badly injured when a smoke cowl fell on top of him in No 3 Shed after an engine had dislodged it. He was never the same again. Later in life he became blind and was looked after in a retirement home at Clifton.

On Shed duties meant working on foreign engines as well as any of our allocation. This could range from ex-L&NWR Super Ds to 9Fs. Most jobs appeared to be piston glands, sands and leaks with some of the jobs tackled outside the Shed. At times as an Apprentice 'On Shed' we assisted Drivers to move engines off the ash pit into whatever Shed the Running Foreman required. This meant setting points, moving the turntable and sometimes we actually drove the engines a short way from the points up to the Shed - allthough it was best that the Running Foreman did not know about it! I took part in these activities after a couple of years and the variety of engines that I helped to turn off was really remarkable.

This helped the disposal staff who were on a set number of hours or a set number of engines per eight-hour shift. Eight was the number required to be disposed. Once this was achieved the men could go home and any help from the fitting staff was appreciated, although frowned on by authority. Fortunately nothing untoward ever happened and everyone was happy.

A couple of types that I did not move as an Apprentice were the ex-Midland Railway/LMS 4-4-0 Compounds very few of which were still in service and the ex-L&NWR 0-8-0 Class 7F Super Ds, both capable of priming and creating havoc. A Super D could move on 50 pounds of steam but you could not stop them except with the tender handbrake. The footplate staff called them Knuckle crackers due to the restricted space for firing and the ability to catch their hands on the ironwork. You needed an umbrella when operating the brake, which was placed strategically in the roof. Drivers of short stature had to use a box to stand on to reach the controls. Terry Essery, an ex-Saltley Fireman and author, stated that Midland men considered them to be Webb's last revenge on footplate men, although they were actually designed by Bowen-Cooke. A new generation will be able to put this to the test when the NRM example No 49395 of 1921, is put back into steam. According to the ex-L&NWR Fitters, earlier L&NWR engines had even stranger devices. One of these was the push button Top & Bottom Ball Valve Gauge Frame. An apparatus, which could apparently be manipulated to show any water level, you might require. All of these were removed from L&NWR engines after the boiler explosion at Buxton in 1921 although the actual cause of the explosion was a sticking safety valve. Other L&NWR features were the joy valve gear and huge vacuum brake diaphragms. All this apart, the Super Ds were very strong engines and out-lasted the Fowler 0-8-0s (Austin 7s) that were built to replace them. A Super D once collided with an 8F in the Shed yard with the Stanier engine coming off much the worse. The other engines that could give trouble were Compounds, which could prime and move off out of control in seconds, if the boiler was over full. The tale is told of one particular incident in No 3 Shed when a Compound ran off the turntable out of control due to water carry over into the cylinders. The Fireman in charge reversed it rapidly only to travel off the turntable and onto the pit road opposite, thankfully empty, and knock large holes in the opposite Shed wall. Some wag then chalked over the opening in the brickwork the legend 'Jinxs Cafe' after the nickname of the Fireman. One other character occasionally seen around the Shed was the 'Railway Rat Catcher'. He was known by that title and not the more high sounding 'Rodent Exterminator'. He was accompanied by his mongrel dog and sackbag. He was not a member of the Shed staff, but was an employee of the Civil Engineers Department.

A few classes of locomotive had moved from Nottingham by 1957, these were the ex-MR types such as the Compounds 4-4-0s and 3F 0-6-0s. A feature of these 0-6-0 saturated engines was whitemetal piston rod packing which was easier to work with than the usual cast iron type used on superheated engines. Although an old design, these Class 3Fs had good boilers and were well liked by footplatemen. It is sad that none have survived into preservation

During April 1960 a visit was made to the Ministry of Supply Storage Depot at Ruddington, where a couple of steam locomotives were to be checked for gauge. One of these was the Manning Wardle 0-4-0ST No 1847 of 1914 'Olympia' which had been rebuilt by Robert Stephenson & Co in 1941 for use at ROF Ranskill in North Notts. The purpose of our visit with Fitter Charlie Turner was to see if 'Olympia' would travel over BR metals to its new owner, the Steel Supply Company Ltd, Jersey Marine, Swansea, South Wales. The visit was by double deck Barton bus, a type with a side aisle and long bench seats, an example of which is preserved at the Nottingham Transport Heritage Centre, Ruddington.

Other engines on the MOD site at the time were:
'Landore' 0-4-0ST OC (Barclay No 769 of 1896), which was to be scrapped.

'ROF No1' 0-4-0ST OC (Bagnall No 2650 of 1942). New to Ruddington in that year, it was eventually sent to the same location as 'Olympia'.

'ROF No4' 0-4-0ST OC (Barclay No 2124 of 1942) and, like No 1, new to Ruddington in 1942.

'ROF No14, an 0-4-0 (Fowler Diesel No 22979), new to Ruddington in 1943 and later sent to MoS Kings Newton, Derbyshire.

Also an unknown numbered or named 0-6-0ST IC (Peckett No 1691 of 1925) which was originally at MoS Kings Newton,was later sold to D Ward, a second hand locomotive dealer of Burton-on-Trent in April 1960.

'Chelford No1' 0-4-0 (Drewry diesel No 2168 of 1942). Originally ex-MoS Chelford which arrived in 1957 and was still on site in 1963.

This information was compiled with the help of the late Dave Henly of the Great Central Northern Development Association, Ruddington,

BR examination sheets can be seen in Fig 10 and Appendix 10.

BR Class Five No 73000, when all day seemed to be spent trying to get oil into the rear right hand piston valve oil fitting. This entailed winding the lubricator handle on a hot day, a task that appeared to go on forever. My Fitter at this time was Fred Pask. One trip with Fred was to the station to look at No 46157, which was suffering from a burst Fireman's side gauge glass. The glass in this particular gauge frame would burst and after about 20 miles it would go again. We changed the glass but suspected that the gauge frame was out of line. This proved to be the case when the top and bottom fittings were checked using the alignment kit that we had taken with us. The Driver had every right to refuse to take the engine but he was already ten minutes late so he decided to proceed with one gauge glass. GWR engines had one gauge glass, as standard, but this is supplemented by a test cock. Once again 46157 had struck trouble, it later required a new gauge frame due to misalignment.

Another job with Fred was crawling on the top of the tubes of a Black Five boiler in order to tighten up some internal pipes and bolts. During my apprenticeship I occasionally went on footplate trips with my brother, Donald. One was on the Lincoln to Birmingham Fish train with 4F No 44387 of 18B (Westhouses) my footplate ride being from Lincoln to outside Nottingham Loco. Another trip was on BR standard No 75058 (16A) and he took me from Nottingham to Tibshelf and Derby St Marys. Another short trip was with No 46100 'Royal Scot' when it was on local trips due to cracked frames. Most memorable was on Nottingham Black Five No 44861 from Kettering to Nottingham when we went across Harringworth Viaduct and it definitely appears to move as the train goes across!

Fitter Charlie Hooson, a mercurial character, was another of the Shift Fitters who once demonstrated how to renew the bolts on a 'Crab' tender tank vent with a tender full of water, a technique that involved a longer bolt than normal and a long piece of wire. He also managed to smash all the gauges on the same engine when totally frustrated with not being able to obtain a proper vacuum (21') even after changing the gauge twice. All this occurred on the road outside the Fitter's Office which, before 1877, was the other road into No 1 Shed. How Charlie got away with it outside the Foreman's Office I do not know! Sometimes we worked with a regular days Fitters one of whom, Ron Bowler, I got off to a really auspicious start when I offered to help him with a 4F regulator handle that had come loose. Having had all of one week's experience and being aged 15 and 12 days, he quite rightly told me to sit down and **** shut up! One really interesting job carried out with Bob Robinson the electrician was changing some of the main traction motor cables on an English Electric Shunter. This engine had been failing in Nottingham Yard with persistent earth faults. After testing with a 'Megger', an instrument that puts a high voltage across a circuit, it was found to be one of the main cables shorting out. These ran from the control panel down to the traction motors via a conduit on the cab's rear bulkhead. This cable was pulled out with a block and tackle suspended on the cab roof with the new one being pulled through with great difficulty, using liberal amounts of grease, brute force and bad language! There were two of these cables and the second one was pulled out in order to check it, although it did not show a fault, and was found to be in an even worse state. The cause of all this hard work and language was a cab radiator leak. This water had found its way down the cab sheet into the conduit. Once there it had corroded the steel, which then cut its way into the insulation followed by the copper conductor. The highest viscosity oil on a steam loco is that used in the cylinder lubricator, however on an English Electric Shunter (Class 08) and other diesel electric locomotives the traction gear oil is made of even sterner stuff. Resembling blocks of bitumen, it had to be almost boiled in order to achieve some sort of pour point. In cold weather it set like concrete and tripped out the overloads on the engine when power was applied. A sight that could be seen in really cold weather was a shunter being towed with all wheels locked up. This was due to the oil not allowing the reduction gearing to rotate with flats developing on the tyres as a result. Charlie Turner once used some high viscosity oil mixed with other oils in the noisy back axle of a Lanchester car which he promptly took in for part exchange. I often wondered if that car ever moved a wheel again?

Whilst discussing the new traction, it was from the authors' time at Derby Works when the Peaks were in service and the class 47s being built, that very little, if any, faultfinding instruction was provided. The answer to the Manager's question 'Was working at Derby Works a good experience?' was summarised as 'It could have been better'!

When asked to qualify this it was mentioned that after eight months no outstation Apprentice had been given even one hour of theory in the classroom, and therefore apart from recognizing the bits and pieces was not that much wiser about the new forms of traction. No attempt was made to connect the systems together in order to understand the relationships. It was pointed out that it was no use knowing how to remove a main engine when what was required on a dead 'Peak' on the 'Robin Hood' express was an understanding of the whole locomotive. At this point, distant in time, it may seem like sour grapes, but it was symptomatic of the headlong rush into diesel traction without fully considering the support activities on the system as a whole, rather than just where the diesels were allocated. After all they did not conveniently break down outside Derby Works. And break down they did, all over the place.

Indeed E S Cox, in the preface to his 'Locomotive Panorama Volume I', where he discusses the coalescence of the CE and CM Engineers, observed that 'In the long run however this move must result in the emergence of dually experienced engineers, equally competent in mechanical and electrical. The lack of whom in sufficient numbers has made more difficult the great change over to diesel and electric traction.' This also applied to the Locoshed Maintenance staff. On a positive note, one of the more interesting tasks in Derby Works was working with the on site Sulzer Engineer. This involved testing the Peaks on full load with manometers to check pressures coupled up to every conceivable point. We were trying to find out why there were so many crankcase explosions on this type of 12-cylinder engine. This was before the Bicera crankcase pressure release valves were fitted. The 6-cylinder engine fitted to Type 2 locomotives never seemed to have this problem. The result of one of these explosions was quite remarkable with the crankcase doors being blown out and doubled over like cardboard. What most people do not realize is the potential for an explosion in a large crankcase full of oil mist. Eventually the problem was traced to badly fitted free end main bearings, the end away from the generator, that were overheating. Unfortunately a number of Drivers and some works staff were badly burnt by hot oil before the solution was found.

There were a few lighthearted moments in the works such as the time someone clocked on using a steel card which wrecked the clocking on machine. The same piece of steel was use to teach someone a lesson in No 9 Shop. There was one old hand notorious for stealing sandwiches. To teach him a lesson the same steel clocking on card was put between two slices of bread, which had the desired result after the first bite! Then someone's old boots were nailed to the floor in the washroom and when the owner came to put them on he was a bit surprised as they would not move. He also found his tool locker welded up around the door. Great laughs all around! On another occasion the Cutting Up Gang were working on the cab roof of an O4. Rule one, when carrying out this operation is 'don't stand on the piece you are burning or result man and burner in the pit.' This did happen on this engine, fortunately without injury. Whilst at the Works, experience was also gained on building new Type 2s, Stones Vapour Boilers rebuilding AEC and Rolls Royce Railcar engines as well as English Electric Shunter engines.

My First Week at Work

By Roy Padgett

Monday: I reported to the Shed Foreman, Mr Frank Thompson, at 7.30. Frank, I later learned, was one of the two Foremen who worked afternoons and nights weeks. This could go on for years until you could find a promotion. The day Foreman, Mr Croyden, no one ever called him Percy, was on annual leave so Frank was covering. Eventually, I was put with a Fitter John 'Jock' Gordon an ex-St Rollox Works man and Fitters Mate Eric Wheeler. Just before leaving the office the Foreman said 'These engines creep into this Shed very quietly, don't get run over!' That was my induction to safety in the Shed.

The first engine I worked on was No 48666, a Southern Railway built LMS class 8F in No 1 Shed. The job was removal of the crossheads for remetaling. I was given the job of holding a brake stick attached to the dolly with a piece of rope. The dolly was a piece of steel bar approximately three feet in diameter and four feet long. It had to be hit from below with a 14lb hammer. John said, 'Eric's going under the engine to knock the cotter out, so keep your head down'. After about four hits with the hammer the cotter disappeared flying passed my head! The crossheads were then taken to the Coppersmiths for remetaling.

The next job was to change the tender brake blocks. Eric fetched a set of blocks whilst John started removing the old blocks. John showed me how to fit the blocks and when we came to the right hand leading hanger he gave me the block to fit. I placed the block into position at the bottom of the brake hanger. John said 'When you get the block half way up pull it towards you, like I have just shown you The block will jamb, allowing you to reposition yourself for the final lift and when the holes line up keep your fingers out and put the pin in'. We then went under the tender and he showed me a trick of the trade, how to slightly open the cotter prior to fitting. The cotter was placed on the rail the head struck, this had the effect of slightly opening the cotter which made opening easier when it was in the brake block pin. After dinner he took me into No 3 Shed and onto a Black Five in steam. He pointed out all the fittings and demonstrated the injector then let me have a go. I remember thinking to myself 'I will never remember all this lot'. John and Eric were shift men, so they went home at 2 pm. I then went with Dave Simpson and Albert Rudge, the Mate, on No 40557 an ex-Midland Railway 4-4-0 2P from which they were removing the piston valves.

Tuesday: We refitted the crossheads on 48666 and in the afternoon I went back on 40557.

Wednesday: We had a blast pipe to fit on a 4F, which, although a small engine, had a very heavy two ported blast pipe. I later learned that the BR Standard 9F probably had the smallest blast pipe in relation to the size of the smokebox. The blast pipe had been removed to enable the Tubers to renew the boiler tubes. Due to the corrosive environment in the smokebox, the retaining nuts had to be split, which often damaged the threads. John showed me how to use the die nut This was a die that fitted a spanner and was used for running down the threads to restore their shape. He informed me not to let go until it was started on the threads because if I dropped it we would have to start stripping the piston valves out until we found it. I later heard that years ago one of the Shed staff suffered from vertigo and whilst walking around the

Shed he would run people down so they called him 'Die Nut'. He would sometimes suffer attacks when walking round the turntable hole, but somehow he always managed to correct his balance before he actually fell in.

Thursday. We had wash out repairs on 45636 'Uganda'. I was shown how to repack the regulator gland, the first of many regulator glands I was to repack. This was my last day with John and Eric as it was the end of their day week. John went into the work study department some years later. Eric became a very good friend whilst working at Toton until his sudden death some twenty years later. (Between 3rd February 1949 and 24th April 1953 'Uganda' was fitted with one of only five remaining vertical throat plate boilers. This was boiler No 8752. The others were Nos. 8748-8751. This engine also ran with the same tender, No 4624, all its working life).

Friday. I went to work with Charlie Hoosen and Len Chester, his Mate. Charlie was very thin with a hooked nose, sometimes he was called Jake, just like the cartoon character. Len was known and liked by everyone in the Meadows. He informed me that if I required a 3d bet he knew where one could be placed, as most bets were 6d. The job we had was to fit the blast pipe into a Stanier 2-6-2 tank. This was the annular type that had to be split and cleaned prior to fitting. Len said he was going home for his dinner as he lived close to the Shed in Goodhead Street. I asked him if he knew where I could get some paper in which to wrap my, by then, very dirty overalls. When he came back he produced a new butcher's brown paper carrier bag. Len I learnt later provided the butcher with white cloths, and a Mars bar saying to me 'You don't get paid this week so I have brought you a Mars bar'. I often think about Len when I have a Mars bar.

Working on the Drop Pit by Roy Padgett

Access to the drop pit was through No 2 Shed, its actual location being beside the machine shop attached to No 1 Shed. An engine suffering a hot box or worn or loose tyres that required its wheels changing or machining would be placed on the drop pit table. The connecting and coupling rods would then be removed as required after which springs were uncoupled then the horn stays, the bracing between the axle box guides, followed by the sand pipes and then the brake rigging. The table would be lowered by means of four electric powered screw jacks and, as the wheels went down, two more rails automatically slid into place to make up the gap of the missing rails. The safety catch would then be engaged, the loco moved and the wheels raised to rail height. The wheels then would be pushed along to a small turntable which just caught the wheel flanges. Driving wheels on the Stanier 2-8-0 class 8 Fs were extremely difficult to move due to the heavy balance weights and the BR 2-10-0 9F were even worse. They not only had heavy balance weights but there were no flanges on the driving wheels, ie the middle pair. Large wheels on Britannias, some of which had roller bearings, and Jubilees took some stopping when you had them rolling along.

Fortunately we did not have many hotboxes on these, as they had large bearings and a pumped oil supply. When the wheels were in the workshop the axle boxes would be removed and then taken to the machine shop for the brasses to be pressed out. There they would be remetalled and machined to the correct dimensions. If the axle required attention it would be polished by hand and if scored it would be skimmed whilst mounted in the wheel lathe. One loco that received attention on the drop pit was Royal Scot No 46164 'The Artists' Rifleman'. This engine had been reported riding very rough when crossing Harringworth Viaduct. Royal Scots were notorious for riding rough when the trailing coupled wheel axle boxes where badly worn. On arrival at Nottingham Midland the loco was taken off the train. Examination revealed that all four-axle boxes on the driving and trailing coupled wheels had run hot and there were three broken springs. A closer inspection revealed that the trailing coupled wheels, which normally had the axle just protruding through the wheel boss, was approximately a quarter of a foot inside the boss on both sides. The wheels were actually coming off the axle! Ths was no doubt caused by the excessive side thrust of the inside wheel boss against the axle box face. Paul Heyes, the Fitter, looked up at the nameplate saying 'This is a right artist'. The wheels were removed then sent to Crewe and this engine took some time to put back into traffic as we could only take one pair out at a time. Whilst the wheels were away other work was progressed. Waiting for material to be returned, we would shunt the drop pit and do another hot box or request an engine to be

Plate 112
4F No 44215 with sludge tenders. The one next to the engine is being washed out with water from the water column

C Beck

brought to the Shed that required tender wheel changing. When tyres became thin, caused by running with the tender brake applied to assist stopping loose-coupled trains, they often came loose. To economise, wheels would be exchanged between engines having their tyres turned, or re-profiled, in the wheel lathe prior to fitting. Other work carried out by the drop pit Fitter was the repair of sludge tenders. In Plate 112, in a view looking towards the ash plant, we can see LMS Class 4F 0-6-0 No 44215, a long time Nottingham resident. This engine is backed onto a pair of ex-Midland Railway tenders that have been converted into water softening plant sludge carriers. These sludge carriers were taken from ex-Midland Railway Class 2P, Compound and Class 4Fs, and were modified with paddle doors to discharge the sludge collected from the carriage sidings softening plant to the Attenborough dumping ground. It appears that the front tank is being washed out as the water bag is in the tank and sludge is pouring onto the ground. The tender chassis coupled to the preserved Class 8F No 48305 is an ex-sludge carrier. This particular tender was restored at the Great Central Railway at Lougborough. The chassis was found to have axle boxes from various engines and, during refurbishment, the remains of maroon paint were discovered in a number of places. Due to it being full of concrete and uneconomic to repair, the original tank was scrapped and a short 3500-gallon tank ex-Jubilee No 45593 'Kolhapur' was fitted. The tenders were very old Midland Railway six wheel and Lancashire & Yorkshire Railway eight wheel varieties. What with old age and rough shunting the weight of the wet sludge in the tank would shear the mounting bolts. The tenders would be brought inside the workshop part of the drop pit, via the only surviving small wagon sized turntable that was located through No 1 Shed, between the two workshops. The tank was then lifted by the overhead crane allowing new wooden packing and bolts to be fitted.

Wash Outs and Intermediate 'X' Repairs

At ten to sixteen day intervals the engines would have the boiler washed out and an examination. The Examining Fitter would book the repairs and the Fitters would carry them out. These examinations were periodic and carried out at three to five week intervals which would involve the renewing of gauge glasses etc, or the seven to nine week examination, which involved examination of the injector steam valves and the ejectors etc. The Boilersmiths would carry out a firebox examination and renew any broken stays. The engine, if due for one, would receive a boiler exam by the Boiler Inspector, who came from Derby. The inspection was carried out with a long brass rod, up to six feet long, with a piece of asbestos string attached which was dipped in paraffin and lit. Today it would be a Camera/VDU and fibre optic cable. He would then push it into the boiler and carry out his inspection. On completion, the boiler would be sealed up. This was known as being boxed up. At some Sheds replacing the mudhole doors would be a Fitter's job, but not at Nottingham. Occasionally, on washouts, crossheads and eccentrics would be booked for remetaling, sometimes on more than one engine at the same time. Then it would be a race against the clock to get your crosshead to the Coppersmiths for remetaling first. Off you went thinking that you were bound to be first to the Coppersmiths, only to find that he was remetaling a set of cross heads that had been sent down on the first train from Kirkby Shed. After remetaling and machining the Kirkby crossheads, Albert, the Shed Labourer, would push them on a handcart through the streets to the station. This was hard work as the last part, up Queen Drive, is steep.

The Maintenance Staff

Steam

Fitters & Apprentices
Fitters Mates
Boilersmiths & Apprentices
Tubers
Turner
Machinist
Blacksmith
Blacksmiths Striker
Coppersmith/Tinsmith
Whitemetaller
Joiner
Joiners Mate/Painter

Diesel

Fitter & Apprentice
Fitters Mate
Electrician & Apprentice
Electricians Mate

Running Repairs

One Monday I was working with Bob Rowbottom, known as 'Big Hammer' Bob, a man six foot tall and of a large build with a forceful personality to match. He started work at 6 am and I started at 7.30. On arrival he had sorted out the Repairs Cards into his pile and mine. One of the repairs he had given to me was for a Cricklewood (London) 14A Black Five. The problem was that both injectors had leaking steam and water pipes. On examination, I found almost every pipe leaking. So I went back to Bob to report my findings. He went to the engine and tried the injectors himself. He said, 'It got here, it should get back'. The next day, Tuesday, the same engine arrived on Shed, the Driver booking the injector pipes. Again I fetched Bob who came and looked and repeated the previous day's comments. The Black Five returned on both Wednesday and Thursday, the Driver putting in a Repair Card each time, and each time I tried both injectors. Bob asked me what the leaks and blows were like. I informed him they were getting no better. Bob's reply was that it would get back. Friday morning came and Bob was off the running repairs. He had far more important things to attend to selling his football tickets. To give some idea of the force of his personality this next event actually took place. On seeing a Driver who was on his, almost compulsory, football ticket list he called him over, informing him he had last Friday's football ticket. Bob's tickets were 2/6d or 12 and a half new pence, when most tickets were 6d, 2 and a half pence. The Driver handed over the money only to be told by Bob 'You need not bother opening the ticket, the prize was claimed on Saturday night'.

Jeff Marriott was the Fitter on running repairs that morning and again the Black Five turned up. Jeff picked up the Repair Card and read out the repairs. I informed him that the same engine had worked the same job all that week and the repairs had been reported every day and signed off. He asked if it was bad. My reply to him was 'I do not think you will sign it off'. On trying the injectors, Jeff was horrified. We filled the boiler right up, closed the dampers and informed Freddie Bloomer, the steam riser, of what we were about to do. The pipes were removed, which was easier said than done, and taken to the Coppersmith for repair. Eventually the pipes were repaired and refitted.

Fortunately we only had a couple of other engines to attend to. Jeff said 'Put some coal on to make some steam'. The water was by now getting low in the boiler and as soon as there was sufficient pressure, I turned on the water supply and Jeff checked for leaks: there were none. The steam was turned on and, whilst there was no reason to suspect that the injector would not work, the loco having worked in from London, I could see the relief in Jeff's face when he saw the water stop overflowing and heard it going into the boiler, making its distinctive singing noise.

On another occasion I was working with Fitter Vernon Dale. It was a very hot day and the Jubilee No 45609 'Gilbert and Ellice Islands' was even hotter. The repair was a burst tube blowout pipe in the smokebox. the valve for which can be seen on the smokebox side. On opening the smokebox door the char fell out onto us. It was up to the top of the blastpipe and should have been removed on the ash pit. We shoveled the char out, then removed the broken pipe. But fitting it was a different matter. The engine was still warm and the day was getting hotter. Try as he may, Vernon could not get the nut onto the adapter, which was located at the back of the superheater header. Vernon said, 'There's only one thing to do in a situation like this, go and mash'. After a drink and sit down we returned to the smokebox and the nut went on first time!

Whilst working with Barry Lee we had a V&P on another Jubilee No 45611 'Hong Kong'. The loco was on the long pit in the Fitter's corner of No 2 Shed. I started stripping the front covers off and Barry started uncoupling the connecting rods and return crank etc, then the outer crossheads were removed. I loaded them onto a barrow and took them to the Coppersmiths for remetaling. Barry then uncoupled the inside connecting rod and motion followed by the crosshead cotter. Barry then set about breaking the crosshead, in the usual manner with the gibs and wedges. There was no sign of movement and the crosshead appeared to be stuck fast. At this time BR had introduced work-study and we were allowed 52 minutes to remove the crosshead.

Plate 113
Sometimes a visitor on the Edge Hill Goods, un-rebuilt Patriot No 45539 'E C Trench' is seen here at Manchester

K Field

141

52 minutes soon passes when things are going wrong.

A rag was dipped in paraffin wrapped around the cotter slot and set fire to. The cotter was then hit in again to try and ease it, but still no sign of movement. After about an hour he told me to go to see Sid Wright, the Chargehand, for some excess time. Barry went to mash and we both sat down beside the engine waiting for Sid. Along came Sid who was reluctant to give any excess time as it came out of his bonus. He went under the engine. The next minute there was a clatter. Barry and I instantly realised the crosshead had broke. Sid had only given it one hit: the last straw had broken the camel's back. Barry said 'What about some excess time?' Sid's remark as he went off was 'You haven't been trying hard enough'.

The Annesley Push and Pull Tank

In early 1962 I was working on the drop pit with Fitter Paul Heyes and our Fitters Mate on that occasion was John 'Nobby' Clark. Paul came into the drop pit and told us he had arranged for the Annesley 'Push & Pull' tank engine No 41280 that worked DIDO, reputed to mean Day In Day Out, to have its pony wheels changed. An easy job for a Friday morning. Friday morning came and the engine was still in steam on the drop pit as planned. We had never changed a pair of wheels on one of these engines before. This turned out to be a longer job than we thought. It was 3.30 before we had finished. John, who normally did not work on the drop pit, said 'I would prefer not to have any of your snip jobs on a Friday'. (No 41280 was an early withdrawal for this class and was the only one cut up at Derby works in February 1963.)

Side Rods

Working with Paul Heyes again on the drop pit, we came to fit the side rods onto a 4F but they would not fit. Being on the drop pit, it was easy to line up the cranks as the table was capable of lifting the engine on the centre wheel allowing you to spin the outer wheels. Eventually we noticed the number stamped on the rods was not the same as the number on the engine, as some five or six days previously we had completed another 4 F and put the wrong rods on! 'Oh dear' said Paul 'How are we going to explain this one?' After a few minutes he went to see the Driver's Foreman to ask where the first 4F loco was. He was told that it was out working and should be returning later on that day. Paul asked if it could be put on the drop pit next morning as the loco had had extensive repairs carried out to four axle boxes and that he would like to check them. The next morning the loco was on the drop pit, the rods were removed and examined. Fortunately there was no damage and the correct rods were fitted.

Meal Times

At lunchtime Paul Mosley would come round to the engine we were working on and say 'We are dining on such and such today'. This would usually be the oddest loco on the Shed a visiting Midland 3F, Stanier 2-6-0, Eastern Region B1, K3, B16, some with steam reversers, or the engine that arrived mid morning from Edge Hill, returning on the 8.13pm Edge Hill fitted freight. The Edge Hill sometimes produced engines that were not regular visitors to the East Midlands such as Jubilees Nos. 45678 'De Robeck', 45670 'Howard Of Effingham' or Patriot Nos 45539 'E C Trench' and 45518 'Bradshaw', or the unnamed 45551. Jim went home for dinner and on his return he would join us and we would discuss railways.

Plate 114

Ex-MR Class 2F No 58175, built as No 1234 in 1875 by Neilsons seen here on the drop-pit shunt complete with SR target

Paul Mosley

On Wednesdays we would see the latest Brush Type 2 in the D5500 series, later to become Class 31, being delivered passing the Shed about 1.15 pm they passed onto the Eastern Region at the GN exchange sidings. We saw the blue liveried one and D0280 Falcon in a lime green colour which, at the time, seemed strange and an odd engine number. On the point of inter railway transfers, we later found out from one of the older Fitters, that the LNER on taking over the M & GN in 1936 had just added a prefix '0' to the M&GN engine numbers.

One miserable drizzling murky day Paul came round to say we were going on Midland 2F No 58175 (Plate 114) that was on the 'Field Side' It had been stored there for ages. At 12.30 pm we made our way to the engine. On climbing into the cab we asked why he had selected this particular one. His reply was so we could experience an open Deeley cab of a Midland 2F in dismal conditions! Just imagine, he said, working over the GN & LNW Junction from Low Level to Northampton, 22 stops, or working to Bourne on the M & GN. I pointed out that they usually had a fire! After about ten minutes we departed for a class 9F spending the next ten minutes stand with our backs to the wide firebox trying to get warm. I suppose it could have been worse, he could have selected a Johnson half cab loco. Paul eventually went on to the Advanced Passenger Train Project he then became the Commissioning Engineer for the Class 58 locomotives.

Work Study

Prior to the introduction of Work-Study the day Fitters worked long hours which were:

Week I   Monday to Friday 7.30 to 4.30 and Saturday morning 8.00 to 12.00
Week 2   Monday to Friday 7.30 to 4.30 and Saturday morning 08.00 to 12.00
Week 3   Monday to Thursday 7.30 to 5.30
Booked off Saturday

In actual fact, they worked overtime everyday, resulting in the hours being 07.30 to 6.30pm Monday to Friday and every Saturday morning. They would get a Sunday working about every six weeks. The working week was in actual fact five and a half days every week and Sunday, if available. The annual leave was two weeks.

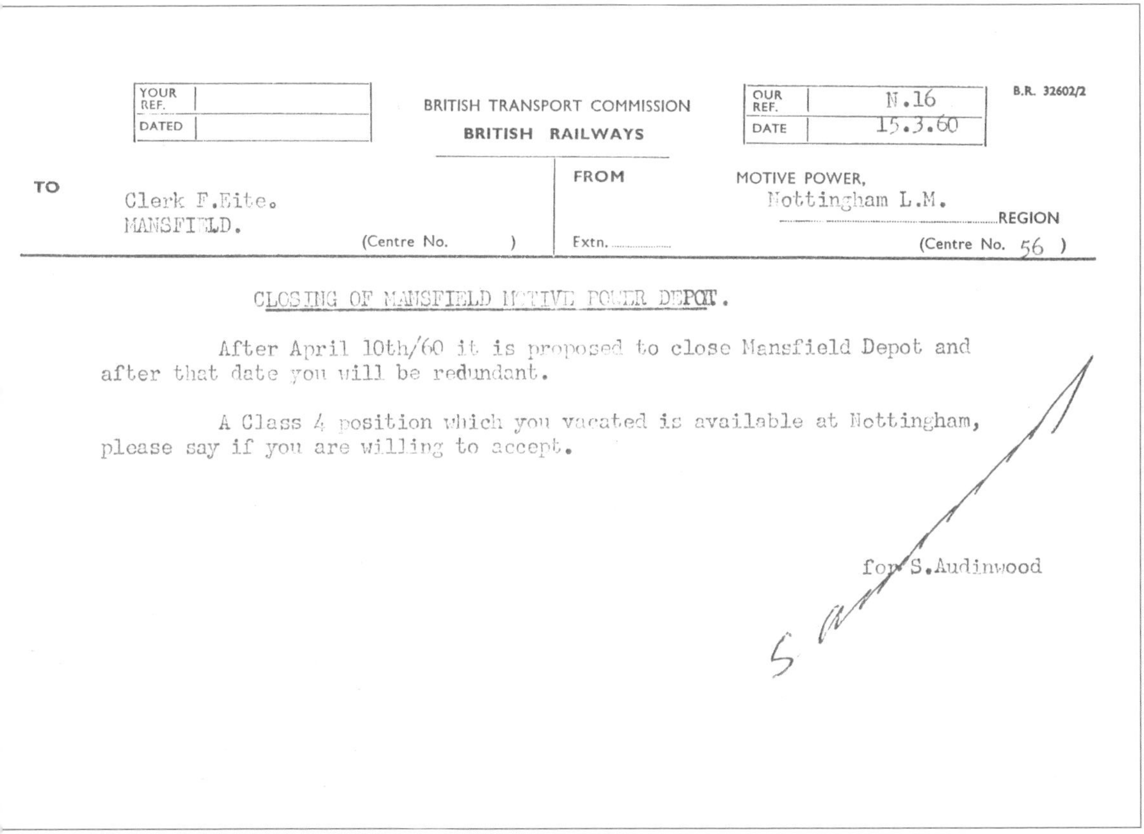

| YOUR REF. | | BRITISH TRANSPORT COMMISSION | | OUR REF. | N.16 | B.R. 32602/2 |
| DATED | | **BRITISH RAILWAYS** | | DATE | 15.3.60 | |

		FROM	
TO			
Clerk F.Eite.		MOTIVE POWER,	
MANSFIELD.	(Centre No.)	Nottingham L.M.	...........REGION
		Extn.	(Centre No. 56)

CLOSING OF MANSFIELD MOTIVE POWER DEPOT.

After April 10th/60 it is proposed to close Mansfield Depot and after that date you will be redundant.

A Class 4 position which you vacated is available at Nottingham, please say if you are willing to accept.

for S.Audinwood

Fig 11
Mansfield MPD Notice of Closure

F Eite

The Apprentice hours were 07.30 to 5.30 Monday to Thursday 07.30 to 4.30 Friday. I remember asking Cliff 'Chummy' Edwards 'Are you any worse off?' his remark was 'Slightly, but I don't want to go back to an 11 hour day and every Saturday it's nice going home at 4.30'. Some staff transferred from the footplate voluntarily when there was a vacancy(Fig 11). Others, such as some of the Stores Issuers, were Drivers who had to come off the footplate due to eyesight or other health problems. They all could tell some interesting tales. How that, as young cleaners, and there would be as many as forty on nights, however hard they tried polishing the axle boxes on the Johnson 'Spinners' the Driver would say 'Who's whitewashed my brasses then?' The Chargehand Cleaner would wipe the back of the spokes with a clean white cloth. Also they would tell how as passed cleaners, working out to Bourne and Saxby on the M&GN, they would be going along up the gradients and the Driver would check the boiler and say 'Don't put any more in'. They would watch the water getting lower and lower in the glass. The Driver kept repeating 'Don't put any water in'. The reason for this was that when going up gradients they required as much steam as possible. The vacuum ejectors were not very efficient and any drop in steam pressure would result in the vacuum falling, allowing the brake to drag. Putting cold water into the boiler would cause the steam pressure to drop, further reducing the vacuum, which would cause brake drag. Which was the last thing you wanted when the engine is down on power due to shortage of steam. They would watch the water get lower and lower, often being just in the gauge frame bottom nut. On reaching the summit the Driver would say 'Put the water in' and they would breathe a sigh of relief as they saw the water rise in the boiler. This was in the 1920s and no doubt the Driver had been doing it since the 1880s. He knew just how far to go without disastrous results such as dropping a fusible plug.

Lou Constantine once told me how, as a young Passed Cleaner, he left Nottingham Midland, first stop Trent. On arrival the fire was in good order, just the right amount of water in the boiler, so he got down off the engine. The Driver immediately said 'What about the lamps'. Instant panic from Lou - he could think of nothing he had done wrong. He had checked that the lamps were correct at Nottingham and there was no need to change them at Trent. Not knowing what he had done, he reluctantly asked the Driver what was wrong with the lamps? The Driver's reply was that they wanted cleaning - 'But we have only come from Nottingham' - 'They still want cleaning!' He never got down again until the Driver did.

Lou was later transferred to Horninglow, the ex-L&NWR Shed at Burton on Trent. His first Driver asked where he had come from. On replying Nottingham Midland the Driver said somewhat disparagingly 'A Midland man!' Although the amalgamation had taken place the staff were still very loyal to their former companies, thinking they were the best. The Driver was a man of few words and firing L&NW locomotives required a different technique to Midland ones. Fortunately for Lou the Driver gave him some tips. One night they were running rather fast and Lou said to the Driver 'You nip along here' the Driver's reply was to screw the tender brake on as they were running away! Eventually Lou parted from the Driver who reluctantly said, 'You will make a Fireman even if you are a Midland man'. Horace 'Sos' Parnham, an ex-Colwick LNW Fireman, recalled how they had relieved a loco at Northampton that was going to London. On looking into the firebox he said there were five knobs of coal bouncing on the bars and when they eventually got going he had never seen side rods go round so fast.

The Machine Shop

The machine shop would be a hive of activity in the morning with connecting and coupling rod bushes being pressed out. The bushes on being pressed out would then be re-metalled in the Coppersmith's shop and then machined. The machining of bushes and eccentric straps, axle boxes, piston packing, clack valves and sand valves etc would take place in the machine shop. Crossheads would pass through the Coppersmiths at great speed, the first ones there would be the first to be re-metalled. This process involved melting the old whitemetal off, and then re-metalling. They then had to be allowed to cool prior to machining. If there were several to machine they would go onto the planing machine a bit too hot. Along with planing cross heads the machinist, Les Dodsley senior, would carry out hair cuts at a shilling a time. His Barber's shop was situated among strategically stacked firebricks in the old workshop. If it ran over the dinner hour they used to carry on saying that it grew in railway time!

There was sufficient work for two Coppersmiths, the older, Len Guyler, who was the Railway Silver Band Master had been in the Royal Flying Corps at the end of the First World War. During World War Two he was called up again but was recalled back to the railway - as everything in those days went by rail he was considered to have a reserve occupation. Len, who had become part of the fittings after a lifetime in the same shop, used to relate that one morning he came to work and as he entered he looked up at the clock, which he had done for the last twenty years, only to find the clock gone. Chalked on the wall were the time and the words 'Time Flies'.

The younger Coppersmith was Bill Orton, an ex-Toton, who like many railway men was redundant on completion of his apprenticeship. He then had to move away. Bill was a good Coppersmith and liked to get involved with anybody's job but his own. Other things such as lunch tins would be soldered up - there was not much plastic in those days. One of Bill's tricks was to pour soap powder into the grindstone water bath, for some unsuspecting Fitter to switch on the machine only to be covered in soapsuds. The drop pit workshop, which was part of the large 1868 repairshop, was very cold on a winter's morning until the stove was lit. It would often be banked up last thing at night. One trick, whilst the Fitter was away at lunch, was to build the fire up, put an air line up the chimney to draw the fire and finally drop coal down the chimney. The Fitter on return would find the whole stove glowing red. All nice and warm but too warm if you had to spend the next two or three hours filing and scraping axle boxes. But that's how it was, never a dull day.

The Coppersmiths Mate was Ruben Carlisle, a small friendly man who had time for everyone. By the afternoon, if all the metalling and pipe repairs had been done, the Coppersmiths would turn their attention to repairing loco and Guards' brake lamps plus handlamps brought in from the yards. In the extremely cold winter of 1962/63 it was almost impossible to find a lamp vessel. Many had been removed from the lamps and resided in the outside lavatories in the Meadows - sufficient heat was given off by one to stop lavatories freezing up. Due to the shortage of lamp vessels, the Coppersmiths and Mate set about making new ones, one marking out, one cutting and one soldering, The trains could not run without them, so it was a bit hectic at this time.

The Blacksmiths

The Blacksmiths was located in the corner of the machine shop and had probably been there since it had been the spring shop in the 19th century. Alec Hunt was the Blacksmith and his Striker was Len 'General' Booth. The routine work was straightening sand pipes, sand pipe stays, rail guards and repairs to the brake gear of locos after being derailed. Alec also carried out oxy-acetylene cutting and burning. You would go to Alec and request his services He either replied 'Where's the engine' or sharply 'No gas'. Which ever reply you received, a few minutes later Len would trundle the oxy-acetylene barrow round to the engine. The majority of burning jobs were in smokeboxes and on the drop pit. Alec was over six-foot tall and if it was a small box you would be handed the gun, called the burner, and given instructions. Len, prior to being the Blacksmiths Striker, related how he had previously been a Tubers Mate. This involved working in smokeboxes which were black and damp. In the early years they used bare gas jets in both firebox and smoke box for illumination. One morning he climbed into the smokebox of a Compound. The gas pipe had been left pushed through the tubeplate and into the boiler. He had just turned round when his Mate pushed his lighted burner through the firebox tubeplate and there was an explosion. Fortunately he was not looking into the boiler but the side of his face was peppered with boiler scale. The accident was investigated and was thought to be the result of steam risers catching the gas tap when replacing their shovels in the storage brackets that were on the same stanchion.

The explosion reminded Len of the First World War. He told me he had seen the white cliffs of Dover going away twice and wondered if he would be coming back a third time. Len also said how, when he started in 1919, the engines were a wine colour, the sheds clean and every Saturday morning the boarding on the turntables would be scrubbed white like a butchers block. When No 46100 'Royal Scot' came to Nottingham he gave me a booklet which had been produced by the LMS of the American tour in 1933 and presented to the company's servants, as they were then known. Even in the 1960s what few letters we wrote would be signed 'Your Obedient Servant'!

Joiner's Shop

The Joiners shop was located in the original 1868 Boiler and Engine House. Its original occupant was used to drive the machinery in the main workshop. Fred Straw was the joiner, again a man who had been made redundant at Colwick, the ex-GNR Shed, he then came to Nottingham. His Mate was Tommy James, T K James the pavement artist. Tommy was an excellent artist who had exhibitions of his work. One of his watercolours was of the joiners shop (Plate 115) faithfully painting in both the boarded up and cracked window. From the picture you can see that the door has two knobs and you could guarantee that every time you went to open the door you got hold of the wrong one! Tom showed me an oil painting he was working on of a sunflower. The main flower in the picture had been painted from the rear! As well as being a painter he was also an excellent sign writer. On one occasion we were sending a pair of Britannia wheels away which had a loose tyre. Tom with loving care painted the engine number, its Shed 9E (Trafford Park) and Return to Nottingham 16A on the edge of the wheel. No chance of loosing that label.

Plate 115
The Joiner's Shop with its two door knobs, in a view looking towards the drop pit

Fred Straw

Royal Scot Class No 46112 'Sherwood Forester' carried the regimental coat of arms above the nameplate. This loco had been exchanged with No 46140 'The Kings Royal Rifle Corps' at the request of the Chamber Of Commerce to work the 8.15 'Robin Hood' express to London St Pancras calling at Manton only to pick up passengers. One day it returned to the Shed minus one regimental crest. In those days things like this did not usually go missing. The other side crest was removed then used as a pattern to make a mould. A new crest was then cast in whitemetal. We could have had one made from brass at Derby but Mr Croydon was the type who would have the Shed make their own. So, after the casting had been finished and cleaned up, it was Tommy James's job to paint it again with loving care. Several years later I saw the crest at a railway exhibition in an Art Gallery on Victoria Street, Nottingham and I wondered if the owner knew its history. (This crest is now in Derby City Museum with the nameplate and the original nameplate and brass badge from the other side at the Sherwood Foresters Museum, Nottingham Castle. To be strictly accurate the badges should have been handed as per Regimental practice, ie one deer looking to the left the other to the right)

There were many charcters around in those days. Two names of Boiler Washers spring to mind, Bill Jelly and Harry Paling. Harry was also an artist taught by Tommy James. One Tuber was Jess Wild, known as 'Ten Men', an extremely conscientious man who was asked on one occasion, when sitting on a rail looking rather tired 'Where's those ten men?'; Jess's reply was 'Most of them have died'. There was also the Shed Labourer, 'Kirkby' Jack, Jack Hague.

Plate 116
Group Photo of the team

Roy Green

The Fire Brigade (Plates 116 and 117)

The Shed had its own fire brigade. It consisted of several Fitters and Mates on a retainer of around £2 10s 0d per annum. Although this does not seem much you would have to wait several years for a vacancy before you could join. Fortunately we had very few fires. On one occasion there was a shortage of overtime but fortunately a minor fire started under the old coal stage so we utilised the 'fire brigade' leaving sufficient work to accommodate everyone on overtime. There was, however, a serious side to the fire brigade. This was the competition that was run between various other parts of the railway in Nottingham. This took place in March and meant practising in February, usually when there was snow on the ground. Trying to save time, the brigade tried to be like the real City Fire Brigade by turning on the water whilst running out the hose, attempting to couple one hose to another before the water arrived. The water usually beat them!

Railcars and the Carriage Sidings

When the diesel railcars were introduced the Fitters were sent on courses. Like all courses some can be very informative but you really only learn through practical experience. Most call outs were to the station, usually for engines shutting down, whose cause was usually through low water. When built, the coolant systems were not pressurised. They were eventually pressurised but it took many years. On a summer's afternoon as many as five trips on foot would be made to the station to top the systems up. A bonus would be a station call at dinnertime when the Fitter would work through his dinner and get paid. On more that one occasion John Bowers would be conveniently standing, signing up some work sheets, outside the Foreman's Office, whilst his Mate Eric would phone from the coal hopper 'Fitters required at the station, and bring a toasting fork'. The toasting fork was used for isolating railcar final drives. The Foreman or Chargehand

Plate 117
Fire Practice at London Road low level station an ex-LNER O4 2-8-0 is passing by

Roy Green

would come out, see John and tell him he was required at the station. John would say 'Do you realise my Mate has gone to mash, but duty calls' He would then disappear before the job was given to someone else. On their return he reminded the Shop Office Clerk that they had foregone a meal break and to show them no meal on their time card.

The internal phones used a version of morse code, just dots and dashes. There may have been seven or eight on the circuit and calls could not be traced. Although the phone would be going dots and dashes all day the uncanny thing was you only ever responded to your call. The Mechanical Foreman's office was four dots.

Plate 118

Ex-Caledonian Railway 4-2-2 No 123 seen here at London Road Low Level Station in
October 1953

Bill Reed

To get onto other parts of the railway system, which at that time was probably larger
than that of the General Post Office, you had to go through the operator. Many
telegrams were sent which would be dictated over the phone using a word or a series
of words from the Telegram Code Book. One of the codes was 'EXPAM' which meant,
'Expert Attention Required Immediately'. (Another was 'GROVE' which was the code
for a Royal Train.)

Railcars stabled over night at Nottingham Carriage Sidings were refuelled by the night
fitting staff. We would go in the van from the Shed and park it in the Nottingham Low
Level Station yard and would walk through the old station. The booking office and
waiting rooms were still being used, mainly as a signal and telegraph department store.
The lighting was gas, although only a few were lit and it did not take much imagination
to realise how poorly lit stations were until the advent of electricity. This station was
built in 1855 to the design of T C Hine, one of Nottingham's prominent Victorian
architects, who had also designed many of the houses in the Park Estate Building.

This was commenced in 1820 and was further developed by the Duke of Newcastle later in the 19th Century. Today, apart from the Royal parks, this estate is the largest gas lit area in Europe. As we walked to the end of the new arrival platform I recalled the visit of the Caledonian Railway Single No 123 which had been exhibited there in October 1953 (Plate 118). There was an odd thing about this station - it was built by the Great Northern Railway, the London & North Western Railway also used it, arriving via the GN and L&NWR Joint line from Northampton. On the opening of Nottingham Victoria Station in 1899 most of the GN trains were transferred from the Low Level station into the new Victoria Station. The GN/GCR would not allow the L&NWR to use the new Station. So from 1899 until 1923 the station was owned by the GN but used mainly by the L&NWR. After the amalgamation in 1923 it was owned by the London & North Eastern Railway and used by the London Midland & Scottish Railway.

On arrival at the Carriage Sidings we would commence fuelling and most nights were very routine. As well as fuelling and doing small repairs and changing the odd starter motor there were other more interesting jobs. Although the facilities were very limited, Joe Vickers would do anything to have the set ready for the morning service. One very bitterly cold and windy snowy night a set failed in the carriage siding with a collapsed final drive seizing up the wheel set. To clear the sidings, Joe, snowing or not, was determined to have the final drive stripped and clear the sidings ready for a full passenger service to commence on time by the morning and have the set ready to go to Derby for a wheel change. This we achieved with one torch, a paraffin lamp and a sheet of sacking between the body and bogie to keep the wind and snow out. Another night we had a call to an ex-LNER B1 in Nottingham Victoria Station where, on arrival and examining the engine, we found a broken cylinder drain tap. Off in the van we went to Colwick Shed for a replacement. Once there we contacted the Chargehand who said we would have to rob one, pointing to a B1 which had suffered a bent con rod. The tap was removed from this engine and taken back to Victoria Station. Whilst we were fitting the replacement cylinder tap a signal on the next road was pulled off. Realising a train was coming, we stepped back. The next minute a BR Standard 9F 2-10-0 burst into the station sounding its whistle, going north at a tremendous speed. They always seemed even faster when you were only a few feet away! It was nice to see a Class 9F in action especially having carried out valve and piston examinations on most of these Annesley based engines. With the Beeching plan in full swing the experience of redundancy brought us together with other redundant railwaymen, one being Colin Randel from Annesley. Even before Beeching, few railway men would start and finish their railway service at the same location. Colin eventually became an MS3 grade, which was an example of how you could reach a senior position starting as a Fitter.

In conversation about the 9Fs I mentioned the B1 we had been called to at Victoria station. Colin Randel had a brother who had been a Fireman and had told him that if the Nottingham Goods South signal was off the Driver could run fast as they knew they had the road through Queens Walk Goods Yard. Then it was over the bridges and viaducts crossing the Meadows through Arkwright Street Station, over Broad Marsh Viaduct, through Weekday Cross Tunnel and into and out of the station then diving into Mansfield Road Tunnel, which was always full of smoke, and, with a bit of luck, a fast run to Annesley. At this point they had got plenty of steam with the road set for them. They would take advantage of this, allowing the fire to thin out as less cleaning would be required on arrival at the ash pit.

Whilst on the subject of the BR Standard 9F, there was a working about 4.30 from Nottingham Eastern Region siding usually known as the GN, Great Northern, which was opposite the Midland Region carriage sidings. The GN yard was lower than the Midland and the loco would have to lift the train in the length of the yard to pass over the Midland lines to Lincoln. This was a tremendous sight and sound and a loco fitted with a single chimney would almost shake the town with its exhaust, but from a loco that was fitted with double chimney there was hardly a murmur.

Engines in Trouble!

The diesel/electric and especially electric locomotives had many benefits over steam. They were so much cleaner plus they had far shorter down time for maintenance However, in one respect they could never match steam and that was reliability. A steam locomotive could be virtually dropping to pieces, and in the end they were, yet they would still keep going. The following stories illustrate how steam locomotives kept moving despite what would seem a catastrophic failure.

'One night about three in the morning whilst we were working down the carriage sidings Joe and I heard a knocking somewhere in the distance. We kept going out of our hut as we realised that it was getting nearer but there was no sign of anything. It must have been two hours later, when a 8F came slowly down the bank from Melton with clouds of steam coming from the front left cylinder end followed by a bang. The engine passed by and on through the station. On returning to the Shed I enquired what they had found. Sid Wright the Chargehand replied that it had knocked the cylinder cover off. Not convinced I went to look at the engine to find that the nut retaining the piston head had come off allowing the piston to knock the cylinder cover off. Further examination revealed that on the backstroke the piston rod had pulled the piston head back into the cylinder casting. That was the bang we had heard on every revolution of the wheels. The loco was scrapped. How many miles had it run like that to get home?' -
                                                                                   Roy Padgett

'I remember well one occasion when I was given a Driver's Report Card stating 'I heard and felt a big bang when coming down the bank, after that the beat (exhaust beat) sounded funny'. I went to examine the 5X loco and discovered that the inside valve gear had somehow come adrift and was wrapped around the crankshaft. Fortunately the centre valve had stuck in the position cutting off the steam supply to the centre cylinder, letting it ride free as if in neutral. Now that was a serious defect and yet the loco had completed its job - I found, in contrast, that most complete failures of electric and diesel/electric locomotives were caused by relatively minor defects. That's progress!'
                                                                                   Les
Dodsley

The Engineer's Department

The Engineer's Department, often known as the Civils, had three diesel shunters numbered in the ED series. Two were standard gauge, ED 3 and ED 5 (Plate 119) one of which worked at the Beeston Sleeper Depot and the other at the Central Materials Depot, Lenton. They were built by John Fowler of Leeds in 1949 and had two engines. One was a two-cylinder donkey engine, which had to be started by hand. This was then

Plate 119
ED3 and ED5 in No 1 Shed Roundhouse at Nottingham on August 23rd, 1963

H Needle

mechanical gearbox and jack shafts. Driving these was a work of art.

They had a three speed gear box, the gear lever almost as big as a steam shunter reversing lever and a clutch pedal about one foot off the floor which had to be depressed when changing gear. A third loco ED 10 was built by Ruston & Hornsby Lincoln in 1958 and had chain drive. It was three-foot gauge and worked on the extensive three-rail system at Beeston Sleeper Depot. There was also a narrow gauge steam loco Service Engine No 1 built by Bagnall in 1911. During the summer months, when the sleeper traffic was heavy, the narrow gauge steam loco would be put in steam. Due to the low roof this engine was not allowed into the workshops, where the sleepers were cut and machined to length. One wet day the loco, on approaching the workshop, failed to stop, being pulled along by the weight of the trams, as the wagons were known, with disastrous results. The chimney, which was approximately three feet tall, struck the low roof and was broken off at the base. To effect a quick repair the two halves were retrieved, brought back to the Shed, gas welded and refitted.

Chapter Nine
The Final Five Years

The five years from 1960 to 1965 saw Nottingham gradually decline from being an active steam centre to a diesel only location. However, much was to happen before then. On the 23rd January 1960 the, now preserved, Black Five No 45407 came to Nottingham and Frank Eite was informed that there was a position for him in the Nottingham Office. By May 1960 there were still 18 ex-Midland Railway engines working out of 16A, five of which, Nos 40411, 40421, 43953, 43954 and 43958, had been at Nottingham all or most of the time since 1925. Of this group No 43953 was destined to be the last ex-Midland Railway locomotive in service, being withdrawn from 12D (Workington) in November 1965 and cut up at Campbells of Airdrie in January 1966. A couple of rare visitors were the ER Pacific No 60038 'Firdaussi' of Leeds, Holbeck (55A) and on 18th August the LMS main line Diesel No 10001 on the 8.20 am to London with D225 taking on the duty the following week.

There was also a threat of a National Railway Workshop strike, which was to have taken place on 17th October. This strike was called off after arbitration (the Gallibald Report) but the Locoshed Fitting Staff were not taken into account. Subsequently there was a threat of strike action by all the RE staff. The footplate staff declared that they would not take engines off Shed that had defects, thus effectively closing down the railway. The system could still run for a short time without workshop output but not on a day-to-day basis without RE (repairing engines) staff. Support from the WE (working engines) staff, was vital and, although the strike by fitting staff did take place, the railway management decided to talk after a couple of days. As an Apprentice I went around on my James 123cc motorbike passing on the strike message. Not everyone had telephones at that time.

(Jim Perkins)

The 13th of October saw the pioneer 8F No 48000 transferred back to Nottingham and the ER L1 No 67769 on Shed for working the Derby-Nottingham trains but it was transferred back to the Colwick on the ER later in the month (Plate 123). The 1960s saw some route changes and additions to Nottingham diagrams these were:
Ratcliffe-on-Soar Power Station
Nuneaton to Coventry and Bedworth Oil Sidings
Lichfield to Brownhills Oil Sidings
Nottingham to Immingham Reception Sidings and Shed plus Lindsey Oil Refinery.
Nottingham to Whitemoor (now the site of Whitemoor Prison) via Sleaford and Spalding
Nottingham to Boston and Skegness
Nottingham to Grantham

The old Nottingham working, since 1845 (when the Nottingham to Lincoln line opened) the Tamworth Mail, was diverted to Crewe and later to Lichfield via Stafford. At this point it is worth relating a few details about this famous, at least locally, working. A description by David Joy of an accident with this train, which took place in early October 1850, can be found in Volume 1 of this series. The incident that Joy describes was when the Mail was diverted onto the Mansfield line instead of heading towards

Plate 120
The Midland Pullman seen here passing through Beeston Station in July 1961

C Beck

Plate 121
A severely damaged Class 8F No 48621 seen here on the field side

T Hewitt

Beeston with a head on collision taking place, fortunately without loss of life.

One hundred years later the engine and men initially worked a Nottingham to Lincoln train then the 8.00 pm Lincoln to Tamworth. The train stopped at Collingham and Newark en-route Whilst at Nottingham the engine came off the train and went onto the loco Shed. The preferred class of engine for this job was a Fowler 2-6-4T such as No 42339 a class which, according to footplate staff, could accelerate better than the Stanier or Fairburn tank engines. A fresh engine then worked to Tamworth via Chaddesden Sidings with a stop at Burton on Trent before arriving at Tamworth High Level Station. At Tamworth the tanks were filled with water, the engine then taking one mail coach down to the Low Level Station. This was an extremely busy place with a movement required across the Up line onto the Down line. Once this movement had been made the coach was backed into the Bay to be loaded /unloaded. After the Irish Mail had gone through, a quick move was made back to the High Level Station. There was then a wait until 2.00 am for mail to be loaded and then it returned to Nottingham where the engine came off and went onto the Shed. The Driver for the return working to Lincoln booked on at 3.00 am and the Fireman at 3.16 am. They were always spoken to by the Running Foreman to check if everything was in order and to pass on any special instructions. This set of men then took the engine to the station and coupled up for the run to Lincoln St Marks.

Plate 122
Damaged 8F No 48621

T Hewitt

Plate 123
The pioneer Stanier Class 8F No 48000 seen here at Boat House Bridge,
Matlock on 2nd February 1953

B Matthews Collection

157

Plate 124
Class 8Fs and a BR 2-6-2T in No 2 Shed

D Newton

At Lincoln two coaches were detached and taken across to Central Station (Eastern Region). It was then back to the Midland side for a bit of shunting and on to the Shed to top up the engines' water tanks This was also water and 'snap' (food) time for the crew. The engine remained at Lincoln and the men worked a Cleethorpes to Birmingham train, usually with a B1. Leicester men took the train over at Nottingham.

1961

The shape of things to come, and a precursor to the HSTs, was the mid-day service from St Pancras to Leicester provided by the Midland Pullman (Plate 120), known as the Blue Pullman which was later extended to Loughborough and Nottingham. It departed from St Pancras at 11.20 am and arrived at Nottingham 1.20 pm, returning at 3.45 and arriving London at 5.45. After the summer service it was withdrawn from the Nottingham route due to low patronage and was eventually sent to the Western Region.

They should have used it on a more prestigious and timely train like 'The Robin Hood'. Talking of modern traction, one of the authors, Jim Perkins, once went with Fitter Les Dodsley to Edwalton Station in order to isolate the engine on a railcar, which had suffered a gearbox fire. The extinguisher contents had left a green coating on everything. It was a CFC called Chlorobromomethane a substance that is not allowed in these more enlightened times. In the summer of 1961 a severely damaged 8F No 48621 could be seen on the Field Side close to Middle Furlong Road. This engine had been in the charge of ex-Mansfield men working empty stock to Queniborough, Leictershire when it was struck on the side by another engine. The damage was so severe it had to go to Horwich works for repair. (Plate 121 and 122)

Another feature of Shed life was the visit by the mobile Mutual Improvement Train. The smell of this vehicle was wonderful, as were its polished metal and woodwork models. It was open to all staff that were interested. Its sectioned exhibits and diagrams revealed the internal workings of the everyday locomotive parts with exhaust and live steam injectors, ejectors, valve gears, ATC/AWS brake systems and many other items being displayed. The insides of those perennial problematic LMS items such as sands and exhaust injectors also were laid bare.

OUR FREIGHT TRAFFIC THIS WINTER

A Message to All Railway Staff from Dr. Richard Beeching, Chairman of the British Transport Commission

Never before has it been so necessary for us to attract to rail all the good traffic which we can get. The best of traffics is coal, and yet for the past two winters we have had to divert coal from rail to road, and pay for doing so, because we were not able to carry it all ourselves.

This winter we shall have a chance of taking more coal than we have moved in recent years. We mean to carry every ton that is offered. This will involve carrying about $3\frac{1}{2}$ million tons a week, compared with last winter's best of 3 million tons. In other words, we must clear an extra 10 to 12 million tons over 20 winter weeks.

You know better than I do what this means. We must, among other things, avoid the hoarding and over-ordering of wagons; they must be moved and cleared quickly and sent back to where they can earn money by being loaded with more traffic.

It will be difficult, but we *must* do it, and with your help we *will*.

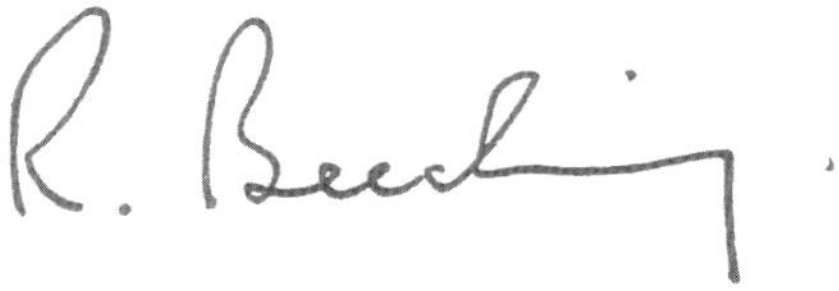

R. Beeching

Fig 12
A letter from Beeching
Jim Perkins

As well as injectors there were other problem items encountered on engines such as bent scoop blades. Objects in the troughs or inappropriate use of the scoop often caused such damage. Another problem area occurred in the water tank. This was when the water left the tank to go to the injectors, between which lay the tank sieves.

Plate 125
LNER B1 Class 4-6-0 No 61003 'Gazelle' waits outside No 3 Shed in July 1962 for its next turn of duty. The coal hopper is prominent in the background as is the old steam crane and a stored 2-6-4T engine

C Beck

Plate 126
Ex-Franco-Crosti Fitted Class 9F No 92024 in a photo taken on the 2nd May 1960
P H Groom

Plate 127

Taken in July 1962, this view shows the Nottingham wheel lathe and drop pit workshop. A set of 4F driving wheels can be seen. These were out of 44137

Jim Perkins

These are particularly inaccessible except on the more modern LMS and BR types and were a difficult job for which an Apprentice was usually the right size. The sieves and float mechanisms on Fowler and Stanier tanks were very awkward to clean or repair and the advent of external tank sieves on BR standard engines made life much easier. These, however, were more prone to frost and collision damage. When they first came out as the LMS Standard engine the Class 4F 0-6-0s could cause confusion as they came in both LH & RH Drive versions. This also meant a reversal of the Scoop & Tender handbrake, which gave even more confusion when tenders were exchanged. Sometimes, a Fireman or member of the Fitting Staff would wind the scoop down thinking it was the handbrake and vice versa. Note: The first LMS built 4F was 4027 and the first LH drive built one was 4207. Was the use of 4207 as the first LH drive engine a happy circumstance of similar numbers or a conscious decision, perhaps we may never know?

Plate 128
The reality of inside motion. No 44137 a Saltley (21A) engine

J Perkins

Plate 129
Ex-Midland Railway No 44137 on 29th August 1962 with its driving wheels removed

G Coltas

Plate 130
A rare drop pit visitor ED5 outside the workshop

Jim Perkins

Plate 131
Gradually being reduced to rust and scrap, ex-LMS Class 4F No 44313.
The bent side rod can be seen on the framing

L Ryder

Plate 132
Bagnall 3 Foot gauge saddle tank in the drop pit workshop

Roger Jones

Stanier 8Fs were usually the easiest of engines to work on, except for the first few which had that dreadful GWR abomination the smoke box regulator, a device as filthy to work on as super heater elements. The first 8F No 48000 was intermittently at Nottingham, as was another one of the first to be built No 48003. However, later members of the class were fitted with a boiler that had the regulator in the dome and 48003 was later fitted with one of these boilers in order to provide a spare boiler in the works which could be made available for 48000-48002 and 48004 to 48011.

There were two Nottingham engines that tended to get mixed up because of similar numbers. They were Nos 44658 and 44856. Unfortunately one day they were stabled side by side in No 3 Shed and the wrong one was prepared! 44658 was the lowest numbered Black Five, although not the oldest, and spent five years at 16A between

December 1960 and December 1964. Its twin had come to Nottingham in March 1960 and stayed until May 1963. One day Nos 44861 (16A) and 44681, a 5A (Crewe North) engine, were to be seen side by side in No 3 Shed. With such coincidences it is not surprising that the wrong engine was attended to in dim lighting, smokey conditions and bad memories. Another time there were two 8Fs having valves and piston exams. One had the dished piston and domed cover, the other had a piston with a nut and hollow cover. The covers were mixed up with the consequence that on moving the engine the domed cover and nut met and the cylinder end was smashed off. This caused severe damage to the cylinder and at that late stage scrapping of the engine was inevitable.

At this time there were an increasing number of ex-LNER engines visiting 16A and a rare visitor at this time, was the named ex-LNER B1 No 61003 'Gazelle' which can be seen next to the old breakdown crane (Plate 125). Also to be seen in this view are the prominent Coaling Tower along with stored 2-6-4T engines. In April 1961 the withdrawn Class 2P engine could be seen in store. These were Nos 40411, 40421, 40487, 40502, 40504, 40557, 40585, 40632, 40682 and 40691, all having been withdrawn in January and February of this year. Most of them were stored next to the outdoor machinery department. Ex-Franco Crosti Class 9F No 92024 can also be seen in the same area as the stored Class 2P locomotives, (Plate 126) one of which has had its vacuum ejector removed, probably for a Class 4F 0-6-0. In an open letter to all BR staff in September 1961 (Fig 12), a certain Doctor Richard Beeching was exhorting all railway staff to work harder. It might be said that Dr Beeching had inherited a poison chalice - others would say he should have downed it in one go! The Allocation for 1961 can be seen in Appendix Four and a 1961 Shed visit in Annex D

1962

Plate 127 shows the interior of the drop-pit workshop taken in June 1962. A very oily set of 4F driving wheels can be seen in the foreground. Despite their oily condition these wheels were removed for repairs to a hot box which had been caused by lack of it!. The engine from which these were taken was in the usual deplorable condition. (Plate 128) with the motion in the typical state of these inside cylinder locomotives and with the underneath of the engine from which the wheels had been removed on view. A rope sling was used to raise some of the dismantled valve gear and was wrapped around the left-hand side of the weighbar shaft. The engine is No 44137 of 21A Saltley.

The Wheel Lathe

The wheel lathe in the corner of the drop pit shop had a pair of ten feet diameter face plates and once had its traverse smashed when it was left unattended whilst turning a journal. It was also responsible for taking an index finger down to the first knuckle off George Peach the Turner. He had miscalculated the size of the balance weight on a set of wheels, which promptly chopped the finger end off as it went by! Gerald Hudson got George to the First Aid point and then to the hospital. He then went back to find the finger end, which was a real mess. He then promptly put it on the drop pit fire only to be asked by the hospital where it was!

Next to the wheel lathe was the Shed air compressor with the access ladder to the overhead crane just in front of it. This area was the 1868 'Outstation Fitting Shop' with only the single wagon road into it remaining from the series of lines that entered through the south wall until the 1920s. When the drop-pit was installed in the 1930s, the north wall had to be opened out to give access for wheels from the wheel drop. The wheels that had been removed from an engine or tender arrived into the workshop via a small turntable, which lead to the south wall entrance. The remainder of the old fitting shop was used by the Out Door Machinery Department as a store. On the north side of the building a short section of pit gave access to the underneath of engines. This pit lay between the drop pit and the small turntable for turning the wheels into the repair shop. It was connected through to No 2 Shed from one end and to a dead end road at the other end. The drop-pit, with its smell of stagnant water, was one of those distinct odours around the Shed.

The Nottingham drop pit also repaired tender wheels for freight engines allocated to Kirby Loco Shed. This Shed had a particular problem due to its location on a plateau, which meant that it was downhill in both directions with fully loaded coal trains. What this meant for loose-coupled trains, was excessive use of the tender brake a consequence of which was loosening of tyres. Repairs were carried out by ordering wheels from Crewe with Nottingham fitting them.

Others aromas to be found were those such as the quenching of copper in the coppersmiths shop and the melting of white metal. These, along with the turning of metal on the wheel lathe, still remain strong memories. But perhaps the strongest and most evocative was of a Shed full of hot engines with smoke and sulphur mixed with oil and water with LNER engines, having a particularly strong fish oil smell.

Some engines were out of service for a long time and one such engine that had stood on the drop-pit dead end for 17 months was the St Rollox built 4F No 44313. Early in 1959 it had suffered a severe wheel slip in Lenton Yard. The Driver, 'Crasher' Wilkinson, tried to control it by applying the sands but, when it gave grip, all rods bent like bananas and all crank pins sheared off (Plate 131). Midland 0-6-0 crank pins were particularly prone to shearing and No 44313 made a forlorn sight for a long time being progressively robbed of bits and became a 'Christmas Tree' to keep other 4Fs in service. These Scottish built 4Fs were very strong and, according to some Drivers, could be classed as 4 and a half F! There is no obvious reason for this, but it could have been due to the methods used to set the valves. Driver Wilkinson could not understand why it was not repaired as it was a very strong engine.

This engine was eventually withdrawn in December 1959 and left Nottingham in May 1960. After storage at Clay Cross, it was cut up at Wards, Killamarsh, in October 1960. This belief in strong St Rollox 4Fs is also mentioned in Bob Essery's 'Working with Midland Locomotives' where he describes the experiences with No 44190, built 1925 and withdrawn September 1963. Bill Jarvie, another Nottingham Driver, originated from the birthplace of No 44313. Other engines that were on the drop-pit for wheel removal were the ex-LNER B1 No 61161 and 'Royal Scot' No 46158, 'The Loyal Regiment' plus Britannia No 70041, 'Sir John Moore'. Class 8F No 48024 can be seen in Plate 133 just in front of the drop-pit and machine shop.

The 3ft Gauge

The narrow gauge No 1 at Beeston Creosote Works was not well maintained and one late winter suffered frost damage to the injector, as well as a fractured cylinder block. During the summer months when the sleeper traffic was heavy the services of this steam shunter were required so the loco was loaded onto a 'Dow Mac' wagon and brought back to the Shed. This was to be the last general repair to be carried out in the original Midland Railway 1868 workshop (Plate 130). The engine was stripped, bearings re-metalled, piston rods turned in the lathe and boiler re-tubed. The major repair was to the cylinder block casting, this was carried out by Gerald Hudson. A replacement injector was also found and fitted. On completion the loco was loaded onto a wagon and taken into No 1 Shed and fired up. At the time Roy Padgett was working with Paul Heyes who carried out the steam test. This involved raising steam until the safety valve lifted. As he was the youngest, he had to be the Fireman. He fetched a barrow of coal and began firing, getting well and truly carried away, until Paul said, 'We're not going far'. The pipe work was checked for blows and the safety valve, a Ramsbottom type, allowed to lift, blowing off at 120 psi. To check the repairs to the cylinder block the regulator was opened to put steam into the cylinder casting. There were no blows or leaks and Gerald's repair to the cylinder block was 100% successful.

Plate 134
Royal Scot Class No 46136 'The Border Regiment' seen here taking on
water in July 1962 with the coal hopper control cabin on the left

J Perkins

Plate 135
Three engines await differing fates with No 46100 Royal Scot being preserved and Nos 47631
and 40165 being scrapped at Birds, Long Marston (Feb 1967) and Cashmores, Great Bridge
(May 1963)

C Beck

Early in July No 46136 'The Border Regiment' was photographed outside the coal hopper cabin having its tender tank replenished before going for coal (Plate 134). The most famous engine to be allocated to Nottingham was a member of this class, 'Royal Scot' itself, No 46100 which was allocated to 16A between December 1959 and September 1962. Withdrawn in October 1962, 'Royal Scot' was in store at Nottingham, then at Crewe Works until June 1963 when Butlins bought it as an exhibit for their Holiday Camp at Skegness. When this engine first came to Nottingham the fitting staff examined the inside valve gear. This was different from our usual 3 Cylinder engines, the Jubilees, in that it comprised 4 slide bars rather than a large cross head and two slide bars as could be seen on the Jubilees and rebuild Patriots such as No 45532 'Illustrious'.

By chance one of the authors saw No 46100 on its way to Skegness being towed across the over bridge, now demolished, near Meadow Lane Crossing. In company with No 46100 whilst in store outside No 1 Shed were the 0-6-0T No 47631 and 2-6-2T No 40165 (Plate 135). At this time, the autumn of 1962, the coal stacks had been removed down to ground level. The evocative photograph in Plate 59 is an inside view of No 3 Shed when No 46100 was in service and shows four engines at rest in the north east corner of the Shed. Of these four engines, three were Nottingham based with the fourth, Black Five No 44663 a Saltley (21A) engine. Two of these engines Nos 44806 and 46100 survived into preservation. In a minor detail No 46100 was unique in that the cab roof guttering strip only came half way across the roof, whereas on all other members of the class the strip was along the whole length.

Although some Royal Scots were being withdrawn others were still to be seen in service. No 46152 'The Kings Dragoon Guardsman' (the original 'Royal Scot') was given a valve and piston exam on 1st December 1962 in No 3 Shed (Plate 136). This engine, along with No 46115 the first of the rebuilt versions to be fitted with smoke deflectors, No 46128, fitted with experimental roller bearing middle big end in 1957, plus Nos 46140 and 46160 were to soldier on until May 1965. No 46115 became the final Royal Scot in service when it was withdrawn in October 1965. That two of this fine class have been preserved is entirely due to individuals with foresight, as the official preservation plans did not include any. Those who decided on what should or should not be preserved must have gone to the Harold Macmillan School of historical awareness: Euston Arch was destroyed in his time.

A 60s Montage

The following evocative photographs by Cyril Beck (1924-1991), who worked at Plesseys, were taken in the period between 1961 to 1964. They show a variety of engines around the Shed and out on the line. During World War Two Cyril served in the West Yorkshire Regiment, being stationed in India and Burma (1941-45). During the drive to push the Japanese out of Burma he had been asked and volunteered to work on the footplate of those locomotives used in that theatre of operation. After the Japanese surrendered he eventually ended up in Singapore. Once again on the footplate, Cyril can be seen in the Driver's seat of 46251 'City of Nottingham' when it was at Annesley for the RCTS tour of Swindon on 9th May 1964 (Plate 137).

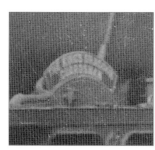

Plate 136

An evocative view, taken on 1st December 1962, of No 46152 also shows its RH valve and cover removed. The piece of timber near the cylinder is supporting the RH crosshead. There must have been some problem with the crosshead cotter as the bottom slide bar has been removed. Other engines are No 42333, a Fowler 2-6-4T, and 75062 BR Standard Class 4

Tony Hill

Plate 137

Cyril Beck on the footplate of No 46251 'City of Nottingham' at Annesley Loco Shed. The small
brass plate below the cab gives details about modifications

C Beck

Plate 138 shows a view across the Shed yard taken in 1963 looking towards the Castle
with Class 8F No 48342 of 16B (Annesley). What is interesting about the Shed plate on
this engine is that it has been welded to make up the correct Shed code. There were so
many engines at Annesley that they did not have sufficient plates to go around, so
anything that was close was altered! Behind the 8F is B1 No 61007. Also in view from
right to left, are Black Fives Nos 45064 of 15A (Leicester Midland) and 44805 of 21A
(Saltley) plus one unidentified ex-LNER Class B1.

Plate 139 shows two Class 9F locomotives: No 92040 of 40E (Colwick) with single
chimney and an unidentified double chimney version both at rest against the buffer
stops on adjacent roads outside No 2 Shed in 1963.

Plate 138
In this Shed yard scene are Nos 48342 (16B), 61007, 44805, 44854 and 45064

C Beck

Although this volume is about the Midland and its successors, the inside view of Annesley Loco Shed (LMR) in 1966 shows the conditions that both engines, by this time nearly all ex-LMS & BR types, and men had to contend with. This atmospheric view in a typical straight road Shed has three Banbury (2D) Britannias in steam, all with nameplates removed (Plate 140).

The final Britannia to be built No 70054 'Dornoch Firth' is seen alongside the last of the class to be named No 70046 'Anzac'. The other engine is either 70050 'Firth of Clyde', 70051 'Firth of Forth', 70052 'Firth of Tay' or 70053 'Moray Firth' all of which were Banbury based at this time, as was No 70047, the only unnamed member of the class. The earlier Annesley allocation of this class had come to Nottingham for concentration repairs but by 1966 Nottingham, by then 16D, was no longer a steam locomotive Shed.

The subject of Plate 141 is the Aston (2J) Black Five No 44942 standing next to the outdoor machinery building.

A very rare photograph taken at Beeston Level Crossing, (Plate 142) shows an engine that should not have been there. This view is of ex-LNER A1 Pacific No 60138 'Boswell' of 50A (York) on a freight train, which had come from the Eastern Region. These engines were not allowed on Midland lines due to their axle weight. They weighed 104 tons as against the heaviest allowed, which were the BR Britannias at 94 tons 0 cwt. This engine was taken off at Trent Station (which was opened in May 1862 and closed 1968) and returned to whence it came in a great hurry!

Photographed alongside the steam crane are Horwich 'Crab' 2-6-0 No 42799 of 16D (Nottingham), and Jubilee No 45647 'Sturdee' of 21A Saltley. (Plate 143) Black Five No

44735 of 9E Trafford Park can be seen in Plate 146 where it is taking water on the exit line from No 3 Shed with No 2 in the background.

Plates 144 to 147: The engine in Plate 144 is the Jubilee Class No 45573 'Newfoundland' of 55A (Leeds Holbeck) which is showing special train code IX24 and is seen on the ash pit and again after leaving No 3 Shed after being turned. Interesting features of these two views are the rail tankers and, from left to right, the Tank House, Fitters Mess Room, 3 Shed, and Electricians Shop in the corner of 3 Shed with the North wall of 2 Shed on the right. Jubilee No 45694 'Bellerophon' of 56A Wakefield and Black Five No 44735 of 9E Trafford Park are both showing special train codes, IT53 for the Black Five and IX23 for 'Bellerophon'. In this view taken on the 31st March 1965, the new traction is in evidence with D5202 moving into No 3 Shed.

Plate 139
Class 9F No 92040 and another Class member at Nottingham in 1963

C Beck

Plate 140
Inside Annesley Locoshed with a trio of very dirty BR Britannias

C Beck

BR Class 9F No 92103 of 15C Leicester (Midland) was in almost ex-works condition when seen in the location used for stabling visiting engines that were waiting for their next turn of duty. In this highly photographed location (Plate 148) No 3 Shed, the Coaling Tower, ODM buildings and its hydraulic accumulator tower can clearly be seen. The Nottingham Black Five No 44861 (Plate 149) is seen at the same location.

1963

The early winter of 1963 was very severe with thirteen weeks of frost and conditions in the Shed were very difficult, with both steam and diesel engines freezing up. For the authors however it meant travelling to Derby Works for eight months' works experience, the bad weather period occurring in the middle of their time away from Nottingham Locoshed. That winter, like 1947, has gone down in railway history and we are thankful not to have experienced it on the drop-pit! Even in ordinary winters the spanners used on the drop-pit had to be warmed up before being handled or attacked with a hammer.

August 28th saw both the Nottingham based Fowler 0-4-0 diesel shunters Nos ED3 & ED5 stabled in No 1 Shed in store (Plate 119). Behind them the 0-6-0 'Jocko' EE

Plate 141
Black Five No 44942 (2J) Aston seen here next to the derelict ODM Boiler House
C Beck

shunter No 12053. These two 0-4-0s, what might be called Diesel Jinties, were part of a batch of five built for the Engineers Department in 1949. They were numbered ED2 to ED6 with the Nottingham engines having builders Nos 4200042 and 4200044. ED5 was scrapped in 1965. ED3 however outlasted the Shed and was not scrapped until 1967. Examples of this type, which were also used at industrial locations, do survive, but none of the BR engines survive.

There were still a few Jubilees in service and Derby (16C) based No 45684 'Trafalgar' was seen in (Plate 150) in No 3 Shed for its next turn of duty. Another member of the class and a visitor from Burton, at that time coded 17B, No 45618 'New Hebrides' could be seen from a passing train whilst waiting its turn to take on coal and water in the summer of 1963 (Plate 151). It was in this summer that the fire brigade turned out in strength to a fire on the diesel stabling road that had been caused by a 9F dropping hot ash. The brigade responded to a reported oil fire, expecting fuel tanks to be on fire, only to find that the Shed staff had extinguished the burning sleepers and ballast! This was quite a turn out with six fire engines and the entire backup!

Plate 142
LNER Pacific No 60138 'Boswell' at Beeston Level Crossing

C Beck

A portent of the future was the demotion of Nottingham Shed from 16A to 16D in September 1963. At this time there was a wholesale change in Shed codes in the area the full list for those in the 16 series being:
16A Toton.
16B Annesley
16C Derby
16D Nottingham
16E Kirkby-in-Ashfield
16F Burton-on -Trent
16G Westhouses
16H Hasland
16J Rowsley
and sub depots
Cromford
Middleton Top
Sheep Pastures   Annex G gives further information on Shed codes.

As related previously, Driver H Smith worked the 1963 RCTS special to Horwich Works on 13th October with 'Crab' No 42896, one of those that had recently been re-allocated to Nottingham after an absence of five years. The 'Crabs', which were of L&Y origin, although built in LMS days, had a cotter return arm crank and these cotters could be difficult to remove especially if they had been necked, ie moved out of line and the hole damaged. This happened to No 42763, which meant the driving wheels had to come out and be sent to Derby for a new crankpin to be pressed in. These 2-6-0s were strong engines although working at 180-psi boiler pressure, which was low for an engine of this type. They were used on many seaside specials. The seats on these engines were like mushrooms, very plain but reasonably comfortable. One engine No 42725 had been given the Rugby Test Plant treatment in the late 1950s. This had pushed its boiler output from 16,000 to 20,000 lbs of steam per hour. It was however an isolated case and no more were modified. As the new main line diesels came into service, re-training was required for both footplate and fitting staff. This created problems as some older hands understandably found it hard going after a lifetime on steam. Training on this new technology was a little belated in respect of Fitting Staff and should have been carried out years earlier, especially for the younger ones. The traffic side had to re-train the Drivers because they ran the service. But apart from the diesel shunters, Fitters with experience of running Shed work had not had much training on the main line diesels. The Driver training at Nottingham was carried out with No D79

(45005) which stood on the No 3 Shed side dead end just outside No 2 Shed. One afternoon Bob Robinson and his team, Jim Perkins and Stan Smith, carried out a test run with this engine to Widmerpool where the breakdown gang were using the steam crane to put a new bridge over the A46 Fosse Way; a bridge that is still in place over the dual carriageway. This line is now being used as a test track for the new Virgin high-speed trains. What is scandalous about the Edwalton Line is its truncation at one end, less than two miles, thus severing Melton from Nottingham with consequent traffic congestion and one less rail route to London. If current plans come to fruition this line will once again be connected to Nottingham via a new line through Cotgrave using the now defunct Colliery Branch. This would give a connection from the Midland Railway Diversion route of 1875 to the Great Northern (Ambergate, Nottingham & Boston & Eastern Junction Railway) of 1850 and would be ironic considering the rivalry that the control of this line created in the 1850s. (See Volume I)

Plate 144
Jubilee No 45573 'Newfoundland' being 'fatted up'. Rail tankers are in the background next to the water tank and the diesel workshop

C Beck

1964

46251 'City of Nottingham' returned to the city after an absence of 18 years, when, on the 9th May, it arrived at Nottingham Victoria to work the RCTS Swindon Works special. Annesley men worked the train and the engine did not come onto Nottingham locoshed. The following year the nameplates and smoke box number plate from 'City of Nottingham', which was scrapped on the 12th of December 1964, were presented to Nottingham City Council, who keep them at the Wollaton Hall Industrial Museum, along with nameplate and number plates from GWR Hall class Nos. 4988 'Bulwell Hall' and 5999 'Wollaton Hall'

In February the WD 2-8-0s Nos 90486/90563 came on loan to Nottingham from Woodford Halse and in December Gorton based WD Nos

Plate 145

No 45573 emeging from No 3 Shed. From left to right can be seen the Water Tank House (Fitters and Drivers Mess Rooms), No 3 Shed, Electricians Shop and No 2 Shed

C Beck

90403 and 90040/90672 (Woodford Halse) followed them. These engines did very little work and can be seen whilst in store keeping company with Type 2 Diesels (Plate 152).

A casual visitor might have thought that there was still some heavy maintenance being carried out on steam locomotives at Nottingham, as the ex-LMS 4F No 44304 was to be seen in No 2 Shed on 26th June 1964 with its internal motion removed along with the buffer beam and apparently undergoing valves and piston repair or examination. This engine had in fact been withdrawn in June of this year then placed in store until November 1964. No 44304 is an engine that disproves the usual rule concerning class 4Fs starting with No 44207, in that they were left hand drive. Built at Crewe in 1926, it was one of a batch of 10 Nos 44302 to 44311, which were built with right hand drive controls. This was at a time when all new 4F 0-6-0 engines were built with what was to become the standard left hand driving arrangement. No 44304 was scrapped at the ominously named, for the steam allocation at least, Slag Reduction Company in December 1964.

In 1964 the design for a new diesel Shed at the west end of the site was being considered (Fig 13). This Shed would have stood across the entrance to No 1 and No 2 Sheds, very close to Furlong House. The Shed was never built due to traffic patterns changing beyond all recognition with the need for a Shed at Nottingham becoming unecessary, Toton being a more desirable location.

Plate 146
Black Five No 44735 taking water

C Beck

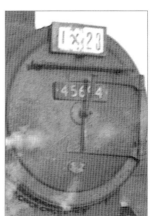

Plate 147
Jubilee No 45694 'Bellerophon' with Black Five No 44735 and Type 2 Diesel D5202

C Beck

The diesel allocation, in Appendix 4, was never to occupy this proposed Shed. It is therefore ironic, that by the time Toton had been built it was apparently in the wrong place! Block Trains were coming into vogue and it was this traffic that resulted in thousands of light engine movements. These block trains did not work into Toton Sidings and were the jobs that the engines were supposed to work to prevent the light engine workings.

Those mainline diesels that were based at Nottingham in late 1964 and early 1965 were placed in and around No 1 Shed. Type 2 locomotives were turned off, or stabled, in the Shed with the Crompton Type 4 locomotives standing outside in almost the same spot where the proposed diesel Shed would have been built. A juxtaposition of mainline diesels and steam locomotives could be seen in this area (Plate 153).

Between August and November 1964 a 9D (Newton Heath) Jubilee No 45564 'New South Wales' was in store at Nottingham. It was in November 1964 that notification of intent to close Nottingham 16D as a maintenance point was issued.

The Shed was still attracting enthusiasts and, on 19th September, the Northern Railfans Club visited 16D. Their train was hauled by BR Britannia Class Pacific No 70051 'Firth of Forth' a 5A (Crewe North) engine.

Plate 148
BR Standard 9F No 92103 of Leicester Midland (15C) seen outside the ODM No 3 Shed, Coal Tower and Accumulator Tower in the background

C Beck

Plate 154, shows No 70051 reversing into No 2 Shed whilst in the foreground is Nottingham Black Five No 45221 and the MIC Coach set. An earlier 4-6-2 Pacific visitor to the Shed was No 70019 'Lightning'. However 70051 was not the final 4-6-2 to come onto the Shed, as a very rare visitor on 22nd December was the BR Clan Class No 72005 'Clan McGregor'. This engine had failed at Leicester with poor injectors whilst on a Carlisle to St Pancras Goods and came to Nottingham for attention. Pacifics other than Britannias were very rarely seen at the Middle Furlong Road Shed. Even rarer were visits by engines from a railway that only ever built one 4-6-2, the Great Western Railway. However, this was to change, as in March 1965 ex-GWR 4-6-0 engine No 7029 'Clun Castle' came to Nottingham.

1965: Final Year of Steam at Nottingham.

In this the final year of Nottingham as an active steam location, Ian Allen organised a rail tour for one last visit which took place on 27th March. This was something a bit special and was planned down to the minutest detail (Figs 14 and 15). The engine, as can be seen in the document, was the Castle Class No 7029 'Clun Castle'. It should be noted that a special mention is made 'The locomotive may be turned on Lenton Triangle'. This was due to the weight restrictions on the turntables at Nottingham, which were nearing the end of their working lives (Plate 155).

20th February saw the Netherfield Spur re-opened, a piece of track that had originally been put in place in 1850 to allow Nottingham to Grantham line trains of the Ambergate, Nottingham & Boston & Eastern Junction Railway to use the 1839, and later 1850, Nottingham Stations. The Nottingham to Grantham Railway joined the Nottingham to Lincoln Line (1845) at this point. Due to rivalry between the Great

Plate 150
Jubilee No 45684 'Trafalgar' of 16C Derby waits in No 3 Shed for its next turn of duty

C Beck

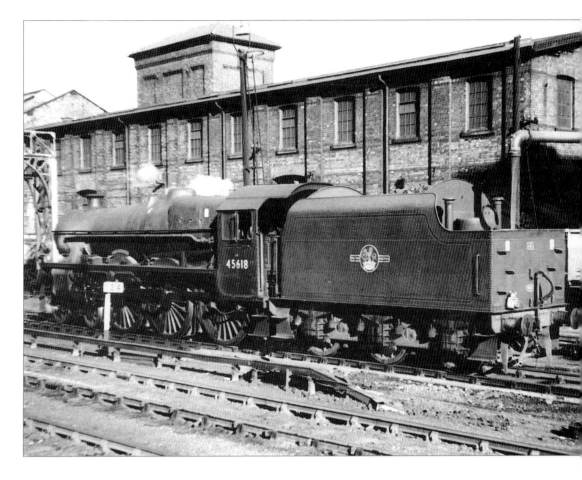

Plate 151
Jubilee No 45618 'New Hebrides' waiting to take on coal, seen from a passing train

C Beck

Northern and the Midland Railway, this junction was disconnected in 1865. The reconnection of February 1965 allowed Grantham trains once again to run into a Nottingham (Midland) Station, the present station having been opened in 1902. The first train to use the new connection was a Football excursion from Alfreton and South Normanton to Kings Cross which was hauled by D1547 (47432), the return working being hauled by D1532 (47009).

Early 1965 saw the final workings of the Leeds Holbeck Class 5X Jubilees into Nottingham. The route for these trains which were known as the 'Hunslet Goods' was from Nottingham Yard via Trowell and the Erewash Valley route, before taking the 'Old Road' via Masborough to Hunslet Yard. A very rare visitor to Nottingham was the Stephenson Link Motion fitted Black Five No 44767, since preserved, which was taken in No 2 Shed for turning and gave some trouble to Fireman Bill Davies. The engine got stuck repeatedly even after Bill received help from his Driver, Ted Gasgoine, who

Plate 152
Derelict Austerity 2-8-0 engines keeping company with Type 2 diesels

C Beck

scotched up the tender wheels in order to squeeze up the drawgear to obtain more clearance. This particular Black Five did not seem to fit on the turntable and required the efforts of fitters with jacks to lift the table slightly so that it could be extracted. It was then taken around to No 3 Shed where the turntable was longer. The turntable in No 2 Shed was 50 feet in diameter, whereas 44767 had an overall wheel base of 53 feet 6 and three quarter inches, as did 44748 to 44766, which is four inches longer than the majority of Black Fives, 44658 to 44747 and 44768 to 45499.

There could also be differences in tenders and tender length, but the narrow Fowler tenders were never seen fitted to Black Fives, although they were to be seen coupled up to their cousins the Jubilees and 8F 2-8-0s. By the time No 44767 came on Shed the Locomen's mess room in No 3 Shed had become almost deserted with preparation well under way to decommission No 1 Shed. The final engines to occupy this Shed were ED3 and ED5 and Riddles 2-6-2T 84006. Syd Horne, the Shed Shunt Driver, was most unapologetic when he put a hole in No 2 Shed wall with an 8F. In reply to his admonishment his opinion was 'I have saved the company the cost of pulling it down' It was from this Shed that the final steam locomotive at 16D was removed in the summer of 1965. Another tale concerning 'Trader' was told by one of his Firemen in the early 1950s when 'Trader' was still on the main line. In this instance his Fireman was Bill Reed

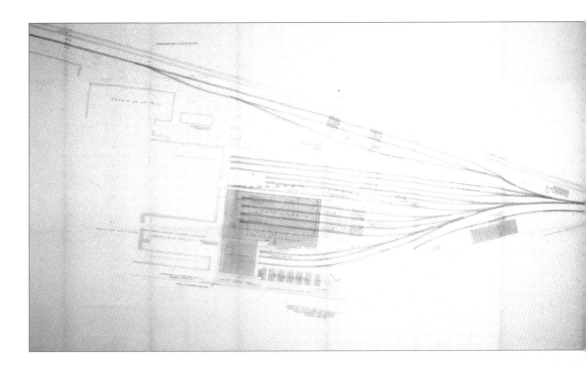

Fig 13
The proposed new Shed
R Padgett

They were working the mid-day Nottingham to Wellingborough coal train with an 8F and were supposed to scoop water on the troughs. But 'Trader' fancied a quick pint so they stopped at Kettering Station and 'Trader' had his pint whilst Bill filled the tender from one of the water columns. Due to this unscheduled stop, Control wanted to know what was going on. Trader's reply is a classic of invention 'Whilst I was looking for the Distant Signal at Kettering I had a sneezing fit and lost my top set of teeth. Due to working a lodging job I could not do without them so stopped to pick them up'! Footplate men knew all the dodges in the book, and a few more besides, but despite Control's incredulity nothing else was heard about the incident.

As well as incidents out on the line, things did not always go well on the Loco Shed as the following tale concerning the coaling of Black Five No 45056 relates. This engine was built at Vulcan Foundry in 1934 and scrapped at Buttigiegs, Newport in 1967. The story, by Bill Davies, is typical of what could go wrong on the coal hopper. All manner of mining debris could be found in loco coal including old detonator wire, broken cutter teeth, and sleepers. A Looe Beach sign was once found on the back of a visiting engine tender and on another occasion, a Southern Railway white target disc, which subsequently adorned No 58175 for some months! One of the disposal activities after coaling was that of dropping the fire. This arduous task was known as the 'Clinker Link'. The more modern engines with rocker grates and rocker ashpans were easy compared to the older engines which required firebar removal or paddling out with a long shovel type implement.

Plate 153
One of the last ex-Midland Railway Class 4Fs in service No 43951 with its diagonal yellow stripe showing. It could not work under the electric wires. It is shown with D7583 outside No 1 Shed. 43951 was scrapped at Cohens, Kettering in Oct 1964

C Beck

One unanticipated outcome of dropping coal from the great height in a coal hopper was the breaking up of coal already won from the ground by mechanized mining into even smaller pieces. This type of fuel was not suitable for the British steam locomotive and although cheaper it would be pulverised by the cutters and trepaners in the mine and was almost dust. Even this was compressed and made into the dreaded ovoids. Any crew seeing a tender full of them would know they were going to have a difficult trip!

The Great Coal Avalanche by permission of Bill Davies (Bedford)

On 11th January 1965 I was informed by Plodder the Foreman [Edgar 'Plodder' Thompson was given this nickname due to coming from Plodder Lane Shed, Bolton (10D)]. That my duty for the day would be firing on the coaling and watering turn, now down to one set of men owing to the impending demise of steam at Nottingham. Harold Tebbut was my Driver who had been grounded off the main line owing to an eyesight defect and now only performed Shed duties. The previous Driver on the 2 till 10 shift had left two engines under the hopper and would now be knocking back pints in the 'Ferry Boat Inn' at Wilford.

The Ferry is only one of the local watering holes. Others were 'The Castle' on Waterway St, which stood opposite Ludlows the bookies on Wilford Street, also known as No 4 Shed!,

There were 'The Navigation' and, around the corner on Canal St, the 'Bowling Green'. The Locomotive Inn' and 'The Magna Carta' were on Wiford Road. Others were the 'Crocus Inn' on Goodhead St, though it was many years since the wild Nottingham Crocus had grown there. On Deering St, named after Dr Charles Deering who is mentioned in Volume I, stood the 'Victoria Tavern' and at the corner of Wilford Road and Queens Walk the 'Cremorne Inn'. There was also the 'Clifton Hotel' on Bosworth Road/Briar Street. Most of these hostelries have gone the way of the Locoshed. Only the 'Navigation', now given a silly modern name 'The Lock & Lace', next to Wilford St Lock on the Nottingham Canal, the 'Queens Hotel' near the station, the 'Cremorne', named after a famous racehorse, the 'Ferry Boat Inn' and the 'Crown' on Arkwright Street remain.

At one time you could sit outside the 'Cremorne' and watch the LNER engines

Plate 154
Visiting Britannia No 70051 'Firth of Forth' with Black Five No 45221 and MIC coaches

C Beck

B.R. 338/3

W 26

LONDON MIDLAND REGION
(Midland Lines)

S P E C I A L   N O T I C E   NO. 283

Nottingham

SATURDAY, 27TH MARCH.

1X20 - Special from Paddington   (Ian Allan)

Barnt Green	pass 12 38	Chaddesden South Jn.	pass 14 11
Kings Norton	pass 12 44	Spondon Jn.	pass 14 14
Camp Hill	pass 12 50	Sawley Jn.	pass 14 21
Landor Street Jn.	arr 12W55	Sheet Stores Jn.	pass 14 22
– do –	dep 13W00	Trent	pass 14 24
Saltley	pass 13 02	Nottingham Midland	arr 14 35
	(3)	– do –	dep 16 05
Water Orton	FL pass 13 11	Trent	pass 16 16
	(3)	Loughborough	pass 16 27
Kingsbury	pass 13 19	Syston	pass 16 35
	(2)		(2)
Tamworth	pass 13 28	Leicester London Road	arr 16W43
	(2)	– do –	dep 16*53
Wichnor Jn.	pass 13 38	Wigston North Jn.	pass 16 59½
Burton-on-Trent	pass 13 43	Kibworth North	pass 17 08
	(3)	Market Harborough No. 3	pass 17 16
Stenson Jn.	pass 13 54	Market Harborough	pass 17 20
Derby Midland	arr 14W01	Kelmarsh	pass 17 30
– do –	dep 14W06		

Western Region C – (BSO, SO, CK, FK, RB, SSO, BSO, 306 Tons)

06 40 Avonmouth to Bromford Bridge to follow from Kings Norton.
05 35 Carlisle to Brent L.W.S. to continue GL Ratcliffe Jn. to Wigston South Jn. and
   follow.

SPECIAL CONDITIONS.

The shoe of the A.T.C. apparatus to be in the "clipped up" position between Wigston and
   Bletchley.
Not to be taken under the bow of an ex Midland Railway Loading Gauge.
The under-clearance to the locomotives to be checked to ensure that they are not less
   than 4½ inches in the fourfoot.
Not to be taken through the crossover in Hazelwell Station.
If taken via Whitacre, speed not to exceed 10 MILES PER HOUR through Whitacre Station
   platform.
Not to be taken into Burton South Bay.
Speed not to exceed 15 MILES PER HOUR through Burton Station Up Platform
Speed not to exceed 25 MILES PER HOUR through Bridge No. 10 between Draycott and
   Borrowash 124 m. 1032 yards.
Not to be taken into Borrowash Down Refuge.
Not to be taken into Nos. 3 and 5 platforms at Nottingham.
Not to be taken through the crossover road in Kegworth Station.
Not to be taken through the crossover roads in Nos. 1, 2, 3 and 4 platforms at Leicester.
Not to be taken through the crossover road in Clipston and Oxendon Station.
Not to be taken through the Up Platform Line at Northampton Castle Station.
Speed not to exceed 25 MILES PER HOUR through Verney Junction Station platform.

The locomotive may be turned on the triangle at Lenton and run to and from Nottingham
   M.P.D. via Wilford Road if necessary.

Power and Guards' arrangements, Sheet 2.

Continued

Fig 14
Clun Castle Visit Special Notice

F Eite

work coal out of Clifton Colliery across Wilford Road into the GCR Queens Drive Yard.)

We walked down to the hopper, watered the first engine, checked the tender doors and coaled her under the hopper, Harold taking the engine onto the ashpit. In the meantime I got the second loco watered and coaled then followed up to the ashpit. Harold was back in the mess room moaning and when the phone rang. 'Plodder' wanted to know why Black Five No 45056 (a 1F Rugby engine) was still waiting at the hopper and would I take care of it?

The tank was well down and took some time to fill especially with the extra care I had to take to get the icy leather bag into the filler. Whilst the tank was filling I went and checked the footplate, noting half a glass of water and 125lbs of steam, and then blew the handbrake [this released both the engine and tender steam brakes] ready to move. By this time, the fatting up had been done and Mick Hindson another Fireman had walked down to give me a hand as another crew wanted the engine. I placed her under the hopper, secured the handbrake, closed the cab doors and went into the hut to operate the electrical controls. The coal kept flowing and Mick and I got talking about a forthcoming lodging turn he was going on to Crewe. We failed to notice how slowly the tender was filling with coal. Too late, it suddenly dawned on me what I had done - I had forgotten to secure the tender doors which had been left open by the previous Fireman when the supply of coal had been taken from the back of the tender. We rushed to the footplate and there was a sight I won't forget in a hurry - about four tons of coal completely covering the cab floor, hiding the fire hole doors and even covering the Fireman's seat. I climbed over the cab doors and surveyed the mess. To add to my consternation the water was now sinking rapidly in the boiler and steam pressure was considerably reduced. There was only one thing for it. That was to get stuck in and clear behind the cab door so that we could move the remainder of the coal off the footplate and onto the ground.

- 2 -

NO. 283 (Continued)

SATURDAY, 27TH MARCH.

1X20 - Special from Paddington (Continued)

Power and Guards' arrangements.

Western Region P (7029 "CLUN CASTLE") Locomotive throughout.
Western Region, Worcester M.P.D. Locomen work to Nottingham and L to
    Nottingham M.P.D.   RELIEF 14 55 by OOC men. Return home as required.
Western Region Old Oak Common M.P.D. Locomen travel as passenger to
    Nottingham and RELIEVE WOS men at 14 55 M.P.D. dep 15 30 to
    Nottingham dep 16 05 1X20 to Paddington.
Nottingham M.P.D. Arrange driver travel as passenger 9.30 Nottingham to
    Birmingham arr 11 19½ and conduct WOS men Landor Street to
    Nottingham and L to M.P.D.
Leicester M.P.D. Arrange driver travel as passenger 13 30 Leicester to
    Nottingham arr 14 21 and conduct OOC men 15 30 L Nottingham M.P.D.
    to Northampton - Return home as required.
Western Region G. to Landor Street Junction. Return as required.
Saltley G. work 1X20 Landor Street Junction to Nottingham and Nottingham
    to Leicester London Road arr 16 43. Return as required.
Leicester G. Relieve Saltley G. and work to Northampton and home as
    required.

The following to acknowledge immediately on receipt of this Notice
    by telegram to "TRAINS NP DERBY" using the code "ARNO S.N. 283" :-

M.P.D. - Leicester Midland, Nottingham, Worcester, Old Oak Common.

D.M.   - Rugby (D.C.), Leicester, Nottingham Victoria, Derby (D.C.),
          Birmingham.

Y.M.   - Leicester Midland, Beeston, Nottingham, Chaddesden,
          Burton-on-Trent, Water Orton, Saltley.

S.M.   - Market Harborough, Kibworth, Wigston Magna, Leicester London Rd.,
          Syston, Loughborough Midland, Trent, Sawley Junction, Spondon,
          Beeston, Nottingham, Lubenham, Derby Midland, Repton & W.,
          Burton-on-Trent, Tamworth H.L., Kingsbury, Castle Bromwich,
          Saltley, Birmingham New Street, Kings Heath, Kings Norton,
          Northfield, Barnt Green.

DERBY.   E.E.COWELL,
23RD MARCH, 1965.   LINE MANAGER.

Fig 15
Clun Castle Visit
F Eite

First however, the initial clearance had to be done under the hopper, because we could not move the engine with coal everywhere. It even covered the handbrake. We accomplished this in a record ten minutes, making one hell of a mess under the hopper, which would not please the coal man in the morning but too bad! The race against time had begun, to avoid dropping a plug, steam and water having dropped further. Standing on piles of coal I drove

her out into the open next to a wagon of coal, and then proceeded to heave the footplate clear and place a few shovels of coal on the fire to make steam to get the injectors on. As the water was now in the bottom nut (of the gauge frame/glass) and even in our elevated position, tiptoes were necessary to see the water level. Whilst we were furiously working away Mick's Driver, Ted 'Gassy' Gasgoine, arrived on the scene and after weighing up the situation realised that things were just about under control, so merely satisfied himself by gloating over our self imposed predicament.

Sarcastic comments came from the floor while we shoveled away, for as fast as we cleared an area another avalanche came through the wide-open tender doors. Finally we were able to force them shut with the aid of 'Gassy', who had been a professional boxer in his time. As a bonus to our misconduct 'Gassy' made me clear up all the coal into a wagon whilst he had his mate coal the engine again and clean the front down [the floor /boiler cladding and fittings in

Plate 155
GWR Castle Class No 7029 'Clun Castle' on the ash pit at Nottingham

C Beck

Plate 156
D107 at Derby works after Leen Valley runaway at Bestwood Park. Driver Ted Ritchins and
Secondman Mick Hindson jumped off.
Ted died suddenly not long after this incident

Bill Davies

the cab]. After this incident I went home very tired and much wiser, in that before coaling an
engine make sure the tender doors are firmly closed and properly locked and remember that
the coal capacity of Black Five cab is considerable!

Note: Mick Hindson was involved with Driver Ted Ritchins in the Bestwood Park Crash
when a Peak D107 (45120) (Plate 156) had run away due to the weight of the loose
coupled coal train it was hauling overpowering the brakes. They ran into the rear of
another coal train. The impact demolished the Guards Van on the other train and
smashed the cab on D104 back to the engine room bulkhead. The compression was so
severe that a pen in Mick's pocket had been completely flattened without even a crease
in it. Fortunately the crew jumped clear and the Guard on the other train was away
from his van. Ted Ritchins died not long after and Mick left the railway.

One of Bill's first jobs when he started work at Nottingham was to remove a blockage in one of the coal hoppers, which were later to deposit all the coal described in the incident above.

Unblocking the Coal Hopper
by Bill Davies

A rope was attached to my waist and I was lowered into the hopper to attempt to break up a mass of coal that had jammed and stuck itself together into a solid immovable mass. Encouragement was shouted from the assembled audience some twenty feet above whilst I was swung around attacking the blockage with my boots and a coal pick. Just as I thought my efforts had been in vain, the mass of coal started to crumble eventually crashing down into the lower part of the hopper, whilst I swung around with no foot or hand holds in sight! My escape from this earlier attempt at abseiling was to scramble over the top railing and then down the very steep open step stairway with trembling legs. It took several days of hard lathering to remove all the coal dust! Other escapades included putting a detonator down the chimney of a brazier fire which, when it exploded, almost frightened to death the West Indian Labourer sleeping on the bench next to it.

Tricks were played all the time in those days. A young Fire Dropper could be led on when told that tenders such as the one on Ivatt Mogul No 4304 which had been swept clean and shining were how Drivers liked to see them at the end of a run! Both the coal episodes with No 45056 and the visit by No 7029 were almost, but not quite, as we shall see, the last recorded steam related events at 16D, as Nottingham locoshed closed to steam on 15th April 1965.

Chapter Ten
The Last of Steam

This summary is from the diary of Bill Davies and other sources and shows some of the final steam workings in and out of Nottingham Locoshed and the Sidings.

1965
1st January
No 75071 (6C) on the Halewood and No 45626 'Seychelles' (55A) on the Hunslet with the 16D Black Five No 44658 (16D) returning from Crewe Works after repair.

6th January
No 45326 (10A) on the Halewood.

8th January
No 75062 (5D) on 13.05 Lincoln and No 45593 'Kolhapur' (9D) on 18.26 to Derby and No 42886 (10H) to Melton.

10th January
No 78042 (16A) on Carriage Shunt (2.00am)

13th January
No 48218 (10J) & 48766 (2F) on Shed.

21st January
No 42114 (1G) on Shed.

25th January
Bill had a difficult day with three engine failures! Speke Junction Black Five (8C) No 45386 (Injectors) D11 & D153 with flat batteries due to engines being frozen.

1st February
No 78023 (16D) on Carriage Shunt.

15th February
No 48262 (8H) floorboards collapsed whilst being fatted up before going on a Wollaton Colliery tripper so engine failed as a consequence. Driver not happy!

1st April
Last week of steam at Nottingham with 'Austerity' 2-8-0 No 90730 (41E) being Bill Davies' final steam engine on the Locoshed. These engine were notorious for giving a rough ride due to their lack of balancing. One engine 90527, of 27B Aintree and scrapped in June 1963, was experimentally fitted with riveted steel plates on the driving coupled wheels giving 40% reciprocating balance, which enabled this engine to run at 40 mph without the usual fore and aft shunting effect.

Plate 157
The last working steam locomotive Class 4F No 44458 to come off Nottingham MPD seen earlier at Lenton South Junction

B Matthews Collection

Nottingham closed to steam on Monday 5th April 1965 and the 2 till 10 shift on the last three days saw the following engines prepared and disposed.
(Information from Bill Davies as written down by Driver Fred Jones)

Thursday 1st April
No 90730 (41E).

Friday 2nd April
Nos. 45207 (55D), 48414 (15B), 48465 (9L) and 92020 (8H).

Saturday 3rd April
Nos 43082 (41E), 44458 (55E), 48126 (55B), 78044 (16A), and 78062 (16D). It was on this day that the final serviceable steam engines were sent to Toton and Derby the last one off Shed being No 44458 (Plate 157) of 55E with steam no longer allowed in the Shed from that point in time. So it was this class 4F No 44458, built at Horwich in 1928 and withdrawn from 55E in November 1965, that was the last Midland design on the Shed in steam. Although steam had finished at the Middle Furlong Road Shed the work carried on with diesels and the occasional visiting steam engine which could not use the turntable and had to use Lenton Triangle. Steam locomotives would never again be prepared at Nottingham.

However, on Monday 5th April, No 48160 of 55B came onto the loco and was turned in No 2 Shed. The Kirkby crew who had not heard about the closure of Nottingham for steam were denied coal and water even though there was plenty of coal in the hopper and the water cranes were still used for filling up boiler water tanks on the diesels. Nottingham men still worked trains with steam engines and could be rostered on engines from foreign depots as diverse as York, Colwick, Normanton, Frodingham and Leeds Holbeck.

The last working steam engine allocated to Nottingham was No 47231 (Plate 159) an 0-6-0T of Midland Railway vintage. Built in 1899 to a design of Samuel Johnson it lasted until 1966. It was one of three survivors of this class, the others being Nos 47201 and 47202, and was withdrawn from Westhouses in March 1966. No 47231 was built as MR No 2752 at Vulcan Foundry (works No 1784) and renumbered No 1931 in 1907. Further renumbered in 1934 as No 7231, it became No 47231 in 1948. It was a non-condensing version of this class and originally had 4 feet 6 and a half inch driving wheels, 18 feet by 26 feet cylinders and a total weight 48 tons 15 cwt. It was re-boilered in 1926 when the wheel diameter was increased to 4 feet 7 inches. Cashmores of Great Bridge, Birmingham cut up this engine in April 1967.

Plate 159
The last working engine allocated to Nottingham MPD the ex-MR 0-6-0T
No 47231

C Beck

Officially the last steam engine on Shed was another 0-6-0T the Beardmore (Glasgow) built No 47645 (Plate 160) of 1929 which was towed away to Wards at Killamarsh by D120 on 13th July 1965. So it came about that the last Nottingham engine was a true 'Jocko'. These 0-6-0T 'Jockos' that worked at Beeston Yard, which was closed on the 12th June 1965, had extended coal rails to their bunkers so that they could stay out longer before having to return to the Shed for coaling. The survival of both 47231 and 47645 at Nottingham was due to the need to shunt the Creosote Works and other transfer goods such as Nottingham Yards to the Eastgate Council Depot. No 47231 had been on loan to Clifton Colliery some years before for which purpose it had acquired a cut down chimney.

The changing scene saw D184 (52A) and D1824 (Driver Training) on Shed. A minor incident was with ex-LNER B1 No 61196 off the road at Lenton South Junction. Steam was still to be seen in the Yard and passing by with No 76099 (5D) turning up on 9th June. An old established turn was to Attenborough Junction, Chilwell COD Chilwell and Beeston followed by light engine to the locoshed for which D7502 was used on 23rd June. At this time Beeston Yard, although closed was very busy as a storage point for a large number of wagons, a situation which needed almost continual shunting.

Plate 160

This LMS 0-6-0T No 47645 was the last steam engine in the Shed where it was stored. The No 46251 had been chalked on and the name 'City of Nottingham' added

Bill Davies

On 28th June the Jubilee No 45600 'Bermuda' (9D) turned up in the West Yard where it was watered and then turned on the Triangle. Short Rest jobs were still being worked and on 29th August Driver Bill Woods took Type 2 engines D5265 and D7526 to Blackpool North via the Erewash Valley, Sheffield (conductor), Royston, Mirfield, Sowerby Bridge, Todmorton, Rochdale, Bury, Bolton, Leyland and Preston and returned via the same route.

The 7th September saw 8F No 48185 (16E) being prepared to work the Melton Mowbray tripper (Trip No 19) to Pedigree Petfoods. On the 19th September the very last steam engine to come onto Nottingham Locoshed arrived. This final visitor was 15A (Wellingborough) Class 8F 2-8-0 No 48609 which had turned up to drag a dead diesel (D143) which had been waiting outside No 1 Shed for movement to Toton, a move that took place at 4.00am on 16th September. On the 14th of the month Black Fives Nos 44665 and 44835 (both 16B Annesley based engines) and 45071 (8C Speke Junction) were noted proceeding light engine to Colwick Locoshed.

Plate 161
D8057 and D8062 with brake tender. D8062 was an early withdrawal after collision damage in 1976 and was cut up at Derby works in 1979

Reddish

Plate 162
Inside No 2 Shed. Type 2 diesels D5235 and D5199 along with three other unidentified members of the class

Reddish

Steam was still to be seen around Nottingham and specials were also to be seen passing, two of which came in April and October. On each occasion the engines were Britannia Pacifics No 70052 'Firth of Tay' in the April and on 2nd October No 70012 'John of Gaunt'. Both engines were based at 5A (Crewe North) and were specially prepared. Due to the route taken in April, 70052 was taken off at Nottingham and serviced at Toton as no steam maintenance staff remained at 16D. The onward route of this special took it onto the Mansfield Line and then to Lincolnshire where it was hauled by Class 4F No 44401(16E) and B1 No 61406.

The new Type 1 and Type 2 diesels were kept inside No 1 Shed and in the Yard. Amongst the former were, D8057 (20057) and D8062 (20062) plus brake tenders and the latter D5235 (25085) and D5199 (25049) (Plates 161 and 162).

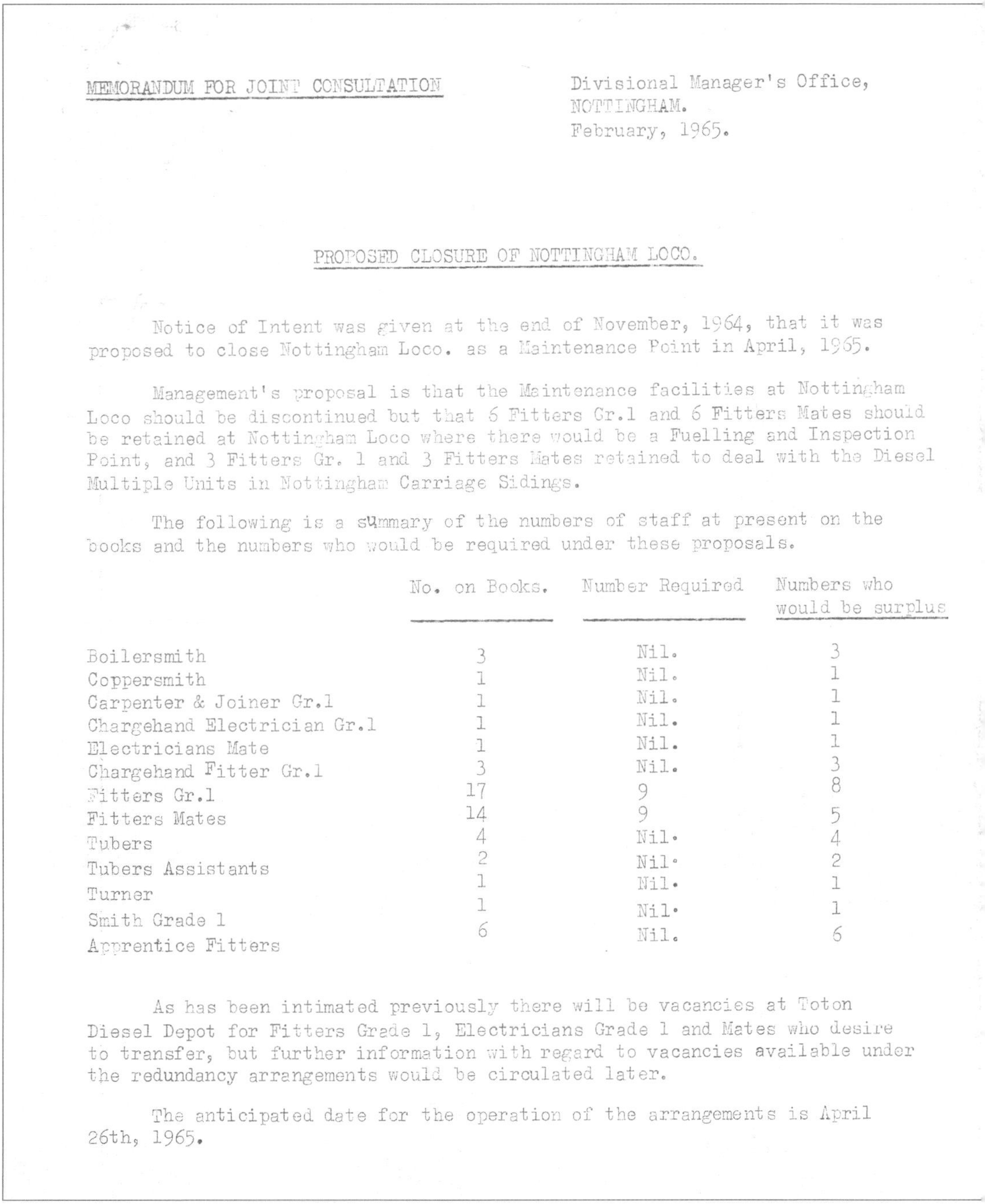

MEMORANDUM FOR JOINT CONSULTATION

Divisional Manager's Office,
NOTTINGHAM.
February, 1965.

PROPOSED CLOSURE OF NOTTINGHAM LOCO.

Notice of Intent was given at the end of November, 1964, that it was proposed to close Nottingham Loco. as a Maintenance Point in April, 1965.

Management's proposal is that the Maintenance facilities at Nottingham Loco should be discontinued but that 6 Fitters Gr.1 and 6 Fitters Mates should be retained at Nottingham Loco where there would be a Fuelling and Inspection Point, and 3 Fitters Gr. 1 and 3 Fitters Mates retained to deal with the Diesel Multiple Units in Nottingham Carriage Sidings.

The following is a summary of the numbers of staff at present on the books and the numbers who would be required under these proposals.

	No. on Books.	Number Required	Numbers who would be surplus
Boilersmith	3	Nil.	3
Coppersmith	1	Nil.	1
Carpenter & Joiner Gr.1	1	Nil.	1
Chargehand Electrician Gr.1	1	Nil.	1
Electricians Mate	1	Nil.	1
Chargehand Fitter Gr.1	3	Nil.	3
Fitters Gr.1	17	9	8
Fitters Mates	14	9	5
Tubers	4	Nil.	4
Tubers Assistants	2	Nil.	2
Turner	1	Nil.	1
Smith Grade 1	1	Nil.	1
Apprentice Fitters	6	Nil.	6

As has been intimated previously there will be vacancies at Toton Diesel Depot for Fitters Grade 1, Electricians Grade 1 and Mates who desire to transfer, but further information with regard to vacancies available under the redundancy arrangements would be circulated later.

The anticipated date for the operation of the arrangements is April 26th, 1965.

Fig 16
Closure Notice
F Eite

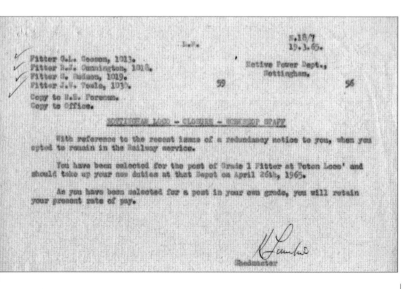

| YOUR REF. | | BRITISH RAILWAYS | OUR REF. | N.18/7. | B.R. 3/2 |
| DATED | | L.M. ____ REGION | DATE | 14.1.65. | |

TO Mr. D. Lill.
✓ Mr. F. Eite.
  Mr. C. Redfern.
  Mr. F. Mumby.   (Centre No.   )

FROM

Motive Power Dept.,
Nottingham.

Extn....59........   (Centre No. 56)

TOTON NEW DIESEL MAINTENANCE DEPOT — SALARIED STAFF COMPLEMENT

Arrangements have been made for Consultation Meetings in connection with the above to be held on 26th and 27th January, 1965, as follows :-

26th January	27th January
Staff Side Preliminary Meeting. 10.30am. Conference Room, Alan House, Nottingham.	Full Meeting, 9.30am. Elizabethan Restaurant, Co-operative House, Parliament St., Nottingham.

Please arrange to attend in the capacity of Staff Representative. You have already been supplied with a copy of the precis, etc.

FOR R.

Shedmaster

Fig 17
Closure Notice

F Eite

L.M.

S.18/7
19.3.65.

Fitter G.L. Geeson, 1013.
Fitter R.J. Cunnington, 101?.
Fitter G. Dudson, 1019.
Fitter J.W. Teele, 103?.

Motive Power Dept.,
Nottingham.

59   56

Copy to H.S. Foreman.
Copy to Office.

NOTTINGHAM LOCO — CLOSURE — WORKSHOP STAFF

With reference to the recent issue of a redundancy notice to you, when you opted to remain in the Railway service.

You have been selected for the post of Grade 1 Fitter at Toton Loco' and should take up your new duties at that Depot on April 26th, 1965.

As you have been selected for a post in your own grade, you will retain your present rate of pay.

Shedmaster

Fig 18
Closure Notice

F Eite

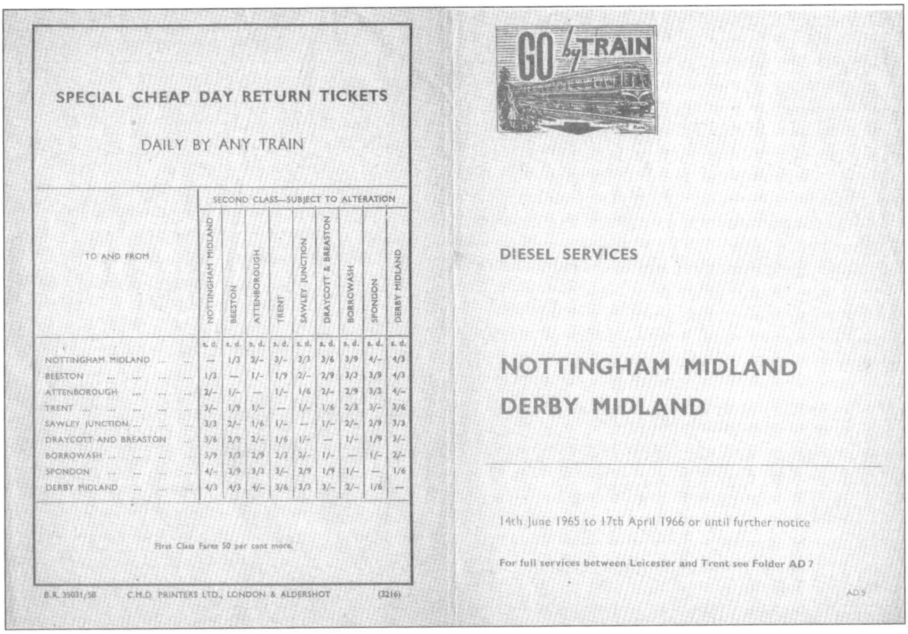

SPECIAL CHEAP DAY RETURN TICKETS

DAILY BY ANY TRAIN

GO BY TRAIN

DIESEL SERVICES

NOTTINGHAM MIDLAND
DERBY MIDLAND

14th June 1965 to 17th April 1966 or until further notice

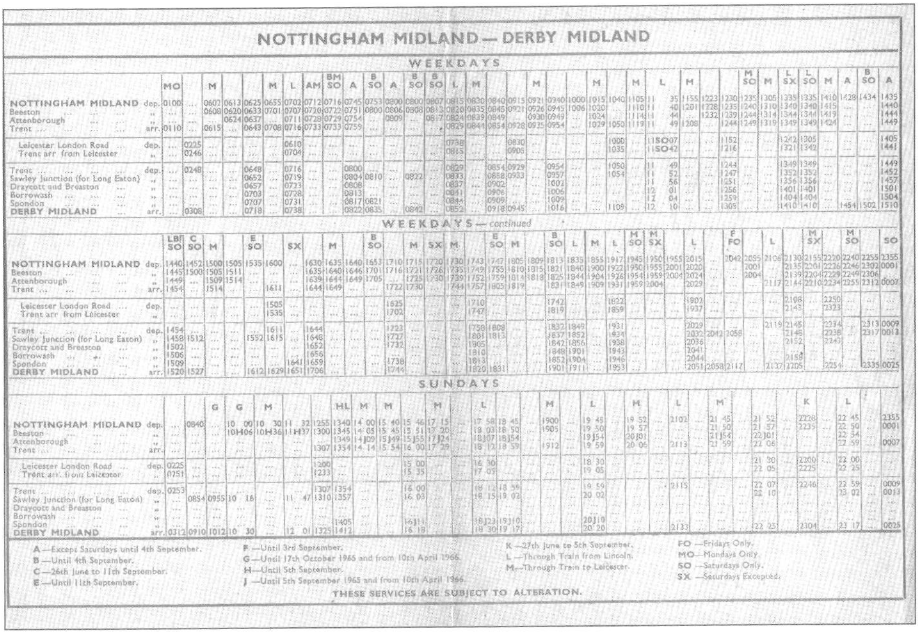

For full services between Leicester and Trent see Folder AD 7

NOTTINGHAM MIDLAND — DERBY MIDLAND

Fig 19
Services from Nottingham to Derby

Jim Perkins

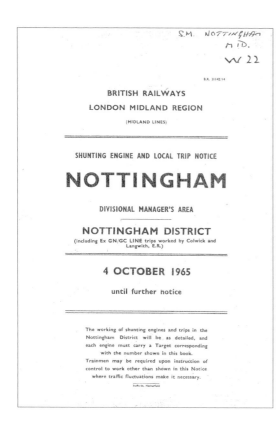

NOTTINGHAM DIVISIONAL MANAGER'S AREA
NOTTINGHAM TRIP ENGINES

Nos. 1 to 9
SPARE

No. 10
NOTTINGHAM YARD NORTH

350 h.p. Diesel Shunting Locomotive.

Engine leaves M.P.D. 05 45 (MO)
Shunts continuously 06 00 Mons. to 06 00 Suns.

No. 11
NOTTINGHAM YARD EAST

350 h.p. Diesel Shunting Locomotive.

Engine leaves M.P.D. 05 45 (MO) Opld.
Shunts continuously 06 00 (Mon) to 14 00 (Saturdays)
Sundays 08 00 to 16 00 (Q)

TESTS FITTED STOCK AS REQUIRED.

No. 12
NOTTINGHAM YARD EAST

350 h.p. Diesel Shunting Locomotive.

Engine leaves M.P.D. 14 00 SX.
Shunts 14 15 (SX) to 06 00 (MX)

TESTS FITTED STOCK AS REQUIRED.
Shunts Wilford Road Cattle Dock.
Works internal trips in Yard.

No. 13
NOTTINGHAM YARD WEST

350 h.p. Diesel Shunting Locomotive.

Engine leaves M.P.D. 05 45 (MO)
Shunts 06 00 Mondays to 22 00 Saturdays.
TESTS FITTED STOCK AS REQUIRED.

No. 14
NOTTINGHAM COAL YARD (A)
NOTTINGHAM YARD (B)

350 h.p. Diesel Shunting Locomotive.

Engine leaves M.P.D. 06 00 (MO)
Shunts 06 15 to 18 00 (SX) (A)
06 15 to 13 45 (SO) (A)
18 00 to 21 45 (SX) (B)

No. 15
BESTWOOD PARK

350 h.p. Diesel Shunting Locomotive.

Engine leaves M.P.D. 06 00,
Shunts 06 30 to 21 45

Nos. 16 to 24
SPARE

No. 25

06 20 to 20 45 (SX)
06 20 to 13 05 (SO)

	Arr.	Dep.
Nottingham M.P.D.		06 20 LE
Nottingham G.Y.E.		06 45
Beeston South Jn.	07 00	07 20
Beeston Goods Yard	07 30	08 00
Beeston South Jn.	08 05	08 10
Beeston Boots	08 15	08 25 ENV
Nottingham G.Y.E.	08 40	09 30
Beeston Boots	09 45	10 00
Beeston Goods Yard	10 10	12 40
Nottingham G.Y.E.	12 55	LE 30
Nottingham M.P.D.	13 05	
Nottingham G.Y.E.		13 30 ENV SX
Beeston Boots	13 45	14 30 SX
Nottingham G.Y.E.	14 45	15 30 SX
Beeston South Jn.	15 45	18 18 SX
Nottingham G.Y.E.	18 35	19 20 SX
Beeston Boots	19 45	20 30 SX
Nottingham G.Y.E.	20 45	LE SX
Nottingham M.P.D.	20 55	

Accompanied by Shunter ex Nottingham Yard.

No. 26

08 45 to 21 40 (SX)
08 45 to 16 45 (SO)

	Arr.	Dep.
Nottingham M.P.D.		08 45 LE
Lenton South	08 53	

Feed N.W.P. Station and clear empties to Clifton Colliery.

	Arr.	Dep.
		10 20
Colwick	10 49	11 47
Lenton South	12 35	
Nottingham G.T.W.) Feed and clear ROF and		
Nottingham N.S.) Nottingham Ballast Sdgs.		
Lenton South	.....	14 10
Colwick	14 54	15 42
Nottingham N.S.	16 45	LE 30
M.P.D.	16 56	.....
Nottingham N.S.	17 10	18 00 ENV SX
Lenton South	18 00	SX
Bucknall	18 53	20 20 SX
Lenton South	21 00	SX

Work as required 21 00 to 21 40 SX
thence to Nottingham M.P.D. 21 55.

Fig 20

Other sheets from this document are printed on the following pages

Jim Perkins

Developments now moved rapidly with the rails in both Nos 1 and 2 Shed being removed in November 1965 leaving only 3 Shed and the Yard still open.
Some of the documents that were part of the management process of closing the Shed and dealing with staff issues can be seen in Figs 16, 17 and 18. These official notices dated 14th January, February and 19th March 1965 show the arrangements for salaried staff together with the numbers and grades of the fitting staff and their possible transfer to the new Toton Diesel Depot.

For most of the fitting staff there was work elsewhere but the old hands went into retirement. Apart from a few men, the Working Engines (footplate) staff still worked out of the Shed until they transferred to the Train Crew Office at Midland Station. Fig 19 shows the Nottingham to Derby local services for June 1965 to April 1966 still calling at such stations as Draycott & Breaston and Borrowash. As well as main line passenger and freight workings there were still the local shunts and trips to be worked and Fig 20 show those which were published in BR 31142/14 of 4th October 1965.

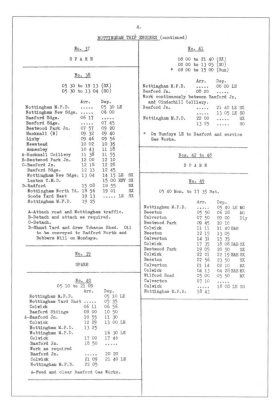

Fig 20 continued

Jim Perkins

1966

Steam was by this time becoming a rare sight at Nottingham with the days between visits gradually lengthening. These were to be seen only in the various yards and passing by the Shed. The following table is the record of these visits.

17th January
No 42727(9B) in the West Yard (1.30pm)

18th January
No 48364 (16E) passed on a Wellingborough to Kirkby conveying coal empties.

24th January
No 45675 'Hardy' (55A) on 8.10 am Clay Cross Pickup.

27th January
No 61022 (55A) on the Clay Cross Pickup.

28th January
Tragedy in Nottingham Carriage sidings when Albert Taft the Foreman Shunter was killed whilst coupling up buckeyes. He was trapped between two corridor gangways.

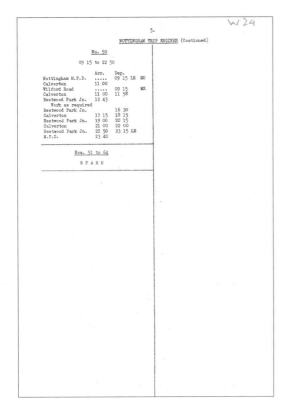

Fig 20 continued

Jim Perkins

29th January
No 62012 (50A) was de-railed on catch points at Lenton South whilst it was turning on the triangle when in charge of Westhouses men who took the wrong signal! This appeared to be a repeat of the incident with No 61196 in April of the previous year.

30th January
The Class 8F No 48381(15A) passed on tripper to Colwick as it had done on the 21st, 22nd and 23rd.

2nd February
Class 9F No 92145 (40B) passed Shed.

7th February
No 92206 (50A) on the Clay Cross pickup and No 48364 (16E) passing locoshed.

8th February
No 44932 a Derby based engine (since preserved) passed.

9th February
Saw No 61131 (50A) on the 8.10 am Clay Cross pick up.

7.

COLWICK (E.R.) TRIP ENGINES (Continued)

No. 16
06 20 to 17 56 SX
06 20 to 11 50 SO

	Arr.	Dep.	
Colwick M.P.D.	....	06 20 LE	
Colwick		06 35	
Nottingham Vic.	07R08	07R18	
A-Ruddington	07 35	11 00	
Nottingham Vic.	11R15	11R25	
B-Colwick	11 50	....	
Colwick M.P.D.	....	13 15 LE	SX
Colwick		13 30	SX
Nottingham Vic.	14R04	14R19	SX
C-Queens Walk	14 27	14 40	SX
D-Ruddington	14 55	14 56	SX
Hotchley Hill	15 10	16 45	SX
E-Ruddington	16 57	16 58	SX
Nottingham Vic.	17R19	17R29	SX
Colwick	17 56	.... LE	SX
Colwick M.P.D.	....		

R - Run Round.
A - Trip and Shunt as required, Ruddington, East Leake, Gotham, Hotchley Hill by arrangement with Station Master, Ruddington, on day to day basis.
B - To bring 40 empties
C - Attach empties
D - Pick up shunter.
E - Set down shunter.

All trains to Ruddington and Hotchley Hill to convey BRO each end.

No. 17
07 42 to 15 04 (SX) 14 30 (SO)

	Arr.	Dep.	
Colwick M.P.D.	....	07 42 LE	
Colwick		07 57	
Bestwood Colliery	09 00	....	
Bestwood Jn.	....	12 05	
Hucknall Town	12 16	12 42	
Linby Colliery	12 48	12 58	
Newstead Colliery	13 08	13 55	SX
Colwick	15 04	....	
Newstead Colliery	....	13 30	SO
Colwick	14 30	.... LE	
Colwick M.P.D.	....		

No. 18
03 45 to 09 30 (Daily)

	Arr.	Dep.	
Colwick M.P.D.	....	03 45 LE	
Colwick	....	04 02	
Nottingham Vic.	04R36	04R46	
Queens Walk	04 55	08 45	
Nottingham Vic.	08R55	09R05	
Colwick	09 30	LE	
Colwick M.P.D.	....		

R - Run Round

8.

LANGWITH (E.R.) TRIP ENGINES

No. 11
09 55 to 16 35 (SX) 16 25 (SO)

	Arr.	Dep.	
Langwith M.P.D.		09 55 LE	
Langwith	....	10 10 EBV	
Skegby	10 26	10 27	
Silverhill	10 37	11 25	
Skegby	11 35	12 25	
Langwith	12 50	13 45	
Pleasley Colliery	14 03	14 18	
Skegby	14 30	14 45	SX
Sutton-in-Ashfield Town	14 55	15 30	SX
Summit Colliery	15 39	16 05	SX
Langwith	16 35	....	
Skegby	14 30	14 45	SO
Summit Colliery	15 00	16 00	SO
Langwith	16 25	.... LE	
Langwith M.P.D.	....		

No. 32
10 19 to 16 00 (Daily)

	Arr.	Dep.	
Langwith M.P.D.		10 19 LE	
Mansfield C.S.	10 47	11 20	
Kirkby South Jn.	12 10	12 20	
Kirkby Bentinck	12 30	13 05 EBV	
Newstead Colliery	13 25	14 05	
Kirkby Bentinck	14 25	14 55	
Kirkby South Jn.	15 05	15 15	
Mansfield C.S.	16 00	16 20 LE	
Langwith M.P.D.	16 46		

No. 46
14 20 to 18 55 (SX)

	Arr.	Dep.	
Langwith M.P.D.		14 20 LE SX	
Langwith	....	14 35 EBV SX	
Annesley (Wagon Shops)	15 30		SX
SHUNT 16 00 to 18 00			
Annesley (Wagon Shops)		18 15	SX
Langwith	18 55	.... LE	SX
Langwith M.P.D.	....		

DERBY,
OCTOBER, 1965.

E. E. COWELL,
LINE MANAGER.

Fig 20 continued

Jim Perkins

10th February
No 48532 (9L) passing Shed.

11th February
Saw No 61306 on the 0810 Clay Cross with Nos. 92059 (8B) and 48381 (15A) seen passing the locoshed.

14th February
No 48609 (15A) passing with D1509 to be seen on the Shed

15th February
No 48342 (16E) passing.

22nd February
Saw No 43141(55E) on the Clay Cross Pick up and the Black Five No 44824 (55A) dragging B1 No 61003 'Gazelle' to Sheffield (22nd) with No 48185 (15A) passing Shed and Black Fives 44946 (56D) and 45392 (1H) working trains.

24th February
8F Nos. 48492 (15A) & 48195 (16G) were seen passing.

Plate 163

The formal group photo. From Left to right: George Woodward - Running Foreman Class 2; Arthur Key - Running Foreman Class 2; Charles Redfern - Running Foreman Class 1, who has contributed to this story; William Wright - Chief Clerk; Arthur Place - Boilersmith Supervisor; John Thompson - Shedmaster; Bert Hunt - Running Foreman Class 1; Frank Thompson - Mechanical Foreman, whom we first met in Volume 11; Edgar Thompson - Running Foreman Class 1; Derrick Cleveley - Diesel Instructor

C Redfern

3rd March

No. 45190 (16C) on the Mansfield Parcels and during the rest of March the following engines were to be seen around and about the Nottingham area Nos 48177 (16G), 48204 (16G), 48211(10J), 48381(15A), 48225(16E) and 48267 (16E) and 48258 of 16G.

Plate 164
And a more relaxed shot taken afterwards with Type 4 Diesels, a Stanier 2-6-4T and a
Black Five in view

C Redfern

14th March
Driver Bert Daykin went light engine to Colwick on his last day at work with No 48258
of 16G.

18th March
No 48541(16E) to Kirkby Summit.

A sign of the times was the increasing number of dead engine movements on a one
way ticket to the scrap yard. Wednesday the 21st March saw No 48382 towing
ex-LNER engines Nos 63674, 63644 and 61145.

During April there were still Class 8F 2-8-0s working and Nos 48440 (6C), 48284 (16E)
48315 (15A), 48687 (15A), 48673 (16E), 48507 (16G), 48369 (5D), 48258 (16G),
48621 (16E) 48092 (16E), 48193 (16A), 48393 (16G), 48219 (16G), 48186 (16E),

48119 (16E), 48442 (16E) 48395 (16E), 48267 (16E), 48317 (16E) and 48124 (16E) could be seen in the area.

7th April
The Ivatt Mogul No 43125 (55E) worked the 8.10 am Clay Cross pickup.

20th April
9F power was still to be seen with No 92139 (2E) at Lenton North.

There were no entries for May.

The first week of June 1966 saw a variety of engines working the Clay Cross pick up with ex-LNER engines

Plate 165
The last steam hauled train into Nottingham from Manchester Central. Black Five No 45284 seen here on 31st August 1967

Bill Davies

Nos 62062 and 61017 'Bushbuck' on the 2nd and 3rd respectively with ex-LMS power in the form of Black Five No 44876 (2B) on the 17th.

A tragedy occurred this week when the Nottingham Fireman Jeff Campbell was killed in a motorbike accident at Great Yarmouth. This was a second choice holiday for Jeff as his first choice was the Isle of Man TT, an event that was cancelled, as it was in 2001, by outside events. In 1966 there was a seaman's strike which prevented the ferries from sailing.

A rare visitor on 14th June was BR Britannia No 70003 'John Bunyan' which worked the Chaddesden tripper. While on the 18th what was once a familiar class of engine re-appeared when Jubilee No 45562 'Alberta' (55C) worked the Bradford-Poole service (Plate 166).

There were now fewer sightings of steam with the record for July showing only:

1st July
The Black Five No 45050 (5D) on the Clay Cross pick up.

12th July
Nos 48282 (16E) and 48137 (15A) at London Road with No 45324 (16B) on the West Yard to Trent job.

28th July
Austerity No 90074 (56A) on the Clay Cross pick up.

The final BR train to work into Nottingham with steam was on the 31st July when Black Five No 45284 (8A) substituted for a failed diesel on the 10.07am Manchester Central to Nottingham service. Despite the traction change the train was only ten minutes late. Trafford Park men had brought the train in and Dennis Ancliffe conducted them around Lenton Triangle in order to turn the engine. No 45284 (Plate 165) then worked the 4/45 Nottingham to Manchester Central Service. When 16A closed forever in December 1966, the Footplate men and some Office Staff moved into an office on Station Street, now the Central Trains Offices, next to the site of the 1852 Shed. The new set up was called a Train Crew Office, and Running Foremen became 'Train Crew Supervisors'. For all the staff it meant a different way of working and for the Supervisors no more walking around the Sheds supervising, Drivers, Firemen and support staff such as Steamrisers, Fire Droppers and Tube Cleaners. All those labour intensive grades which along with the repairing engines staff, made up the complement that went with

Plate 166
A fine sight, the Jubilee Class No 45562 'Alberta' seen here on the Bradford to Poole working
on 17th June 1966
C Beck

Plate 167
Seen here passing Lenton South Signal Box, BR 9F No 92203 and Class 4 No 75029

C Beck

the running of up to one hundered and fifty steam locomotives for over a one and a quarter centuries, had been consigned to history.

Of the remaining Fitting Staff, some transferred to the Carriage Sidings Shed that was in use for a short time, others went to Etches Park and then Toton. Others retired, and those who had tired of railway work went to other industries such as the Coal Board at Clifton Colliery, CEGB at Wilford Power Station and the Royal Ordnance Factory in the Meadows. Eventually the first two were closed and demolished leaving only the ROF occupying its site next to the old Loco Shed area. This site also closed in 2002 leaving Furlong House as the only link to the railway history of the Meadows area.

A group photograph was taken of the supervisory staff in the summer prior to closure of Nottingham Shed (Plates 163 and 164). This panoramic view taken close to the end of No 2 Shed has most of the Shed Yard fixtures on view. Amongst the steam and diesel locomotives are a water column, ash plant, signals, wagons and Mansfield Junction Signal Box, itself soon to disappear under the Power Signaling scheme based at Trent. The line to the left is the dead end where many locomotives were photographed, the line to the right led into No 3 Shed which at the time this photograph was taken was the only one being used. The diesel road can be seen extending from the dead end road. To the upper right of the group is the site of the second, coal stage, which was demolished in the 1930s. A few steam hauled trains went by the site in 1967 and then on 6th April 1968, the BR standard locomotives Nos 92203 (8H) and 75029 (5D) passed the site en-route to preservation, having been purchased by the artist David Shepherd (Plate 167). It was, after 127 years, the end of regular steam operations at Nottingham. Many thousands of engines and men had passed through its three engine Shed sites since 1839 when the first contractor's engines had built the line and then the Midland Counties 2-2-0 Bury locomotives began to work the trains. It will never again be like the 1950s or early 60s when the sheer variety of engines and workings was truly amazing.

A list of those steam and diesel locomotives with a Nottingham connection that still exist can be seen in Appendix 6.

Demolition

Taken from the Castle in the summer of 1962, Plate 168 shows the extent of the Shed site in the East Yard and the Cattle Dock area. The withdrawn No 46100 'Royal Scot' and a Caprotti Black Five can be seen to the left of the ODM building. Engines waiting for repair on the drop-pit can also be seen. Apart from the white building in the middle of the view, W J Furse Ltd and St Georges Church, none of the buildings in this photograph remain, the site and surroundings having been transformed beyond recognition.

Plate 168
A view of the site from the Castle taken in 1962
John Bailey (Bramcote)

Plate 169
The last Shed standing No 3 with a Type 2 diesel sticking its nose out on what was the crossing road to No 1 Shed

D East

Plate 170
Entrance to No 3 Shed from a similar view to Plate 145

D East

These two photographs follow the demolition of the Shed during 1967. (Plates 169 and 170)

Demolition of the last Shed, No 3, was in March 1968. The outdoor machinery buildings and their distinctive hydraulic accumulator tower stood for some years after. The Midland Railway builders plate of 1895 (Plate 172) came off one of the old 0-6-0 chassis that served as pumping engines for these hydraulic accumulators.

Plate 171
The Coal Tower no longer connected to the Shed
Bill Reed

Plate 172
The Midland Railway Builders' Plate
Jim Perkins/ A Grice

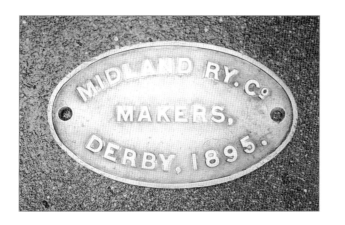

Plate 173
Class 56 No 56069 next to the Carriage Sidings Shed

D Towle

Chapter Eleven
After Steam

For a short time there was a fourth Nottingham locoshed when a diesel Shed was in use at the carriage sidings (Plate 173). This eventually became an engineer's facility and is still used for this purpose. There were still a few incidents in the area that demanded attention from the Toton beakdown crane, which was manned by many ex-Nottingham men, as the view in Plates 176 and 177 show. This scene is at the entrance to the carriage sidings and shows a de-railed 0-6-0 diesel shunter with another one in attendance, plus the Toton Crane RS1106/35. This scene was taken in 1968. Behind it is the Great Northern Station of 1855, later known as London Road Low Level Station, which served the GN until Nottingham Victoria was built.

An altogether much more serious incident occurred in the early morning of 16th December 1971. A special freight train carrying 260 tons of coal from Bestwood Colliery to Derby Gas Works ran head on into a Liverpool to Nottingham parcels train. This occurred just as the coal train crossed from the Mansfield Line at Lenton South Junction. According to the inquiry the signals had been correctly set for the coal train when the parcels train had run past signals in what today would be called a SPAD (Signal Passed at Danger). Others however, especially Drivers, were not and are still not convinced it was Driver error. Unfortunately the Driver was killed so could not be called to testify. The locomotives involved were D7605 (25256) on the parcels train and D8115 (20115) and D8142 (20142) on the coal train. (Plate175)

The Future

Up until 1999 all servicing on the Regional Railways, later Central Trains, stock was carried out in the open alongside the refueling line, facilities that were worse than the 1839 arrangements. So much for progress! However new developments were put in hand in late 1997 when it was decided that a new Shed would be built in the East Croft on the site of the old carriage sidings to service multiple units used by Central Trains. This then has become the fifth Shed (Plate 179). There is also once again a Midland Company at Nottingham, which although known as Midland Mainline has its engines and rolling stock painted green, just as the Midland Counties Railway of 1839 and the Midland Railway in its early days.

In another ironic twist of fate, it is St Pancras and not Kings Cross or Marylebone, the terminus of the former Great Central Railway, that will be the northern gateway to the Channel Tunnel and Europe.

At this point it is perhaps fitting to look at the three steam locomotive Shed sites that have been described in these volumes as they were to be seen at the end of the 20th Century

Plate 174
View of Carriage Sidings

D Towle

Plate 175
Lenton South crash
Bill Davies

Plate 176
A Shunter off the road
Bill Davies

Plate 177
Shunter being re-railed

Bll Davies

1839 Site

Black Five No 45110, whose final BR Shed was 10D on a steam special is shown passing the site of the 1839 Engine House. This Engine House can be seen in a painting by Denys Brindley on page 27 of Volume I. Just behind the photographer can be found the original stone rail blocks that were laid when the Engine House was built. These are built into the north retaining wall of the Tinkers Leen River a full description of which can also be found in Volume I.

Plate 178
1839 Site with preserved Black Five No 45110 passing on a special
Jim Perkins

Plate 179
The new Central Trains
Shed being built. London
Road Low Level (ex-GNR)
station is to the left
Bill Reed

1852 Site

In this view looking down from London Road Bridge the original boundary wall can be seen in the background.

Plate 180

The Future

Taken from the opposite direction to the floods photograph (page 108 in Volume II) the view in Plate 181 shows the only remaining part of the Middle Furlong Road site that can be seen. This is the piece of wall in front of the new building in the middle of the photograph. The tarmac road surface is the only part of Middle Furlong Road that remained.

Plate 181
Middle Furlong Road
Jim Perkins

Plate 182
Ex-LNER 4-6-2 No 60009 'Union of South Africa' passing the site of the 1839
Engine House
Jim Perkins

About Volumes I, II and IV

Although this is the end of the trilogy, ie the telling of the story, a fourth Volume of photographs will be compiled. This will tidy up a few loose ends and be a collection of all those photographs that could not be included in Volumes I, II and III. The first volume began the history of the Midland Railway in Nottingham from an age that seems very remote to those living in the 21st Century. In comparison to what was to come, the locomotives of the Midland Counties Railway of 1839, which were described in Volume I, seem very primitive. But technology must have a starting point and developments were rapid. By the end of the period covered by Volume I the Midland Railway had become a large organisation with the greatest changes and tests yet to come. With two World Wars, grouping in 1923 with some of its rivals into a new railway that still had Midland in its title, followed by economic depression and locomotive problems that eventually led to almost wholesale change and was completed by Nationalisation on January 1st 1948.

This volume covers the period most of us remember, so we are nearly at the end of our narrative, which has taken over a decade to bring to fruition and has taken much time and effort. The three volumes of this history deal with a story the authors thought worth telling - whether it has been well told must be the reader's decision. Technology has always forced the pace of change, with the decline of traditional industries mirrored in the decline of the railway and it might seem obvious to say that the end of the Locoshed was the end of an era.

But that is how those who worked there would feel and it was the people who made it work. Just as we might wonder what it must have been like to experience the last days of the great windjammers and before them the stagecoach, the time will come when all the men and women who kept the enterprise running have departed, leaving future generations to contemplate what it was like in those far off days, when steam traction was an every day affair. Indeed, when we see photographs of people with whom we worked and remember the camaraderie along with engines we worked on at long departed locations, it is as if the last forty years just fall away.

Knowing what we know now would we do it all again? The answer is a most emphatic yes. All our hard work is nearly done as the well known and well used words of 70004 spoken by 34002 at 4085 in Act III Scene II of 6021 so eloquently put all things nostalgic.

'O call back yesterday
Bid time return'

Plate 183
The sun shines through the No 1 Shed windows as the old Pay Office and the turntable are being dismantled
Dave East

End of Days

*'It is with the heart that one sees rightly,
What is essential is invisible to the eye'*

Antoine de Saint Exupery, The Little Prince

Annex A

Shed visit 15th August 1948 (from the Chris Banks Collection)
Time of visit given as 10.00 am.

Stanier 2-6-2T: Nos 40140, 40147, 40163, M178 and 40193.

Johnson/Fowler 4-4-0 2P: Nos 40394, 40417, 40427, 40498, 40504, 40533 (16B), 40540 and 40546.

Deeley 4-4-0 4P (Compound): No 41032

LMS 4-4-0 4P (Compound): Nos 41084 (17A) and 41096.

Johnson 0-6-0T: No 41682.

LT&S 4-4-2T 2P: Nos 41911, 41914, 41916, 41917, 41921 and 41926. Previously: Nos 2093, 2096, 2098, 2099, 2101, 2103, and 2109.

These 'Crooners' were freight tank engines fitted with steam reversers. One of their jobs was the dinnertime pick-up from Nottingham Yard to Beeston. This was a long train and had to be pushed out of the yard by an 0-6-0T 'Jocko'. Another duty was the Beeston to Radford Yard trip working.

Fairburn 2-6-4T 4P: Nos 42229, 42680 and 42686.

Fowler 2-6-4T 4P: Nos 42333 and 42373. In some areas these were known as 'Riverside Tanks'

Hughes/Fowler 2-6-0 5MT: No 42823.

Johnson 0-6-0 3f: Nos 43239 (16D), 43310 (18D), 43389, 43458, 43587 (16D), 43637, 43651 (16B), and 43274.

Deeley 0-6-0 3F No 43805.

Fowler 0-6-0 4F: Nos 43859 (16B), 43879 (15A), 43898 (16B), 43942 (20C), 43962, 43969, 43997 (16D), 44004 (16D) and 44022 (19E).

LMS 0-6-0 4F: Nos 44030, 44039, 44155 (16B), 44158, 44215, 44247, 44275, 44278 (15B), 44412, 44533, 44546 and 44578.

Stanier 4-6-0 5MT (Black Fives): Nos 44918 and 44984 (14B).

Stanier 4-6-0 5X Jubilee:

Nos 45554 'Ontario', 45598 'Basutoland' (14B), 45612 'Jamaica' (14B), 45640 'Frobisher'

LMS 0-6-0T 'Jocko' Nos 47552, 47629 and 47637.

Stanier 2-8-0 8F: Nos 48003, 48006 (16C), 48027, 48064, 48122 (2C), 48170, 48282, 48375 (15A), 48476 (1A), 48635, 48639, 48651 (15A), 48653, 48675 and 48696.

Aspinall 0-6-0 3F: Nos 52121 and 52123. These ex-Lancashire & Yorkshire Railway engines were usually stored in the winter, coming out again in the summer when traffic built up. Apart from the loco coal workings onto the Midland Railway coal stage of 1868 they worked the 'Shining Light' which was the name given to the Beeston Drag, ie the Yard to Yard at Beeston.

Johnson 0-6- 2F: Nos 58248 and 58275. These engines were previously numbered 3177 and 3511.

Of these 92 engines 68 were Nottingham based.

Plate 184
Class 4F No 44223 turning on No 1 Shed turntable. The photographer was standing with his back to No 2 Shed. One of the Shed road number plates that were attached in 1868 can clearly be seen in the left hand pit

G Coltas

Annex B

Shed visit of 22/08/1954 (Graham Kaye, Widnes)

This Shed visit was on a Sunday when nearly all engines were on Shed, the variety and range of types is, in retrospect, amazing with engines ranging from elderly ex-MR types up to BR Standards with the odd ER B1. Within ten years such scenes were to be a thing of the past and Nottingham was to show a very meagre steam allocation. The list is repeated as taken down. The visit would appear to have started in 3 Shed, where all or most of the tender passenger engines were turned stabled:

All engines are allocated to 16A except where shown.

3 Shed
Nos 44861, 45088, 45113 (8A), 45354 (8B), 45040 (21A), 73000, 73002, 73053, 45636 'Uganda' 45620 'North Borneo', 45667 'Jellicoe', 40454, 40395, 40458, 40493, 40553, 40487, 40900 41185, 41144 and 41108 (20A)

There are 21 engines on this list, which would leave 3 spare roads in No 3 Shed. According to earlier records 40900 was out of service.

2 Shed
This was the main tender freight engine Shed but at the week end passenger tanks were stabled here.
Nos 48136, 48218, 48170, 48293, 48614, 48635, 48282, 48064, 48312 (1A), 48000 (16C), 48333 (15A) 48770 (16C), 48639, 48763 (21A), 48206, 48648 (1A), 48009 (16C), 42140, 42174 (17A), 42228, 42184, 42361, 42339, 42333 and 42373
Drop-pit Roads
Nos 41940, 41943, 58056, 78020, 61070 (50B) 46502 and 42873 (17D)

1 Shed and its outside roads
Nos 43371, 43253, 43729, 43558, 43249, 43773, 43378, 43192, 43401, 43757, 43817 (21A), 43657 43781, 43240, 43634, 44112 (17A), 44401, 44195, 44132, 44313, 43954, 44097 (35C), 44158 and 43962,

Outside 2 Shed
Nos 43970 (16C), 44320 (15A), 44021 (16C), 44169 (22A), 44151, 44472, 44546, 43928 (22A) 44211 (21A), 44582 (20A), 43847 (17A), 44578, 44585, 44215, 43983 (16D), 43040, 58133, 58137* 47623, 47277, 47630, 47422 and 41779 Both Nos 58133/58137 and later 58175 were frequently seen with white wheels. This was due to them working the sludge tank trains to the dumping ground near Long Eaton.

Diesel Roads
Nos 12101, 12058, 12097, 12098, 12099, 12069, 12102 and 12100.

Of the 102 Steam Locomotives shown here there were 2 Class pioneers, 73000 and 48000, sadly neither of these engines have survived. The diesels have fared better however, with both 12098 and 12099 surviving.

The visiting engines came from a wide area :
1A   Willesden (London)
8A   Edge Hill(Liverpool)
8B   Warrington
15A   Wellingborough
16C   Kirkby
16D   Mansfield
17A   Derby
17D   Rowsley
20A   Leeds Holbeck
22A   Bristol
35C   Peterborough and 50A York

This 50B B1 duty was sometimes carried out by a B16, some of which had steam reversers, similar to the un-rebuilt Bullied Pacifics and Schools class. The author, Jim Perkins, remembers a demonstration of this feature by the Nottingham Fitter Charlie Hooson one day in 3 Shed on a really filthy example of this class No 61413. The B16/3 variant No 61444 (Plate185) was also a regular visitor. This engine had been modified in 1944 to take 3 sets of Walschaerts Valve gear, one of seventeen out of a total class of 69. There were other variants to be seen with Gresleys derived motion, known as B16/2, total 7. ER engines seem to have a particular smell about them very different from the LMS and BR standards. It must have been something to do with the oil used or the fish trains.

Plate 185
No 61444

A Bwandi

Annex C

Shed visit to 16A of 07 April 1957 by P Hayes, Canada.

40411, 40454, 40461 (recently transferred from 5C), 40504, 40542, 40553, 41712, 42137 (15C), 42161, 42333, 42335 (15C), 42764, 42784, 43033, 43040, 43240 (3E), 43249, 43369, 43371, 43378, 43401, 43558, 43729, 43856 43888, 43917, 43918, 43954, 43958, 43972, 44018, 44020 (17A), 44021, 44030, 44095, 44112 44131, 44132, 44151, 44158, 44195, 44223, 44227 and 44230 (21A), 44313, 44412, 44414, 44472 44480, 44533, 44538 (17B), 44555, 44562 (17B), 44578, 44585, 44861, 44918, 45088, 45224 (26A), 45242 (8A), 45554 'Ontario', 45611 'Hong Kong', 46502, 47277, 47631, 48053, 48103 (18D), 48206, 48217, 48218, 48372 (2B), 48377, 48448 (6C), 48632 (1A), 48639, 48653, 48666, 48709,, 58137, 58175, 75056 and 62571* (ex-LNER Class D16) which was being tested between Lincoln and Derby.

Diesel Shunters: 12096, 12097, 12098, 12099, 12100, 12102, 13084, 13085, 13246, 13247, 13290 and 13291.

Shed visit to 16A of 28th July 1957 (Diary of a Train spotter by M G Harvey)

40079 (16C), 40411, 40454, 40461, 40487, 40493, 40542, 40553, 40632, 41712, 42140, 42185, 42331, 42339, 42342, 42361, 43040, 43249, 43558#, 43729, 43856, 43903 (16B), 43917, 43918, 43928, 43958, 43962, 44010 (18D), 44018, 44021, 44030, 44033, 44131, 44132, 44151*, 44158, 44195, 44215, 44245 (19C), 44313, 44401, 44414, 44457 (19A), 44555, 44578, 44745 (22A), 44918, 45088, 45152 (66B), 45554, 46497, 47277, 47631, 48053, 48064, 48108, 48117, 48129 (1A), 48218, 48260(8A), 48279, 48282, 48313 (15B), 48337 (55D), 48377, 48528(9F), 48635, 48639, 48644 (15A), 48666, 48675, 58137, 58175 (Plates X), 62564, 73002, 73067, 75056, 75063, 92122 (15A)*
This engine had a blue spot on the cab side denoting a tall chimney which restricted the engine to certain lines.

Note 1: When built as Nos 4577 and 4578 had come to Nottingham the last of this pair had a high sided tender with an extra panel for working the Blackpool jobs.
No 44578 was also unusual in having its cranks set opposite to normal ie RH lead instead of LH lead.
Note 2: No 43558 was fitted with CWA (Carriage Warming Apparatus for working Chilwell Depot trains)
Note 3: No 58175 was the last in a long line of Midland 2Fs to be stationed at Nottingham and those allocated since 1945 had been:

Nos
58133 Scrapped from 16A in Dec 1955
58135 Scrapped from 5B in Sep 1961
58175 Scrapped from 16A in Dec 1961
58201 Scrapped from 16A in Aug 1958
58210 Scrapped from 16A in June 1946
58248 Scrapped from 16A in June 1951
58252 Scrapped from 16A in Dec 1951

58258 Scrapped from 17B in Jan 1954
58275 Scrapped from 16A in June 1950
58291 Scrapped from 11A in Feb 1961 and
58303 Scrapped from 9F in Nov 1953

One, LMS No 23602 did not receive a BR number being scrapped in Jan 1948.
The very last two in service were Nos 58143 and 58148, which went from 21B and
17B respectively in Nov 1963 this class then became extinct.

Diesels
Nos 12049, 12050, 12051, 12097, 12098, 13083, 13084, 13085, 13246, 13247 and
13290.
Total 90 Locomotives

The following weekend, the 4th September, a reduced number of engines were to be
recorded although this is probably only a part list:

44414, 44472, 44585, 44286 (9F), 43917, 44578, 44412, 44195, 43249, 44131, 43729,
44018 (17D)
44132, 44480, 48053 (20C), 48108, 48447 (19A), 48639, 48709, 48600 (1A),
48382 (16C), 44918
45233 (26A), 44846 (14B), 45088, 40447, 40504, 40461, 40537, 42339, 42333, 42185,
42140, 42161 (17A), 46501 (16D), 42564 (40A), 45560, 45620, 40096 (16D),
75061 (15C), 43033, 42902 (17D), 42784 (17B), 13083, 12098 and 41712.

Total 46 Locomotives
Other engines that were the responsibility of 16A but which rarely came on Shed :
0-6-0 Fowler diesels: ED3, ED5 and narrow gauge steam No1.

Annex D

Shed Visit 08/06/1958 Graham Kaye

There were a number of ex-LNER engines to be seen on this visit:

68976 (38A), 43928, 48217, 43962, 43856, 48675, 44223, 42867, 48653, 48170, 42185,
48108, 63792 (16D) 61136 (14D), 40487, 43972, 44585, 48117, 44546, 44401, 44215,
44020, 48053, 44313, 40493, 48666, 40580, 48639, 42326, 75062, 45667, 42161, 45650,
42333, 40632, 12097, 45263, 75063, 73143 (17C) 40542, 42361, 42140, 43124, 64739
(16D), 44021, 48457, 44204, 48377, 48272, 44575, 44158, 48553, 44806*, 44577,
44414, 44412, 44095, 48763, 44195, 44139, 44151, 48696, 43729, 45620, 12049,12051,
12052*, 13247, 44753, 40501, 13083,13084,13085, 41078,13290,12098*, 13246, 48770,
48223, 41712, 44858, 43251, 48267, 58175, 47277, 48672, 43558, 43032, 47631, 75076
and 42339.
* Now in Preservation.

Annex E

Shed Visit 02 January1961 M Whatmough, Lincoln

Nos 40073, 40079, 40165, 40168 and 40182 (All 16B)

Nos 40411, 40421, 40487, 40502, 40540, 40557, 40632, 40682 and 40691 (All W/D by 03.61)

Nos 42054, 42112 (9E), 42140 and 42185,

No 42935 (1A)

No 43251 (18A) in store having been withdrawn in December 1959

Nos 43954, 44030, 44195, 44252 (16B), 44394, 44480 and 44533

Nos 44664, 44756 (55A), 44856 and 44858 (both 21A), 45215 and 45223 (Both 16D) and 45240 (5A) Note: In June 1953 No 45223, along with Nos 45051, 45061, 45130, 45216, 45221 and 45350, had gone to the Southern Region to temporarily replace Merchant Navy Pacifics

Nos 45568 'Western Australia' (55A), 45611 'Hong Kong' and 45620 'North Borneo'

Nos 46100 'Royal Scot', 46112 'Sherwood Forester', 46140 'Kings Royal Rifle Corps' 46157 'The Royal Artilleryman' and 46164 'The Artists Rifleman' (41C)

Nos 48334 (16B), 48393, 48413 (16B), 48653, 48671 (15A), 48675 and 48696

Nos 73142, 75056, 78013 and 78028

Diesels:
Nos 12052, 12098, D3246 and ED5 still lettered BRITISH RAILWAYS

Annex F

1965 The Final Year of Shed Visits - M Whatmough, Lincoln

3rd January 1965
Diesels: Type 4: D43, D59, D65, D94, D139 and D141
Shunter: D3241 and D3861
Type 2: D5195, D5201, D5203, D5235, D5252, D5253, D5258, D5273, D5283, D5294, D5296, D5297, D5298, D7511, D7583, D7590 and D7591

Steam 4F 0-6-0: Nos 44170 (55E) and 44433 (15E)
Black Five 4-6-0: Nos 44658 and 44918
Jubilee 4-6-0: No 45593 'Kolhapur' of 9H now preserved

4F 0-6-0T: No 47231 The last steam locomotive allocated to Nottingham 16D and 47645 which, although a Toton (16A) engine, was in store at Nottingham and was destined to be the last steam locomotive to be moved off the Shed when it was taken to Wards of Killamarsh in July 1965.

8F 2-8-0: Nos 48530, 48538, 48551 and 48763.
Britannia Pacific 4-6-2: No 70004 'William Shakespeare' (In Store)
Austerity 2-8-0: Nos 90075 and 90647.
BR Class 9F 2-10-0: Nos 92075 (In Store) and 92156.

16th January 1965 - M Whatmough, Lincoln
Diesels: D43, D49, D61, D72, D3861, D5187, D5258 and D7596.

Steam: Fairburn 2-6-4T: No 42075
4F 0-6-0: Nos 44113, 44170 (In Store) and 44433 (In Store)
Black Five 4-6-0: Nos 45388 and 45450
8F 2-8-0: No 48184 (In Store)
BR 2-6-0: No 78023
Austerity 2-8-0: No 90075
BR 9F 2-10-0: Nos 92075 and 92213

8th May 1965 - M Whatmough, Lincoln
Diesels: No 12052 and D5187, D5200, D5209, D5229, D5255, D5260, D5270, D5283, D5296, D5581, D7521, D7539, D7542, D7580, D7581 and D7590

Steam (1 only) 4F 0-6-0T: No 47645 emblazoned with the legend 'City of Nottingham' which was towed away to Wards, Killamarsh on 13th July 1965.

18 July 1965 - J Curtis, Nottingham
Diesels Only In order seen: D5263, D1833, D5261, D11, D70, D5295, D7522, D139, D7547, D7527, D7578, D5264, D7554, D5296, D1630, D7539, D5271, D7500, D7543, D5294, D51, D7534, D5262, D5272, D7509 and D142

Annex G

Shed Lists

BRITISH RAILWAY SHED CODES FROM 1950   (MIDLAND REGION)

1A	WILLESDEN	closed to steam on 27/9/65
1B	CAMDEN	no steam allocation after 11/9/63 closed completly on 9/9/63
1C	WATFORD	closed to steam 29/3/65
1D	DEVONS ROAD	(bow) closed to steam on 25/8/58 closed completly on 10/2/64
1E	BLETCHLEY	from 2/3/52 closed to steam on 5/7/65
(sub)	LEIGHTON BUZZARD	from 2/3/52 closed to steam on 5/11/62
(sub)	NEWPORT PAGNELL	
1F	RUGBY	from 9/9/63 closed to steam on 25/5/65
1G	WOODFORD HALSE	from 9/9/63 closed to steam on 14/6/65
1H	NORTHAMPTON	from 9/9/63 closed to steam on 27/9/65
2A	RUGBY	recoded 1F from 9/9/63
	TYSELEY	from 9/9/63 closed to steam 7/11/66
(sub)	MARKET HARBOROUGH	recoded 2F from 10/55
(sub)	SEATON	recoded 2F(sub) from 10/55
2B	NUNEATON	recoded 5E from 9/9/63
	OXLEY	from 9/9/63 closed to steam 7/11/66
2C	WARWICK	closed on 17/11/58
	STOURBRIDGE JUNCTION	from 9/9/63 closed 11/7/66
2D	COVENTRY	closed on 17/11/59 used for storage of locos
··	BANBURY	from 9/9/63 closed on 3/10/66
2E	NORTHAMPTON	from 2/3/52 recoded 1H from 9/9/63
	SALTLEY	from 9/9/63 closed to steam on 6/3/67
2F	MARKET HARBOROUGH	from 10/55 recoded 15F during 2/58
	WOODFORD HALSE	from 2/58 recoded 1G from 9/9/63
	BESCOT	from 9/9/63 closed to steam from 28/3/66
(sub)	SEATON	from 10/55 recoded 15F(sub) during 2/58
2G	WALSALL	(diesel depot) from 9/9/63
2H	MONUMENT LANE	(diesel depot) from 9/9/63
2J	ASTON	from 9/9/63 closed on 11/10/65
2K	BUSHBURY	from 9/9/63 closed on 12/4/65
2L	LEAMINGTON SPA	from 9/9/63 closed on 14/6/65
2M	WELLINGTON (salop)	from 9/9/63 closed on 8/3/64
2P	KIDDERMINSTER	from 9/9/63 closed on 8/8/64
3A	BESCOT	recoded 21B during 5/60
3B	BUSHBURY	recoded 21C during 5/60
3C	WALSALL	recoded 21F during 5/60 (closed to steam on 9/6/58)
3D	ASTON	recoded 21D during 5/60
3E	MONUMENT LANE	recoded 21E during 5/60

```
4A          BLETCHLEY         recoded 1E from 2/3/52
   (sub)    LEIGHTON BUZZARD recoded 1E(sub) from 2/3/52
   (sub)    AYLESBURY
   (sub)    NEWPORT PAGNELL recoded 1E(sub) from 2/3/52 closed on 1/6/65
   (sub)    OXFORD
   (sub)    CAMBRIDGE
4B          NORTHAMPTON       recoded 2E from 2/3/52

5A          CREWE NORTH       closed to steam on 25/5/65
   (sub)    WHITCHURCH
   (sub)    GRESTY LANE       (ex-G.W.R.) from 9/60 closed on 17/6/63
5B          CREWE SOUTH       closed to steam on 6/11/67
5C          STAFFORD          closed to steam on 19/7/65
   (sub)    COALPORT
5D          STOKE             closed to steam on 7/8/67
5E          ALSAGER           closed on 18/6/62
            NUNEATON          from 9/9/63 closed on 6/6/66
5F          UTTOXETER         closed on 7/12/64

6A          CHESTER           closed to steam on 5/6/67
6B          MOLD JUNCTION     closed on 18/4/66
6C          BIRKENHEAD        recoded 8H from 9/9/63
            CROES NEWYDD      from 9/9/63 closed to steam on 5/6/67
   (sub)    BALA              from 9/9/63 closed on 18/1/64
   (sub)    PENMAENPOOL       from 9/9/63 closed on 18/1/64
6D          CHESTER
            (NORTHGATE)       closed during 12/59
            SHREWSBURY        from 9/9/63 closed to steam on 6/3/67
6E          WREXHAM (RHOSDDU) recoded 84K during 2/58
            CHESTER (G.W.R.) from 2/58 closed during 1959/60
            OSWESTRY          from 9/9/63 closed on 18/1/64
6F          BIDSTON           closed on 11/2/63
            MACHYNLLETH       from 9/9/63 closed to steam on 12/12/66
   (sub)    ABERYSTWYTH
            (V.O.R.)          from 9/9/63 closed during 1968
   (sub)    PORTMADOC         from 9/9/63
   (sub)    PWLLHELI          from 9/9/63
   (sub)    ABERYSTWYTH
            (ex-CAMBRIAN)     from 9/9/63 closed on 12/4/65 later converted
                              for V.O.R.use
6G          LLANDUDNO
            JUNCTION          from 5/52 closed on 3/10/66
6H          BANGOR            from 5/52 closed on 14/6/65
6J          HOLYHEAD          from 5/52 closed to steam on 12/12/66
6K          RHYL              from 5/52 closed on 11/2/63
   (sub)    DENBIGH           recoded 6K(sub) during 5/52

8A          EDGE HILL         closed to steam on 6/5/68
8B          WARRINGTON
            (DALLAM)          closed on 2/10/67
   (sub)    WARRINGTON
            (ARPLEY)          closed on 27/5/63
```

8C	SPEKE JUNCTION	closed on 6/5/68
8D	WIDNES	closed during 5/50
	WIDNES (C.L.C.)	from 22/5/50 closed on 13/4/64
8E	BRUNSWICK (C.L.C.)	from 5/50 recoded 27F during 2/58
(sub)	WARRINGTON (C.L.C.)	
	NORTHWICH	from 2/58 closed on 4/3/68
8F	WARRINGTON (C.L.C.)	from 5/50 recoded 27F(sub) from 2/58
	SPRINGS BRANCH	from 2/58 closed to steam on 4/12 67
8G	SUTTON OAK	from 2/58 closed on 19/6/67
8H	BIRKENHEAD	from 9/9/63 closed to steam on 7/10/67
8K	BANK HALL	from 9/9/63 closed on 10/10/66
8L	AINTREE	from 9/9/63 closed on 12/6/67
8M	SOUTHPORT	from 9/9/63 closed on 6/6/66
8P	WIGAN (L.&.Y.)	from 9/9/63 closed on 13/4/64
8R	WALTON-ON-THE (HILL)	from 9/9/63 closed on 15/12/63
9A	LONGSIGHT	closed to steam on 14/2/65
9B	STOCKPORT (EDGELEY)	closed on 5/5/68
9C	MACCLESFIELD	closed on 12/6/61
	REDDISH	(electric depot) from 9/9/63
9D	BUXTON	recoded 9L from 9/9/63
	NEWTON HEATH	from 9/9/63 closed to steam on 1/7/68
9E	TRAFFORD PARK	from 5/50 recoded 17F during 12/56
	TRAFFORD PARK	from 2/58 closed to steam on 4/3/68
(sub)	GLAZEBROOK	from 5/50 recoded 17F(sub) during 12/56
(sub)	GLAZEBROOK	from 2/58 as signing-on point only
9F	HEATON MERSEY	from 5/50 recoded 17E during 12/56
	HEATON MERSEY	from 2/58 closed to steam on 6/5/68
(sub)	GOWHOLE	from 5/50 recoded 17E(sub) during 12/56
(sub)	GOWHOLE	from 2/58 as sign-on point only
9G	NORTHWICH	from 5/50 recoded 8E during 2/58
	GORTON	from 2/58 closed to steam on 14/6/65
(sub)	DINTING	from 2/58
(sub)	GUIDE BRIDGE	from 2/58 as sign-on point only
(sub)	ARDWICK	from 2/58 as sign-on point only
9H	PATRICROFT	from 9/9/63 closed on 1/7/68
9J	AGECROFT	from 9/9/63 closed on 10/10/66
9K	BOLTON	from 9/9/63 closed on 1/7/68
9L	BUXTON	from 9/9/63 closed on 1/7/68
9M	BURY	from 9/9/63 closed on 12/4/65
9P	LEES (OLDHAM)	from 9/9/63 closed on 13/4/64
10A	SPRINGS BRANCH	recoded 8F during 2/58
	CARNFORTH	from 9/9/63 closed to B.R. steam on 7/8/68
10B	PRESTON	recoded 24K during 2/58
	BLACKPOOL	from 9/9/63 closed on 2/11/64
(sub)	BLACKPOOL NORTH	from 9/9/63 closed on 10/2/64
10C	PATRICROFT	recoded 26F during 2/58
	FLEETWOOD	from 9/9/63 closed on 14/2/66
10D	PLODDER LANE	closed on 10/10/54
	SUTTON OAK	from 10/10/54 recoded 8G during 2/58

10D	LOSTOCK HALL	from 9/9/63 closed on 7/8/68
10E	SUTTON OAK	recoded 10D from 10/10/54
	ACCRINGTON	(diesel depot) from 9/9/63
10F	WIGAN (C.L.C.)	from 20/5/51 closed on 24/3/52
	ROSE GROVE	from 9/9/63 closed on 7/8/68
10G	SKIPTON	from 9/9/63 closed on 3/4/66
10H	LOWER DARWEN	from 9/9/63 closed on 14/2/66
10J	LANCASTER	from 9/9/63 closed on 18/4/64

11A	CARNFORTH	recoded 24L during 2/58
	BARROW	from 2/58 recoded 12E from 5/60
11B	BARROW	recoded 11A during 2/58
	WORKINGTON	from 2/58 recoded 12F from 5/60
(sub)	CONISTON	closed during 1/58
11C	OXENHOLME	recoded 12G from 5/60
11D	TEBAY	recoded 12H from 5/60
11E	LANCASTER	from 7/10/51 recoded 24J from 3/57

12A	CARLISLE (UPPERBY)	recoded 12B from 2/58
	CARLISLE (KINGMOOR)	from 2/58 closed to steam on 1/1/68
12B	CARLISLE CANAL	recoded 68E from 7/10/51
	PENRITH	from 10/55 recoded 12B(sub) from 2/58
	CARLISLE (UPPERBY)	from 2/58 closed to steam on 12/12/66
(sub)	PENRITH	from 2/58 closed on 12/6/62
12C	PENRITH	recoded 12B from 10/55
	WORKINGTON	from 10/55 recoded 11B from 2/58
	CARLISLE CANAL	from 2/58 closed on 17/6/63
	BARROW	from 9/9/63 closed to steam on 12/12/66
12D	WORKINGTON	recoded 12C from 10/55
	KIRKBY STEPHEN	from 2/58 closed on 20/11/61
	WORKINGTON	from 9/9/63 closed on 1/1/68
12E	MOOR ROW	closed on 31/7/54
	BARROW	from 5/60 recoded 12C from 9/9/63
	TEBAY	from 9/9/63 closed on 31/12/67
12F	WORKINGTON	from 5/60 recoded 12D from 9/9/63
12G	OXENHOLME	from 5/60 closed on 18/6/62
12H	TEBAY	from 5/60 recoded 12E from 9/9/63

13A	TRAFFORD PARK	recoded 9E from 22/5/50
(sub)	GLAZEBROOK	recoded 9E(sub) from 22/5/50
13B	BELLE VUE	recoded 26G from 22/5/50
13C	HEATON MERSEY	recoded 9F from 22/5/50
(sub)	GOWHOLE	recoded 9F(sub) from 22/5/50
13D	NORTHWICH	recoded 9G from 22/5/50
13E	BRUNSWICK (C.L.C.) recoded 8E from 22/5/50
(sub)	WARRINGTON (C.L.C.) recoded 8F from 22/5/50
(sub)	SOUTHPORT (C.L.C.) recoded 27F from 22/5/50
(sub)	WIDNES (C.L.C.) recoded 8D from 22/5/50

13F	WALTON-ON-THE	
	HILL (C.L.C.)	recoded 27E from 22/5/50
13G	WIGAN (C.L.C.)	recoded 10F from 22/5/50
14A	CRICKLEWOOD	recoded 14B from 9/9/63
	CRICKLEWOOD	(diesel depot) from 9/9/63
14B	KENTISH TOWN	closed during 8/63
	CRICKLEWOOD	from 9/9/63 closed on 14/12/64
14C	ST. ALBANS	closed on 11/1/60
	BEDFORD	from 9/9/63
14D	NEASDEN	from 2/58 closed on 18/6/62
(sub)	AYLESBURY	from 2/58 closed on 18/6/62
(sub)	CHESHAM	from 2/58 closed on 18/6/62
14E	BEDFORD	from 2/58 recoded 14C from 9/9/63
15A	WELLINGBOROUGH	recoded 15B from 9/9/63
	LEICESTER	
	(MIDLAND)	from 9/9/63 closed to steam on 13/6/66
15B	KETTERING	recoded 15C from 9/9/63
	WELLINGBOROUGH	from 9/9/63 closed to steam on 13/6/66
15C	LEICESTER	
	(MIDLAND)	recoded 15A from 9/9/63
	KETTERING	from 9/9/63 closed to steam on 14/6/65
(sub)	MARKET	
	HARBOROUGH	from 10/60 closed on 4/10/65
(sub)	SEATON	from 10/60 closed by 28/1/61
15D	BEDFORD	recoded 14E from 2/58
	COALVILLE	from 2/58 recoded 15D from 9/9/63
15E	LEICESTER	(ex-G.C.R.) from 2/58 recoded 15E from 9/9/
		closed on 6/7/64
15F	MARKET	
	HARBOROUGH	from 2/58 recoded 15C(sub) from 2/10/60
(sub)	SEATON	from 2/58 recoded 15C(sub) from 2/10/60
16A	NOTTINGHAM	recoded 16D from 9/9/63
	TOTON	from 9/9/63 closed to steam 12/65
(sub)	SOUTHWELL	closed on 10/1/55
(sub)	LINCOLN	
	ST. MARKS	recoded 40A(sub)
16B	PETERBOROUGH	
	(SPITAL BRIDGE)	recoded 35C from 12/8/50
	KIRKBY-IN-	
	ASHFIELD	from 10/55 recoded 16E from 9/9/63
	ANNESLEY	from 9/9/63 closed on 3/1/66
	COLWICK	from 3/1/66 closed to steam on 12/12/66
16C	KIRKBY-IN-	
	ASHFIELD	recoded 16B from 10/55
	MANSFIELD	from 10/55 closed on 11/4/60
	DERBY	from 9/9/63 closed to steam on 6/3/67
16D	MANSFIELD	recoded 16C from 10/55
	ANNESLEY	from 2/58 recoded 16B from 9/9/63
	NOTTINGHAM	from 9/9/63 closed on 4/4/65

```
16E      KIRKBY-IN-
         ASHFIELD        from 9/9/63 closed on 3/10/66
16F      BURTON          from 9/9/63
16G      WESTHOUSES      from 9/9/63 closed to steam from 3/10/66
16H      HASLAND         from 9/9/63 closed on 7/9/64
16J      ROWSLEY         from 9/9/63 closed on 27/4/64
  (sub) CROMFORD         from 9/9/63 closed during 4/64
  (sub) MIDDLETON TOP    from 9/9/63 closed during 4/64
  (sub) SHEEP PASTURE    from 9/9/63 closed during 4/64

17A      DERBY           recoded 16C from 9/9/63
  (sub) DERBY FRIARGATE  from 2/58 as sign-on point only
17B      BURTON          recoded 16F from 9/9/63
  (sub) OVERSEAL
  (sub) HORNINGLOW       closed on 12/9/60
17C      COALVILLE       recoded 15D from 2/58
         ROWSLEY         from 2/58 recoded 16J from 9/9/63
  (sub) CROMFORD         from 2/58 recoded 16J(sub) from 9/9/63
  (sub) MIDDLETON TOP    from 2/58 recoded 16J(sub) from 9/9/63
  (sub) SHEEP PASTURE    from 2/58 recoded 16J(sub) from 9/9/63
17D      ROWSLEY         recoded 17C from 2/58
  (sub) CROMFORD         recoded 17C(sub) from 2/58
  (sub) MIDDLETON TOP    recoded 17C(sub) from 2/58
  (sub) SHEEP PASTURE    recoded 17C(sub) from 2/58
17E      HEATON MERSEY   from 12/56 recoded 9F from 2/58
17F      TRAFFORD PARK   from 12/56 recoded 9E from 2/58

18A      TOTON           recoded 16A from 9/9/63
18B      WESTHOUSES      recoded 16G from 9/9/63
18C      HASLAND         recoded 16H from 9/9/63
  (sub) CLAY CROSS
18D      STAVELEY
         (BARROW HILL)   recoded 41E from 2/58
  (sub) SHEEPBRIDGE      recoded 41E(sub) from 2/58

19A      SHEFFIELD
         (GRIMESTHORPE)  recoded 41B from 2/58
19B      SHEFFIELD
         (MILLHOUSES)    recoded 41C from 2/58
19C      CANKLOW         recoded 41D from 2/58

20A      LEEDS HOLBECK   recoded 55A from 10/56
20B      STOURTON        recoded 55B from 10/56
20C      ROYSTON         recoded 55D from 10/56
20D      NORMANTON       recoded 55E from 10/56
20E      BRADFORD
         (MANNINGHAM)    recoded 55F from 10/56
  (sub) ILKLEY           closed during 10/56
20F      SKIPTON         from 7/10/51 recoded 24G from 3/57
  (sub) KEIGHLEY         from 7/10/51 closed during 1956
20G      HELLIFIELD      from 7/10/51 recoded 24H from 3/57
  (sub) INGLETON
```

```
21A        SALTLEY          recoded 2E from 9/9/63
21B        BOURNEVILLE      closed on 15/2/60
           BESCOT           from 5/60 recoded 2F from 9/9/63
    (sub)  REDDITCH
21C        BROMSGROVE       recoded 85F from 2/58
           BUSHBURY         from 5/60 recoded 2K from 9/9/63
21D        STRATFORD-ON-
           AVON             lost code during 3/53 closed on 22//7/57
           ASTON            from 5/60 recoded 2J from 9/9/63
21E        MONUMENT LANE    from 5/50 closed to steam on 12/2/62
21F        WALSALL          from 5/60 recoded 2G from 9/9/63 (diesel depot)

22A        BRISTOL
           (BARROW ROAD)    recoded 82E from 2/58
22B        GLOUCESTER
           (BARNWOOD)       recoded 85E from 2/58
    (sub)  DURSLEY          recoded 85E(sub) from 2/58
    (sub)  TEWKESBURY       recoded 85E(sub) from 2/58

23A        SKIPTON          recoded 20F from 7/10/51
    (sub)  KEIGHLEY         recoded 20F(sub) from 7/10/51
23B        HELLIFIELD       recoded 20G from 7/10/51
    (sub)  INGLETON         closed by 7/10/51
23C        LANCASTER
           (GREEN AYRE)     recoded 11E from 7/10/51

24A        ACCRINGTON       closed to steam on 6/3/61
24B        ROSE GROVE       recoded 10F from 9/9/63
24C        LOSTOCK HALL     recoded 10D from 9/9/63
24D        LOWER DARWEN     recoded 10H from 9/9/63
24E        BLACKPOOL        from 5/52 recoded 10B from 9/9/63
    (sub)  BLACKPOOL NORTH  from 5/52 recoded 10B(sub) from 9/9/63
24F        FLEETWOOD        from 5/52 recoded 10C from 9/9/63
24G        SKIPTON          from 3/57 recoded 10G from 9/9/63
24J        LANCASTER
           (GREEN AYRE)     from 3/57 recoded 10J from 9/9/63
24K        PRESTON          from 2/58 closed on 12/9/61
24L        CARNFORTH        from 2/58 recoded 10A from 9/9/63

25A        WAKEFIELD        recoded 56A from 10/56
25B        HUDDERSFIELD     recoded 55G from 10/56
25C        GOOLE            recoded 53E from 10/56
25D        MIRFIELD         recoded 56G from 10/56
25E        SOWERBY BRIDGE   recoded 56E from 10/56
25F        LOW MOOR         recoded 56F from 10/56
25G        FARNLEY
           (JUNCTION)       recoded 55C from 10/56
```

```
26A      NEWTON HEATH      recoded 9D from 9/9/63
26B      AGECROFT          recoded 9J from 9/9/63
26C      BOLTON            recoded 9K from 9/9/63
26D      BURY              recoded 9M from 9/9/63
26E      BACUP             closed on 10/10/54
         LEES (OLDHAM)     from 10/10/54 recoded 9P from 9/9/63
26F      LEES (OLDHAM)     recoded 26E from 10/54
         BELLE VUE         from 10/54 closed on 16/4/56
         PATRICROFT        from 2/58 recoded 9H from 9/9/63
26G      BELLE VUE         from 20/5/51 recoded 26F from 10/54

27A      BANK HALL         recoded 8K from 9/9/63
27B      AINTREE           recoded 8L from 9/9/63
27C      SOUTHPORT         recoded 8M from 9/9/63
27E      WALTON-ON-THE-
         HILL (C.L.C.)     from 22/5/50 recoded 8R from 9/9/63
   (sub) SOUTHPORT
         (LORD STREET) (C.L.C.) from 22/5/50 closed on 7/1/52
         BRUNSWICK (C.L.C.) from 2/58 closed 12/9/61
   (sub) WARRINGTON (C.L.C.) from 2/56

28A      BLACKPOOL         recoded 24E from 5/52
   (sub) BLACKPOOL NORTH recoded 24E(sub) from 5/52
28B      FLEETWOOD         recoded 24F from 5/52
```

Appendix One

Allocations in the 1950s

1950

Class 3MT 2-6-2T: 40120, 40140 and 40178

Class 2P 4-4-0: 40415, 40417, 40419, 40452, 40458, 40478, 40504, 40535 40540, 40546, 40552, 40553 and 40560

Note: The first 3 engines were originally MR '2183' Class all of which (Nos 403 -427) had come to Nottingham in April 1914.

Class 4P 4-4-0: 40929, 41015, 41019, 41032, 41082 and 41096

Class 1F 0-6-0T: 41682, 41686 and 41846

Class 2P 4-4-2T: 41917, 41919, 41921, 41922, 41925 and 41926. These were not popular and were known as 'Crooners' due to them moving about all over the place, being a rough riding class of engine.

Class 4MT 2-6-4T: Fairburn designed were 42140,*42184, 42185, 42228 and 42229 Fowler designed were 42333, 42339, 42361 and 42373. This class of Fowler 4MTs were preferred on the Tamworth Mails due to their acceleration characteristics. They could be put on half regulator at 15% cut off, something that a Stanier tank with 25XX boiler did not like. They were one of the few Fowler designs on which the valve gear did not throttle the engine.

Stanier designed 2-6-4Tanks were: 42680 and 42686.

* Denotes short wheelbase version

Class 5MT 2-6-0: 42853

Class 4MT 2-6-0: 43018, 43019, 43033 and 43040. When built, these engines had double chimneys and all steel piping but due to poor steaming characteristics they had to be modified to single chimney. Copper piping replaced the steel due to pipes which kept breaking due to their the rigidity. Also the Automatic Blowdown Valve caused slime on the track when running tender first as the blowdown exhaust was clamped to exactly the rail gauge. There were arguments between the Running Foremen and Mr Percy Croydon, the Mechanical Foreman, about moving the pipe and Percy would not consider it unless authorised by HQ. These engines regularly worked the 5.40am Ollerton Colliery job with 80-100 wagons.

Class 3F 0-6-0: 43192, 43240, 43249, 43300, 43369, 43371, 43378, 43399, 43401, 43538, 43558, 43637, 43711, 43723, 43724 and 43729.

Class 4F 0-6-0 Ex Midland Railway: 43954, 43956 and 43958 and ex LMS Nos 44030, 44039, 44055, 44095, 44113, 44132, 44158, 44215, 44223, 44230, 44247, 44264, 44313, 44401, 44408, 44412, 44414, 44425, 44472, 44480, 44533, 44546, 44577, 44578, 44585 and 44598.

These 4Fs were a mixed bag in regards to builders:

Nos 44030/39 and 55 were built at Derby between 1923-25

No 44095 Kerr Stuart 1925

Nos 44113, 44132, 44158: Crewe 1925-1926 and 44533, 44546: Crewe 1928

Nos 44215, 44223, 44230, 44247, 44264: Derby 1925-1926 and 44408, 44412, 44414, 44425: Derby 1927, 44577, 44578, 44585: Derby 1939 and 44598: Derby 1940:

These later 4Fs had removable axle box underkeeps. The class finished at 44606.

Nos 44313: St Rollox 1927 and 44472 St Rollox 1928

Nos 44401 and 44480: North British of 1927. The only builders not represented are Andrew Barclay (who built very few) and Horwich.

Class 5MT 4-6-0: Nos 44773 44825, 44841, 44861, 44918 and 45059.

Class 5XP 4-6-0

Nos

45554   'Ontario' In the previous year both 'Ontario' and 'Hong Kong'

45611   'Hong Kong' had received 4000 gallon Stanier tenders repatriated from the Middle East. Part of a batch of 39 Class 8F Locomotives and 43 tenders surplus to WD requirements.

45620* 'North Borneo'.

     45636* 'Uganda'

     45640* 'Frobisher'

* Denotes short 3500 gallon tender

All the 16A Jubilees were Crewe built with 6ft 3inch wheelbase bogies ex-LNWR Claughtons other Jubilees were North British with 6ft 2inch wheelbase bogies

Class 3F 0-6-0T 'Jocko's These were gradually, replaced by 0-6-0 EE Shunters.

Nos 47277, 47422, 47438, 47485, 47539, 47552, 47623, 47629, 47631, 47632 and 47637. These engines did a lot of trip working and 47485 was unusual in being fitted with a screw reverser. This engine had come to Nottingham from Devons Road in 1945 and was used mostly on the Nottingham Yard shunt at the Wilford Road end. Built as No 16568 by Vulcan Foundry in 1927 it was one of a few 3F tanks that worked push-pull on branches like Ashchurch-Upton on Severn. No 47485 departed to Burton on 15th March 1952.

Class 8F 2-8-0: 48003 #, 48064, 48102, 48170, 48206, 48217, 48218, 48279, 48293*, 48380, 48381, 48402, 48614, 48639, 48653, 48666, 48675 and 48696+,

Note: One of original batch of 8Fs (12 engines) built with a straight throatplate boiler without a dome and fitted with a Smokebox Regulator. It was the only one of this batch to be modified with a sloping throatplate boiler with dome regulator. This was to provide Nos 48000-8002, 48004-48011 with a spare boiler.

* Involved in the Dolphin Junction (GWR) accident during WWII.

+ 1st 8F to be oil fired and last engine to be converted back to coal.

No 48402 was at one time fitted with mixed wheel sets having 3 sets with integral balancing and the trailing set with built up balancing.

Class 3F 0-6-0 (ex-Lancashire and Yorkshire Rly): Nos 52121, 52123 and 52135. All of these engines had a chip in the chimney top due to hitting the top brace on the coal stage when they pushed wagons up the incline to the coaling area. The Adze that was used to shape the wooden tender brake blocks fitted to these engines, hung on the Shed wall for years after the last engine had disappeared.

Class 1P 2-4-0: No 58020

Class 1P 0-4-4T: Nos 58050 and 58056

58056 was motor coach fitted for the Southwell Branch a service that came onto Nottingham Carriage Sidings on Monday mornings for cleaning.
Class 2F 0-6-0: Nos 58133, 58135, 58201, 58248 and 58252.
Class 1P 2-4-0: No 20155. This last surviving Johnson 2-4-0 was employed at Nottingham on the Shed shunt. A duty that entailed shunting from the Field Side Sidings to the Coal Stage and Coal Hopper and was restricted to this job (at Saltley No 22853 carried out this duty). The permanent Driver on the Shed shunt was Bill Morris who had a false foot (he had lost a foot at Stoke Station) and his Guard was Joe Holland, known as 'One Pace Joe'. Another Driver, Tom Roberts who worked the shunt in Nottingham Yard, had a wooden leg.

1954
By 1954 the new BR Classes had started to be allocated and Nottingham received Class 5 4-6-0s 73000 and 73002. The Ivatt designs of 1946/47 that came to 16A were Class 4 Moguls Nos 43033, 43040 and 43119 as well as the Class 2 2-6-0 Mogul No 46502. There were also diesels at the Shed; these were English Electric 0-6-0 shunters Nos 12058, 12069 and 12096 to 12102. Many of the traditional Classes remained and were either scrapped or moved about, according to traffic patterns.

1958
On September 8 1958 the day that one of the authors, Jim Perkins, started work at Nottingham 16A the allocation was 101. This allocation was to be almost the same as that for 1959 (99) with a few changes such as No 40461 (W/D Feb 1959) replaced by Nos 40421 and 40553 (W/D Nov 1958) replaced by No 40502. No 41712 transferred to 16C Feb 1959. Moguls Nos 42769 and 42784 transferred to 16D in Jan 1959. Also still at the Shed in late 1958 was the last Class 3F 0-6-0 No 43558 which was transferred to 9F in Jan 1959. The lone Ivatt 2MT 2-6-0 No 46502 departed to 17A in Jan 1959. There had also been two 0-6-0T engines Nos 47277 and 47631 but by September only No 47277 remained, No 47631 having moved to 9G in August 1958. This low number of steam shunting engines was a result of the numerous 0-6-0 EE Diesel Electric shunters employed at Nottingham. The Class 8Fs remained almost the same although No 48261 ex-21A was exchanged for No 48053 which went to 15D with one extra 8F the Class pioneer No 48000 coming to Nottingham from 21A in Jan 1959. The BR standard engines also moved on with both Nos 73143 and 73144 moving to Derby in Dec 1958 and Feb 1959

1959
Class 2P 4-4-0
Nos 40411, 40421, 40454, 40487, 40493*, 40502 (The former MR Royal Train engine) 40504, 40534*, 40542, 40550, 40557, 40585 and 40632.

Note: After they had been withdrawn these engines were amongst those stored at Chelleston Quarry Siding on the former Midland Railway, Burton to Ashby Railway and HQ of the Melbourne Military Railway 1939-1945.

Other engines recorded as stored at Spondon Junction but stored at Chelleston on 14 Feb 1960 (David Birt) were:
Compounds: Nos 41062 and 41120
Fowler 2-6-4T: No 42341
Class 3F: Nos 43223, 43241, 43308, 43584, 43587, 43881 and 43939.

Class 3F Tank: No 47214
Class 7F: No 49418
Class 1P 0-4-4T: No 58065. This engine was the penultimate survivor of this once numerous class, none of which survived into preservation, a great loss.

Class 2F: Nos 58132 and 58281.

Class 4P 2-6-4T (Fairburn)
Nos 42140, 42161, 42185 and 42636.

Class 4P 2-6-4T (Fowler)
Nos 42333, 42339 and 42361

Class 4F 0-6-0

Nos 43856, 43859, 43888, 43917, 43918, 43928, 43954, 43958, 43962, 43972, 44018, 44021, 44030, 44033, 44095, 44131, 44132, 44139, 44151, 44158, 44195, 44204, 44215, 44223, 44248, 44313, 44394, 44401, 44412, 44414, 44472, 44480, 44533, 44546, 44555, 44577, 44578 and 44585.

In this year almost the entire ex-Midland Railway Class 3F and the Horwich 2-6-0 'Crabs' previously at 16A had been transferred away. New engines to be seen were the BR Class 4 4-6-0 engines Nos 75056 and 75062 to 75064. The only ex-MR Class 2F 0-6-0 at 16A at this time was No 58175 which had been built as No 1234 in 1875 then renumbered No 3002 in 1907 then as No 23002 by the LMS in 1923. This was the third time No 58175 had been allocated to Nottingham.

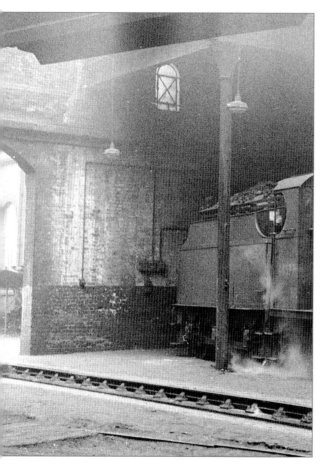

Plate 186
Inside No 1 Shed with Class 4 No 44577. The joint to the left of the switch box is where the archway for the other line into No 1 Shed was situated when built in 1868 (see Vol 1 for details)

T Hewitt

The first was in 1935 followed by a short time in 1943 finally coming to Nottingham from Grimesthorpe in 1955. It went to Toton in March 1960 being withdrawn from there in December 1961 after 86 years service.

Class 5MT 4-6-0
Nos 44806, 44858, 44861, 44918, 44944, 45088, 45253 and 45263

5XP 4-6-0
Nos
45611 'Hong Kong'
45620 'North Borneo' *
45636 'Uganda' *
45641 'Sandwich' *
45650 'Blake'
45667 'Jellicoe'   * These engines were coupled to short 3500 Gallon Tenders.

3F 0-6-0T
No 47277

8F 2-8-0
Nos 48000, 48064, 48108, 48117, 48170, 48177, 48217, 48218, 48261, 48279 ex (WD 566), 48286, 48377, 48614, 48635, 48639, 48653, 48666, 48675, 48696, 48748 and 48763 which were ex-LNER 3543(3143) and 3558 (3158) respectively.

MR 2F 0-6-0

No 58175 which was re-allocated to 18A (Toton) in March 1960, but remained at Nottingham.

BR Standard 4MT 4-6-0

Nos 75056, 75062, 75063 and 75064

No1 the Beeston creosote narrow gauge shunter (preserved)

Total 100 Steam locomotives plus 0-6-0 English Electric Shunters.

Nos 12050 (7137), 12051(7138), 12052 (7139), 12096, 12097, 12098
13083, 13084, 13085, 13086, 13246, 13247 and 13290 (Preserved) Later Class 08
plus the Standard Gauge Beeston Creosote locomotives ED3 and ED5 and the Narrow Gauge ED10.

Total 16

Of these Diesel Shunters: ED10, 12052, 12098 (also12099 which was at 16A from new in 1952 to 1957) all Class 11 and Class 08 No 13290 are preserved.

Total Locomotive allocation:116
A full list of allocations from 1935 to closure can be read in the excellent Steam Archive Services Series produced by Richard Strange.

Appendix Two

The Footplate Staff contained many characters and tales abound about their exploits. One bad winter a Driver who had a farm came to work on a tractor and when the roads were too bad, even for that, he came on a horse. When he asked the Foreman where he could stable his horse the Foreman was up to it and told him to turn it off in No 1 Shed.

Footplate Staff and their nom-de-plumes

When it came to allocating nicknames the WE staff were very inventive and some incident or observation from years before or even childhood attachments could stay for the rest of their railway lives.

Some of the men shown here were legendary at Nottingham and beyond!

Jack 'Sacko' Stead after a notorious Chicago Gangster of the 1920s
Fred 'Cocky' Mould
Len 'Yellow Peril' Cowdell
G 'Spiv' Mason
Albert 'Rolling Tommo' Thomas
Frank 'Comrade' Connell
Bob 'Steady Bob' Hazeldine
Charlie 'Scrooge' Newton
J 'Loose Coupling Jack' Greaves
Jack 'Tank Stamping' Gladwin
A 'Nobby' Keys
Frank 'The Count' Hickling
'Moaner' Smith
'Driver' Smith
'Driver' Brown
'Smiler' Brown
Don 'Docker' Perkins
John 'Sir Willy' Stanton
George 'Pip' Chambers who came from Pipewell , Northants (hence 'Pip'') and became Chairman of Notts County Council
F 'Hopalong' Cassidy (after a well known Western Cowboy character)
W 'Piston Bill' Clarke
'Cowboy' Foreman Hardy, due to his wide legs and large hat
'Rubberneck' Chapman
Harold 'Fireater' Smith, who taught oil firing on the Nottingham oil burning locos of the late 1940s
'Fairy' Marshall
George 'Water Boy' Redfern who could not pass a water column without taking on water.
George 'Weeping' Woodward whose eyes ran if working tender first
Herbert 'Dickie Bow' Walker
H 'Nicky' Beaumont

Stafford 'Staff' Kisby
H 'Umpar' Pikett
J 'Ten Ton Jack' Hinks
T 'Undertaker' Berridge
Sid 'Trader' Horne
Sam 'Fiddler' Leah who played the violin
G 'General' Higgins
J W 'Dunlop' Tyers
Harry 'Lincoln Linnet' Martinson who had a fine singing voice.
Harold 'Ben Hur' Armstrong
Along with the nicknames for individuals other terms were used for various situations and locations:

The Midland was always known as 'DERBY' to any other railway it came into contact with, even if it was a long way from that place and Ell of a Mess was the not so endearing term for the LMS by the LNER the other local system. Midland men always referred to the LNER as the 'Branch Line' at Newark (the Midland were there first) and the Nor West or Wessy, for the former LNWR system.

When engines were short of steam the terms 'down the nick' and 'hard up' were used, sometimes this was caused by using 'Duck Eggs' (Ovoids) instead of coal. This kind of fuel was regularly to be seen in the tender of an 'Iron Lung', a WD 2-8-0. A Traffic Apprentice was known as a 'Thrombosis', ie a bloody clot running around the system and HQ economy men was known as the 'Razor Gang'.

Appendix Three

Fitters and other staff at the Shed prior to 1958

Frank Cresswell, Chargehand
Don Cresswell, Fitter, son of Frank Cresswell who left after coming out of his time c1955
Bernard Blagdon, Tuber
Bill Murfin, Chargehand
Charlie White, Whitemetaller
George Marlow, Machinist
Harry Rearsby, Toolstore Mate
Harold Sedgebear, Foreman Fitter
Joe Roberts, an earlier Mechanical Foreman
Reg Consterdine, Fitter
Alf Smith, Machinist and Tyre Turner
Marshall Lannen
Arthur Grainger
Frank Dearman, Blacksmith
Frank Arnold, ex-Peterborough
Jack Williams, Grade 3 Fitter
Ron Thurly, ex-Peterborough
Harry Towle
Frank Cuckson, ex-Colwick
Fred Tyres, Fitter/Turner ex-Doncaster
Frank Sutton
Jack 'Boxer' Thompson, a grade 3 Fitter.
Harry Pleasant
Jack Stainesby
Paul Bingham
Joe Ormrod

Mates
Ted Smith
George Bratley
Dick Turnell
Lou Ward
Bob Moore
Bill 'Jock' Gralton

Joe Ormrod's son was employed as a cleaner at 16A and was fatally burned whilst cleaning under an engine in No 1 Shed. His overalls, which had become soaked in paraffin, caught the naked flame of a flare lamp and he suffered 100% burns. After this tragedy Joe Ormrod decided to leave the railway.

Herbert Brand Grade 3 Fitter, Grade 3 Fitters were created during WWII when there was a shortage of fitting staff and were limited to certain tasks such as brake block changing etc, although some like Bill Walker had greater responsibilities such as the drop-pit.

Ted Wilcox, Grade 3 and tyre turning
Cyril Ato, Grade 3
Jock Milne
Freddie Plater, Joiner

Fitters and other staff who were at 16A in 1958/1959

Mr Percy Croydon, Mechanical Foreman who came originally from Kentish Town.
Frank Thompson who was a Premium Apprentice at Crewe and had once fired 'Cornwall'.
Tommy Stevenson, Tuber who collected the NUR membership fees.
Frank Mumby, Fitter later Foreman Fitter. Became lifting bay Foreman at Toton.
Tom Wealthall, ex-Colwick
Arthur Wilkinson, Mate
Albert Challons, Machinist
Rubin Carlisle, Coppersmiths Mate
Sid Hill, Fitter son of Sid Hill Chargehand Cleaner
Len Guyler, Coppersmith
Geoff Marriott, 'Necky' Fitter
George Peach, Turner
Grenville Geeson, Fitter
Bill Orton, Coppersmith ex-Toton
Joe Vickers, Fitter
Jock Kerr, Fitter who came from Stirling and his brother
Norman Kerr, Fitter
Fred Pask, Fitter who at one time worked at Ebbw Vale
Keith Stuart, Fitter, son of Driver Stuart.
Cliff Barraclough
Tommy James, Painter and local Artist
Alec Hunt 'Long Pod', Blacksmith
Les Payne, Fitter ex-Saltley, Birmingham and his Mate Danny Sherratt ex-Colwick LNWR and who came originally from the NSR having worked at the W H Smith Bookstore on Stoke Station. His son had died serving in Bomber Command during WWII.

These last two men were the main diesel shunter mechanical maintenance team and had their workshop cum office next to the site of the oil storage tanks for the post World War II oil firing experiment that was paid for by the Ministry of Supply. The shunters had come in 1952 and at one time numbered about eighteen engines. To refuel the shunters the engines own air supply, reduced to 10.5 psi, was used to pressurise a rail tank, which then pushed the fuel through the refueling filling point on the engine. This procedure had to be carefully monitored, as the tank pressure needed to be kept low, at around 10 psi. If this was not maintained and the pressure increased the tank could be overstressed and burst. This did, indeed, happen at Burton Loco Shed and the ex-Foreman Fitter there, the late Joe Benson, described the results as like painting the Shed with diesel fuel! Danny Sherratt was a real 'grafter', small in stature, he managed to work until he was seventy years old. One of his jobs was that he frequently cleaned out the engine compartments on the EE shunters.

A memorable characteristic of Danny when walking along with his two lush (paraffin) buckets was, if spoken to, he quoted his World War I army number, which was 805039, and pronounced 'Eight-Oh-Five-Oh-Thray-Nine'. A time of his life was when he looked after artillery horses on the Western Front, an experience that seemed to be part of his personality, as it was for many who survived that terrible ordeal. He once spoke about the dead bodies moving with lice and rats.

Bob Robinson, an electrician, and his Mate, Stan Smith, who looked after the electrical side of the diesel electrics.

Dave Smith - Stan's son and a schoolmate of Jim Perkins was killed in a car crash in the late 1960s.

Syd Wright, ex-Aston, Chargehand Fitter

Fred Straw, Joiner, ex-Colwick.

Harry Don, Shop Officeman who once had a trial for Aston Villa in the 1920s and who suffered from heart trouble.

Charlie Hoosen, Fitter, ex-Buxton and Rowsley - Charlie was a real character and had the temperament of a short fuse time bomb. He would flare up at the slightest provocation. He also had the habit of fitting tight block cotters which he managed to drive in with a hammer, making the removal of the same a hot spanner or gas axe job (oxy-acetylene), there was no chance of Charlie's cotters falling out!

Norman Hudson, Fitter, ex-Grimesthorpe, Sheffield known as 'Hawkeyes' after spotting a loose eccentric strap on a 3 Cyl Stanier Tank.

Gerald Hudson, Fitter, son of the above and who carried out the last engine overhaul in the 1868 repair shop. This was on the Beeston creosote locomotive No 1.

Bob Rowbottom, Fitter, ex-Stockport and Abergavenny, known as 'Big Hammer Bob', and his Mate, his son, Bob Rowbottom Jnr, known as 'Little Bob' who weighed 28 Stone. Whoever decided to team father and son together had a diabolical sense of humour. This combination was known as Tweedle Dum and Tweedle Dee and weighed in at over 50 stone. According to Fred Pask 'Little' Bob would eat 3lb of sausages for a Sunday lunch because he did not like meat joints. He was two years older than the author, Jim Perkins, at Trent Bridge School and he put a stone on for every year up to the age of 24, and more after that. Both Bobs were great characters and really well known in the Meadows area of Nottingham. 'Big Hammer' Bob was able to navigate anyone around Nottingham by giving all the pub locations.

Vernon Dale, Fitter, whose brother was the Boilersmith Peter Dale

Herbert Cook, Fitter

Brian Cunnington, Fitter, whose father was a Running Shed Foreman at Nottingham.

Bill Walker, a Class 3 Fitter, not time served who worked on the drop-pit and whose Mate was Joe Hoole.

Cliff 'Chummy' Edwards, Fitter

Arthur Hunt, Fitter

Les Dodsley Jnr, Fitter known as 'Young Doddo'

Les Dodsley Snr, Machinist known as 'Ode Doddo'

Chas Turner, a regular days Fitter

Ron Bowler, ditto

Jimmy Towle, ditto

Barry Lee, Fitter who started as a cleaner at Kirkby Loco

Paul Dickens, Fitter, ex-Bescot in LNW days). once related the tale, also mentioned in A J Powells 'Living with Midland Locomotives', Ian Allen 1977, of a set of 4F experimental high duty steel alloy side rods that he had picked up and lifted whilst at Derby Works in the late 1920s. Paul was one of the lamp men or examining Fitters, and had a real sense of humour. One of his favourite funnies was to sit next to you on the Fitter's messroom bench then rock from side to side and ask you 'Is this train going far?' He was one of the staff called out to the Stanton Gate crash and described the scene and the clearing up operations in gory detail.

Dave Simpson, Fitter

Jeff Smith, Fitter, left just before the Shed closed in 1965, now in New Zealand.

Dennis Burditt, Fitter

Harold Wadsley, Examining Fitter

Paul Heyes, Fitter

Les Clamp, Fitter

John Bowers, Fitter

George Piggot, Fitter

George Kirk, Fitter who transferred to Blackpool on getting married.

Jock Gordon, Fitter ex-St Rollox

Andy Waddell, left after coming out of his time, now in Australia.

Fred Straw, Joiner, ex-Colwick LNER

Albert Rudge, Fitters Mate

George Etches, Greaser

Lou Constantine, Fitters Mate

Len Chester, Fitters Mate, who was Tubers Mate at one time.

Jack Roberts, ex-Driver who left footplate due to ill health and worked in tool stores.

Colin Wheeler, Fitters Mate

Eric Wheeler, Fitters Mate

These were brothers and drove the breakdown crane.

Len Booth, Blacksmiths Striker, who was an extremely methodical man and who smoked two Capstan Full Strength cigarettes each day.

Herbert Tinsley, Fitters Mate. According to Herbert he had at least two lucky escapes during his life. The first was when he had been posted home from HMS 'Hood' on compassionate grounds the night before it sailed to meet the 'Bismark'. On the second occasion he was confused due to having influenza. He jumped out of a train at Aylesbury and landed in the only snow drift for miles!

Roy Green, Fitters Mate

Frank Howard, Fitters Mate

George Stanley, Fitters Mate and ex-Fireman.

Horace, Fitters Mate,

'Sos' Parnham, ex-LNWR Colwick Fireman

Dicky Dawkins, Fitters Mate

George Edridge, Fitters Mate

Vin Whitehead, Fitters Mate

Cristin Jacobus, van De Merwe, a South African of Dutch origin who came to the Shed in 1960 and worked as Fitters Mate with John Bowers. A great lad, but an out-and-out racist, he once had a go at Charlie Salmon after he had come out of a smokebox. He mistook all the soot for a West Indian and even he had to laugh about it afterwards. He took the job whilst on his round the world travels eventually joining the merchant navy on a passenger ship. A couple of tales are told of when he helped change a chimney on a Jubilee and walked around the rim in plimsols. He also started work without a cup and was given a demand for the stores to get one. This was one of those practical jokes such as going for a bucket of steam, a rubber hammer for soft coal and a straight 'S' hook. The joke, however, backfired as Harold 'Rubber Neck' Monk the storeman actually gave him a new cup. One outcome of the chimney changing story was that the rough casting was not painted and the engine left the Shed with a rusty chimney. This was frowned upon by authority and Norman Hudson related that whilst standing around the Fitters' fire in 2 Shed that he had seen it passing the Shed and it did look a **###### !!

Boiler Smiths Gang - Known as the Black Gang most of them were semi-skilled Tubers and Tubers Mates, who were unskilled, removed blast pipes and renewed tubes and Fitters replaced the blast pipes.
Alf Bearpark, ex-Crewe Works who came to Nottingham in World War Two.
He travelled on a Monday and stayed all week returning on Friday.
George Ockelford, Foreman Boilersmith
Jack Ainsworth
Ron Shaw, Boilersmith
George Place, Boilersmith
Charlie Farr, Boiler Inspector ex-Crewe
Arthur Place, Foreman Boilersmith
Peter Dale, Boilersmith
Tony Archer, Boilersmith
Bernard Corden
Charlie Salmon
Charlie Carlisle, Tuber, brother of Reuben Carlisle
Jess Wild, known as 'Ten men'.

Apprentice Boilersmiths
Maurice Green

Apprentice Fitters
Dave Fell who died in 2002
Mick Kent
Keith Riley
Paul Moseley
Mick Hopkins, now in Australia
Jim Perkins
Tony Coy, now in Canada
Roy Padgett
Derek Towle
Dave Coverley
Cliff Swainson, went on to work at Colwick, along with Jim Perkins, as an RSI then at Nelson St Derby and finally to C I E (Irish Railways). Cliff died in 2001.
Dave Palmer
Terry Cooper from Leicester
Edwin Clark
John Wooley

Appendix Four

Nottingham Allocation Summer 1961

Class 4MT Tank engines
Nos 42054, 42091, 42140, 42161, 42185, 42587 and 42636

4Fs
Ex-MR Nos 43870, 43888, 43917, 43918, 43928, 43953, 43954 and 43958

Ex-LMS Nos 44030, 44033, 44047, 44131, 44132, 44139, 44151, 44158, 44195, 44215, 44223, 44248 44304, 44394, 44401, 44472, 44577 and 44578

Black Fives
Nos 44658, 44664, 44806, 44856, 44861, 44918 and 45407
Jubilees class 6P
Nos 45611 'Hong Kong', 45620 'North Borneo'. This engine ran with the same tender (No 4603) throughout its working life.
45641 'Sandwich'
45667 'Jellicoe'
'Royal Scot' class 7P
Nos 46100 'Royal Scot' W/D, 46112 'Sherwood Forester', 46118 'Royal Welch Fusilier', 46157 'The Royal Artilleryman'

3F Tank
No 47631

8F
Nos
48000, 48024, 48064, 48099, 48170, 48193, 48211, 48217, 48261, 48279, 48286, 48377, 48393, 48401, 48490, 48604, 48614, 48638, 48639, 48640, 48653, 48666, 48675, 48696, 48663 and 48748 (Note: engines 48705 to 48772 were originally built for the LNER)

BR Standard class 4
Nos 75055, 75056, 75062, 75063 and 75064
BR Standard class 2
Nos 78020, 78021, 78028 and 78029

Diesels 0-6-0
Nos 12050/51/52/96/97/98, 13290
D3083/84/85, D3246/47, D3859/60/61

15 Diesels
84 Steam
Total 99

Allocation - Winter 1964-1965 from Frank Eite

Diesels	Steam
D138 to D147	Nos 42184, 42230, 42284 and 42588
D3083 to D3085	Nos 43954, 43964, 43975 and 43994
D3246/D3247	Nos 44658, 44861, 44918, 45221 and 45444
D3290	Nos 47231 and 47645
D3696	Nos 48024, 48045, 48046, 48143, 48165, 48184, 48187, 48214, 48217, 48393, 48401
D3859 to D3861	48490 (one of six 8Fs once fitted with self cleaning smokebox apparatus), 48638, 48696 and 48763
12050 to 12052 12096 to 12098	Nos 78023, 78042, 78044, 78055 and 78062

D5193/D5195/D5199

D5201, D5203, D5224, D5231, D523, /D5239, D5252, D5253
D5258, D5264, D5273, D5282 and D5283

D756, D7580, D7585, D7590, D7591 and D7597

Total 48 Diesel
35 Steam
Total 83

By the 30th of October 1965 only 19 Locomotives were based at Nottingham :

12050 to 12052, 12063, 12069, 12096 to 12098.
D3083 to D3085, D3246, D3247, D3290, D3296
D3859 to D3861 and D3863.

Appendix Five

Extracts from Frank Eite's Diaries 1955 to 1957

These extracts show the great variety of work carried out and are typical of a Locoshed of that period. The beginning of the narrative concerns the railway strike, which was a tragedy for the railways and eventual caused a loss of traffic to the roads. Engine numbers are shown without the 4 prefix. Notes: E&B these mean Engine and Brake. LE means Light Engine and, 'as booked' means working job as planned. Spike was the sidings next to the Lenton PW (CMD) both of them being located in what was known as the Klondyke Area. This low ground had been built up by decades of loco ash.

Tuesday 31 May 1955
Fred, Bill, Graham and I went to sign on today, Graham was on picket at 4 till 6

Wednesday 1 June 1955
I went down to the strike HQ with Bill and Fred came down with Graham. We had a speech from a fellow called Bevin. Fred was on picket at 12 noon until 3 pm. I went on at 3 pm until 6 pm.

Thursday 2 June 1955
Bill and I were on picket outside the main gate from 3am to 6am. I went to bed at 8am and got up at 10 am. Bill and I then went to sign on

Friday 3 June 1955
Bill and I went to sign on. Fred went to sign on when he collected his wages. I went in the afternoon to collect mine - £13 5s 11d with £5 15s 9d back pay.

Saturday 4 June 1955
We went to collect our strike pay which was £2

Monday 6 June 1955
Bill and I went to sign on again. Fred came down later. Bill and I are on picket from 2 till 4 tomorrow

Tuesday 7 June 1955
Bill and I were on picket from 2 till 4. Fred was on from 8 till 10. There is still no settlement yet although something is expected Thursday or Friday.

Wednesday 8 June 1955
I went down with Bill to sign on again. Fred and I went to the strike HQ and saw a concert put on by local talent Roy Sansom who sang two songs and Sam Leah played the fiddle.

Thursday 9 June 1955
Bill, Fred and I went together to sign on. I went on picket from 8 till 10 pm

Friday 10 June 1955

We went to sign on this morning, but a little later because we had to wait for some income tax rebate, mine was £1 6s 0d. Bill, Fred and I went on picket from 6 to 8.

Saturday 11 June 1955

We went to collect our strike pay - £2.

Monday 13 June 1955

Fred and I was on picket from 10 till 12 noon

Tuesday 14 June 1955

Fred and I went to sign on again. Bill came down later as he was 12 till 2 picket. Whilst in Lyons having something to eat the strike was called off. We went to find out what jobs we are and Fred is 1.32 am and I am 12.30 pm the Holwell

Wednesday 15 June 1955

Time On	Time Off	Job	Engine	Driver
12/30	7/20	593	4477	Pickering

First day back after strike, the Holwell was cancelled so we prepared 4477 and took a train of empty vans to Toton, was relieved at the centre. We prepared 8108 at Toton loco and worked a train of sugar beet to Wilford road then home

Thursday 16 June 1955

Time On	Time Off	Job	Engine	Driver
12/15	8/45	593	8217	Pickering

As booked today, prepared the engine then LE to Beeston and loaded to Holwell 31=38 arrived at 3/00 but did not leave until 6/00 for Beeston and then LE to Wilford Road and relieved

Wednesday July 1955

Time On	Time Off	Job	Engine	Driver
8.50	5/0	122	553	Pickering

Walked to the station and relieved the Horse Dock and was relieved ourselves at 4/25. The Queen to Nottingham for the Royal Show. I took some snaps of her on the steps leading out of the station

Sunday 17 July

Time On	Time Off	Job	Engine	Driver
6/27	1.50	275	5554 (Ontario)	Pickering

Passenger to Kettering and relieved 9/30 from London at 11/1 arrived Nottingham 12.32 Shed

Wednesday 27 July

Time On	Time Off	Job	Engine	Driver
8.45	4/45	Spl M970	5088	A Lea

Engine prepared LE to the Carriage Sidings the left Nottingham at 10.00 for Blackpool on the City of Nottingham Holiday Express. We were relieved at Cheadle and came home on the passenger;

Friday 20 July

Time On	Time Off	Job	Engine	Driver
8.30	3/50	785	4526, 4777	Pickering

Caught the 9.6 to Trent and relieved the Alsager - Beeston at Sheet Stores. Took two loads of cattle to GN then Shed. Relieved the Cricklewood - Nottingham, shunted them at Spike then Shed again

Thursday 4 August

Time On	Time Off	Job	Engine	Driver
7/30	3.30	404	8696	Pickering

Walked to Beeston to relieve 44T took a load of cattle to Plumtree the E & B to Hucknall, brought 28 loads of slack for Wilford Power Station and was relieved at Lenton South.

Sunday 20 August 1955

Time On	Time Off	Job	Engine	Driver
4/37	11/50	223	1185 and 5620 (North Borneo)	S Morey

Prepared the engine and worked the 6/15 London as far as Bedford and worked a train back via Leicester 11/17 in Nottingham

Monday 29 August 1955

Time On	Time Off	Job	Engine	Driver
9.00	5/00	785	92022	Pickering

Went passenger to Trent to relieve a Brent-Beeston. We had one of the Franco-Crosties class 9Fs, we then went LE to Toton to dispose of it then back passenger. Relieved the Basford Gas then Shed

Tuesday 30 August 1955

Time On	Time Off	Job	Engine	Driver
11.47	6/50 at Wellingborough	616	8673	Pickering

Prepared the engine LE to Beeston and loaded to Wellingborough with 57=57 we had a tender full of slack the steam came below 150 lbs but we kept going, was relieved at Findon Road

Monday 5 September 1955

Time On	Time Off	Job	Engine	Driver
8/54	3.30 at Birmingham	674	3369	Beswick

Prepared the engine LE to Yard West and departed with 39 loads of goods 15 fitted at 10/40 right away to Washwood Heath arriving on time at 12.35 LE to Saltley loco disposing of engine

Tuesday 6 September 1955

Time On	Time Off	Job	Engine	Driver
4/50 at Birmingham	9/35	406	3369	Beswick

Prepared the engine then LE to Water Orton and departed at 5/45 with 45 goods for Beeston and arrived at 8/30 LE to the Shed. The lodging house at Saltley is not as good as Wellingborough, the meals are not as good and it is not as clean.

Thursday 29 September 1955

Time On	Time Off		Job	Engine	Driver
8.50	4/50		122	454	W Towle

Walked to the station and relieved the horse dock, Walter didn't come down right away so the Shunter drove to No 3 platform and A Keys who is the new Firing Instructor he came up to the engine. Later I drove half on my own while Walter went to the Embankment to play football.

Monday 17 October 1955

Time On	Time Off		Job	Engine	Driver
8.16	3/16		534	9074	Pickering

Walked to Wilford Road and relieved the Lloyds-Kirkby the engine was a Wessie [L&NWRly] although she steamed fairly well and two good injectors we had 57 empties but only just made it through the tunnel. We disposed of it and came back on the 1/26 passenger

Tuesday 18 October 1955

Time On	Time Off	Job	Engine	Driver
10.28	6/30	593	3936	Pickering

Walked to Yard West and relieved the Melton pick up we shunted at Edwalton, Plumtree, Widmerpool, Old Dalby and Holwell and was relieved in Melton station at 5/10 then home on the passenger

Tuesday 22 November 1955

Time On	Time Off	Job	Engine	Driver
11.45	7/5 at	616	8763	W Clark

Wellingborough Prepared the engine LE to Beeston and loaded to Wellingborough. Sands were not working and we nearly came to a stand in Stanton tunnel. We were in the loop at Old Dalby so both of us crawled between the frame underneath the boiler and got all four front sands working. We arrived at Neilson Sidings at 6/30 and was relieved

Saturday 26 November 1955

Time On	Time Off	Job	Engine	Driver
5.20	2/10	197	935, 2132	Pickering

Engine prepared and worked the 6.30 Lincoln and the 9.30 back. Walked back to the loco and prepared 2132. Worked the 12/15 to Newark and 1/10 back. Engine to the Shed

Sunday 27 November 1955

Time On	Time Off	Job	Engine	Driver
9.45	7/35		4414	J Badder

Went in a brake to Melton Junction, relieved our man on the GN branch worked between Great Dalby and John O' Gaunt then back to Wilford Road

Tuesday 20 December 1955

Time On	Time Off	Job	Engine	Driver
9.00	5/00	785	92021 (Crosti)	Pickering

At first we were going to Staythorpe but the booked men who had made over 12 hrs turned up and went instead. We relieved the Brent-Kirkby and we went to Kirkby with a Franco Crosti and 53 empties, this is the engine that has been to Derby and has had the blast made sharper. We came back on the passenger and then went to Beeston with a Billsthorpe.

Sunday 1 January 1956

Time On	Time Off	Job	Engine	Driver
12/13	8/55	90	2361	Pickering

Walked to the station and relieved an engine which had been 6.10 Chesterfield and back. We went Derby-Melton-Nottingham-Loco. Have completed my 46 weeks with George. I am now the Senior Fireman in the middle Wellingborough Link.

Monday 2 January 1956

Time On	Time Off	Job	Engine	Driver
7/7	4.5 at Wellingborough	626	8008	C Morton

Prepared the engine LE to Beeston and took 61=65 to Wellingborough. Instead of the booked time of 30 mins from London Road to Widmerpool it took 56 mins. We just crawled along at times. The fire becoming very dirty and when we arrived at Neilson's we only had 100 lbs of steam.

Tuesday 3 January 1956

Time On	Time Off	Job	Engine	Driver
4/25	2.35	627	8008	C Morton

at Wellingborough
Engine prepared took 15 empties to Burton Latimer then 9 goods to Kettering, from there we had 54 right away Toton via Syston was relieved on the bank at Trent Station at 12.00. We then went by bus to Toton and brought 4215 back to Nottm

Friday 6 January 1956

Time On	Time Off	Job	Engine	Driver
7/7	3.50	626	8644	C Morton

at Wellingborough
Prepared the engine LE to Beeston to load to Wellingborough. The engine was better than the first two trips although we still had Belgium coal it is very large and hard as rock. We arrived at Neilson's in decent shape with plenty of steam and a boiler full of water.

Wednesday 11 January 1956

Time On	Time Off	Job	Engine	Driver
.				

The members of the MIC quiz team were B Willis, .F Brunton, A Dabel, J Townsend, R Wilcox and G Twiggor. Bill Clark and myself were in reserve. We all went to Chesterfield to compete against Leeds 64 Sheffield 40 our marks were 46 1/2.

Monday 26 March 1956

Time On	Time Off	Job	Engine	Driver
7/7	2.25	626	8709	J A Taylor

at Wellingborough
Prepared the engine LE to Beeston and took 52=57 to Wellingborough. We were right time nearly everywhere and gained a few minutes over Harringworth. We passed

London Road at 9/10 and was inside at Neilson's at 12.45. We then disposed of the engine

Saturday 21 April 1956

Time On	Time Off	Job	Engine	Driver
4.0	12/0	4847, 4861	73000	Ted Jones

Prepared the engine for the Chilwell-London and two engines for the Ilkeston-London also one for a Barnsley football special.

Sunday 13 May 1956

Time On	Time Off	Job	Engine	Driver
8.25	10/30	SPL	4215	R Hawkins

Engine prepared passenger to Buxton arrived at 1/10. Short Rest and left again at 7.05 arrived Nottm at 10/5. First SR Sunday Rest day working since August 1953

Friday 18 May 1956

Time On	Time Off	Job	Engine	Driver
1/30	8/55	58	2829	J Pounder

Prepared the engine LE to Beeston and loaded to Holwell we had 42=48 and the engine was fitted with a motion similar to a Caprotti One of five fitted with Reidinger Valve Gear and we were flat out all the way. I thought it would stick. We came back with 47 for Beeston and then to the Shed

Tuesday 5 June 1956

Time On	Time Off	Job	Engine	Driver
6.0	1/30		7631	B Daykin

Prepared the engine and then across to West Box to relieve the diesel, we shunted for 2 1/2 hours and then came back to the loco for some bags of sand for Beeston. [These were transported on the framing] We returned to the locoshed again.

Saturday 7 July 1956

Time On	Time Off	Job	Engine	Driver
7/30	3.30	64881	3033	Pickering

Our engine had come to the Shed so we prepared a NE engine and went LE to Lincoln bringing back 3033 LE

Friday 13 July 1956

Time On	Time Off	Job	Engine	Driver
4.5	11.30	691	2818	Ted Jones

Prepared the engine LE to Beeston No 7 and took 68 empties to Wollaton and we came away at 7.30 with 45 coal, we put about 30 off in the Clifton top sidings, then to Beeston. We took another 60 empties as far as Lenton North. We assisted to coal a Blackpool engine and right away home.

Sunday 15 July 1956

Time On	Time Off	Job	Engine	Driver
5.45	12/45	441	8108	Pickering

Two loads of cattle to Edwalton, 50 slack to Sneinton curve, 49 goods to Spike, then to Shed.

Tuesday 31 July 1956

Time On	Time Off	Job	Engine	Driver
8.51	4/40		73002	G Green

Walked to the station and relieved an Army Cadet special from Repton & Willington. Departed from Nottm at 10.30 passed Melton junction at 10.58 and Manton 11.25 arrived Wisbech for relief at 11.55 came home passenger.

Thursday August 9 1956

Time On	Time Off	Job	Engine	Driver
1/30	9/30	579	8108	Pickering

Prepared the engine LE to Beeston and loaded to Holwell with 48 wagons and departed with 58. We were held at Wilford Road for 40 mins. Yesterday Bernard Willis received cuts on the face near his eyes when something flew off a passing express. He spent the night in Chesterfield hospital

Saturday 8 September 1956

Time On	Time Off	Job	Engine	Driver
2.15	10.15	176	5554 (Ontario), 2161, 3972	F Hickling

Prepared 6.40 London, 4.45 LE Melton and 7.25 Blackpool LE to Edwalton ES to Nottm and was relieved, the we relieved a train from Mansfield and took the engine to the Shed.

Thursday 13 September 1956

Time On	Time Off	Job	Engine	Driver
4/25 at Wellingborough	2.15	62786	14C	Morton

Engine prepared loaded from Old Yard to Burton Latimer and then to Kettering. We called in at Kirkby and from there we had 87 for Toton. In Glaston we nearly slipped to a standstill, we nearly choked and it was like a Turkish Bath. We were held at Langham for the 7/10 from London and one or two others, was relieved at Toton rode in with the engine.

Monday 17 September 1956

Time On	Time Off	Job	Engine	Driver
8.16	4/16	4005	3961	Pickering

Walked to Wilford Road and relieved the Lloyds-Kirkby. Didn't get a chance to clean the fire although it wanted doing and we had 57 empties on. We came to a stand between Annesley and Kirkby a light engine came from Kirkby and pushed us into the sidings. We came home on the passenger. We prepared an engine for the London-Leeds

Wednesday 19 September 1956

Time On	Time Off	Job	Engine	Driver
9.0	5/0	785	4100/8409	Pickering

We caught the 9.25 to Trent to relieve a special from Garston to Beeston. We went to Trent again on the 1/20 and relieved a Birmingham to Beeston took the engine on the Shed. I went to the MIC room and Rex Bernard and myself had a discussion on various topics. A new express has begun to run from London at 12/25 first stop Nottingham arriving at 2/33 in 2 hrs 8 mins. This week a lot of the expresses have had minutes knocked off their running time.

Friday 5 September 1956

Time On	Time Off	Job	Engine	Driver
3.25	11.55	514	8136/64719	Pickering

Prepared the engine and worked the 5.5 Willesden as far as Leicester. We then relieved a Northampton-Beeston, an Eastern Region engine but she steamed very well.

Tuesday 9 October 1956

Time On	Time Off	Job	Engine	Driver
11.47	6/55	616	8217	C Stewart

Prepared the engine LE to Beeston and loaded to Wellingborough with 50=55 and arrived at 6.20. This is the first day with my new Mate, I expect to be with him for a year.

Wednesday 24 October 1956

Time On	Time Off	Job	Engine	Driver
4.40	11.50	172	452/3048	C Stewart

Prepared the engine and worked the 6.26 to Derby, Charlie went in the first compartment and F Cassidy drove. We then went to Chadd to bring 11 coaches for a London.

Thursday 20 December 1956

Time On	Time Off	Job	Engine	Driver
5/5	1.5	706	8170	C Stewart

Engine prepared LE to Beeston and onto Wollaton with 16 empties. We came away with 49=50. The 7.20 express didn't pass Wollaton until 8.50 and we left at 9.00. We stood on the Lenton-Radford goods line from 10.00 until 11.50 and we were relieved at Lenton North at 12.00 by Graham Hazeldine. This is the third day and night of the foggy weather and I have been driving all the time, no sign of it lifting yet.

Wednesday 26 December 1956

Time On	Time Off	Job	Engine	Driver
5.15	12/10		3040	S Downing

Prepared the engine LE to the carriage sidings and worked the first passenger to Mansfield we only had one passenger and the snow was about 3' deep. We came home LE, arriving at the loco at 10.00. The Foreman asked us to recondition it for the 2/30 Sheffield and do another bit of work for him.

Tuesday 1 January 1957

Time On	Time Off	Job	Engine	Driver
11.47 at Nottm	6/20 at W'Boro'gh	616	8675	C Stewart

Prepared the engine LE to Beeston and loaded to Wellingborough. We passed London Road at 1.50 and Melton Junction at 2.47. We scooped at Brentinby and was on the loop at Wing for 2.56. Express relief was wailing at Neilson's sidings and so I signed off earlier than ever before. I have been twelve weeks with Charlie.

Thursday 3 January 1957

Time On	Time Off	Job	Engine	Driver
11.47	7/35	616	8675	C Stewart

at W'borough

Prepared the engine and then loaded from Beeston to Wellingborough. We didn't get such a good run as last time and Charlie nearly ran by the signals at Kettering Junction

Friday 4 January 1957

Time On	Time Off	Job	Engine	Driver
5.17 at	11.25	617	8699	C Stewart

Wellingborough

We relieved our booked time at Findon Road at 6.30 and put them all off at Holwell, from there we went LE to Old Dalby for 55 empty vans for Wilford Road sidings and then to the Shed

Wednesday 9 January 1957

Time On	Time Off	Job	Engine	Driver

Today the quiz team went to Derby to compete against Leeds and Saltley. The scores were Leeds 64 Nottingham 60 Saltley 54 out a possible 72. I had questions on hand signals to Driver. Disadvantages of superheated steam. Will wheels lock on a passenger train when brake is applied at high speed? When is shunting strictly prohibited? The ASLEF have accepted a 3% wage increase

Thursday 10 January 1957

Time On	Time Off	Job	Engine	Driver
1/35	9/35	589	8004	C Stewart

Prepared the engine LE to Beeston for a train to Holwell, it was the biggest I have ever had 44=58. I drove back and we were relieved at Beeston North. There was a Lecture in the MIC room on signalling and it was given by Mr Barres. Mr Audinwood the Depot Superintendent seems to have taken a great interest in MIC work since we did so well yesterday.

Friday 11 January 1957

Time On	Time Off	Job	Engine	Driver
1/35	9/40	589	8666	C Stewart

There was a shortage of power this afternoon so we had to relieve an engine which had been to Codnor Park and came back LE over the Trowell branch. We did not leave No7 until 3/40 that meant waiting at London Road until 4/25 and following the Bourne passenger. We arrived Holwell at 5/30 just mashed and started back, leaving at 6/15. We had to be put across the road at Edwalton for two expresses. After putting 8 off at Mansfield Junction we arrived at Beeston at 8/55 and was relieved at Wilford Road.

Saturday 26 January 1957

Time On	Time Off	Job	Engine	Driver
10/45	10.15	580	3627	L Bramley

Prepared the engine LE to Beeston for a train of Bordesleys, we are booked around by Leicester but now it is going regularly over the Castle Donnington branch. There was no relief at Leicester Junction so we carried on to Washwood Heath arriving at 6/00 and came home on the 7/25 passenger

Friday 1 February 1957

Time On	Time Off	Job	Engine	Driver
8.50	4/50	122	553	C Stewart

We walked to the station and relieved the Horse Dock Shunt and was relieved at 4/15. I met Mr Jones outside the lobby and from what he says there might be some changes in the MIC committee, he seems to be causing quite a lot of strife

Monday 4 February 1957

Time On	Time Off	Job	Engine	Driver
4.00	1.40	361	4480	C Stewart

Engine prepared LE to Yard West goods to Beeston E & B to Wilford Road 9 loads of bananas to Manvers Street. E & B to Yard West, we then took the loco wagon and was relieved

Tuesday 5 February 1957

Time On	Time Off	Job	Engine	Driver
3.50	9.20 at Wellingborough	608	3856	C Stewart

Prepared the engine and loaded from Beeston to Wellingborough. We passed London Road at 4.55. Melton Junction at 6.00. The Scotsman was very late, about 1 hour, so after taking water at Melton Station we had a straight run to Nielson's Sidings arriving outside at 8.20. We did not dispose of the engine although we had plenty of time. I went out at 11.00 until 1/30 with Fred Mather our guard. I went to bed at 3/00 and got up at 9/00

Sunday 10 February 1957

Time On	Time Off	Job	Engine	Driver
12/13	9.15	90	2339	C Stewart

Walked to the station and relieved J Townsend we then worked the 12.40 to Derby, 5.35 to Nottingham, ES to Melton and 8.13 back to Nottingham, ES to the sidings and LE to the Shed. We held the MIC Annual General Meeting, I was elected Vice Chairman, Fred [brother] is on the committee. We are also to have a quiz team selection committee, comprising C Jones, J Tyres and G Twigger

Tuesday 19 February 1957

Time On	Time Off	Job	Engine	Driver
9.0	4/0	785	4983	C Stewart

Our first job was to relieve the Normanton at Wilford Road, we were told to relieve the Bradford-London 10.27 from Nottingham. We had eight coaches and arrived Kettering at 11.45. We came back passenger with Stan Buckby who had conducted the 11.21 from Nottingham

Thursday 21 February 1957

Time On	Time Off	Job	Engine	Driver
9.00	5/00	785	4578	C Stewart

We first relieved the Rufford-Beeston and then on the 1/10 passenger to Trent for 4151 but we missed it, instead we relieved the Willesden-Beeston with a Super D our last job was to prepare 4164 for a special to Derby

Friday 22 February 1957

Time On	Time Off	Job	Engine	Driver
9.00	5/00	785	5398/3118	C Stewart

We relieved the Edge Hill in Spike at 9.25 and the took four loads of cattle to Lowdham, back E & B to Wilford Road Sidings and again to the Shed. Our next job was to relieve the London-Nottingham, shunt at Spike and again to the Shed

Monday 4 March 1957

Time On	Time Off	Job	Engine	Driver
3.25	1/30	573	8320/9277	C Stewart

Prepared the engine and took a Willesden train as far as Leicester. We should have been home passenger but a special train of empties from Watford to Beeston wanted relief. It took exactly three hours to get to Beeston from Leicester

Tuesday 5 March 1957

Time On	Time Off	Job	Engine	Driver
3.25	11.25	573	8748/8332	C Stewart

Prepared the engine and loaded to Leicester again we were relieved at 7.15 in the station and a train of empties from Watford was waiting for us but we didn't know, and it was finally 8.30 when we relieved them. We were at Trent within one hour of leaving Leicester

Wednesday 6 March 1957

Time On	Time Off	Job	Engine	Driver
3.25	11.10	574	8673	G Stevens

Prepared the engine and loaded to Leicester we waited until 9.45 and then caught the 9.53. Fred and I went to a lecture given by Mr Barber on the standard examination, Fireman to Driver. There were about twenty present including Harry Greaves who has been appointed Firing Instructor to Toton after being a Grade 4 Clerk and previously a Fireman in the No1 passenger link at Nottingham.

Friday 15 March 1957

Time On	Time Off	Job	Engine	Driver
5/50	2.50	706	457/4030	C Stewart

Engine prepared LE to Beeston and on to Wollaton with 29 empties, we came away with 45, in spite of not arriving in Beeston until 11.00 we still went as booked to Hucknall, there is not many sets of relief about because of the extra trains owing to the petrol rationing

Sunday 17 March 1957

Time On	Time Off	Job	Engine	Driver

I went to hear a lecture by Mr Barber on Appendix Instructions, I being elected deputy chairman had to act as Chairman in place of John Townsend

Time On	Time Off	Job	Engine	Driver
11.41	7/00	548	8709/8064	L Eliot

This is my first day in the top Wellingborough link No5C and is the highest I have been since I came on the job in 1948. We relieved the Lloyds-Kirkby and brought the back to Nottingham, we then went after a Billsthorpe-Beeston and home

Time On	Time Off	Job	Engine	Driver
4/45	12.10	660	4187	D Branston

We should have prepared an engine and loaded from Beeston with a train for Warwick, but that part was cancelled, and we went on the passenger. After a three hour wait we relieved our booked job, the 8/55 from Water Orton and arrived at Wilford Road at 11.28

Monday 6 May 1957

Time On	Time Off	Job	Engine	Driver
4.43	11.30	382	4412	R Gascoyne

Engine prepared LE to Yard West to load to Long Eaton on the Ilkeston pick up E & B to Ilkeston, one wagon back to Trowell E & B to Stanton Gate, LE to Nottingham.

Sunday 26 May 1957

Time On	Time Off	Job	Engine	Driver

Fred and I went on a trip with the MIC to Crewe Works, in the party (which included six Toton men) of about fifty. We left Nottingham at 9.45 and arrived Crewe Works after a meal at 2.15 Leaving again at 4.30 to catch the 5/35 back arriving Nottingham at 9/10

Saturday 1 June

Time On	Time Off	Job	Engine	Driver
8/45	4.00	597	64895	D Bonser

The engine was prepared for us, LE to Beeston and loaded to Peterborough we were relieved at Brentingby and home in the back of the London-Leeds

Monday 3 June

Time On	Time Off	Job	Engine	Driver
12.50	8.50	755		S Hardy

We brought about seven engines in off No1 Independent and that's all. This is the earliest time I have been on duty for about six years and I don't think much to it.

Sunday 9 June 1957

Time On	Time Off	Job	Engine	Driver
8.17	2.50	2896		W Stanton

Engine prepared, relieved our man at Wilford Road Sidings ES to Castle Donnington, stopped at about six places, water and conductor at Cheadle arrived at Blackpool at 1/30. Signed on again at 6/00 prepared the engine. Left Blackpool at 7/30 made the same stops back, right time at Castle Donnington.

Sunday 14 July 1957

Time On	Time Off	Job	Engine	Driver
11.00	6/00		58137	K Timsom

We walked to Mansfield junction to relieve the ballast which was relaying the points and crossovers at the exit to loco

Saturday 24 August 1957

Time On	Time Off	Job	Engine	Driver
8/45	4.00	597	64763	E Bacon

Engine prepared although we had time to turn it out, LE to Beeston for the 10.20 Peterborough, we only had 26 on. It rained all the way to Saxby and the engine cab top leaked. We came back in the brake of the London-Masborough

Wednesday 4 September 1957

Time On	Time Off	Job	Engine	Driver
11.55	9/25		8137	E Bacon

We prepared 3115 on the ash pit and took it down to the station to work the 1/35 to Kettering, and then relieved a train of empty stock for Peterborough. We were relieved at Wisbech Junction at 6/15. We travelled home via Grantham and Nottingham Victoria

Friday 13 September 1957

Time On	Time Off	Job	Engine	Driver
11.47	6/50 at Wellingborough	616	8510	Marshall

Prepared the engine loaded from Beeston to Wellingborough with 52=60 and they were very heavy indeed, it was the worst trip to Wellingborough that I have had for a very long time. We had to stop at Gretton IBS to fill the boiler, we also had a tender full of briquettes. I was in bed at 9/30

Tuesday 24 September 1957

Time On	Time Off	Job	Engine	Driver
3/13	10/35	171	4219	

Prepared the 6/10 London and then passenger to Lincoln. I fired the engine and Aleck Dabell drove whilst Bill Kirk rode in the coaches. Back with the 8/55. There is a rumor that eight Firemen are being moved back in a fortnight

Wednesday 2 October 1957

Time On	Time Off	Job	Engine	Driver
7/28	3.28	345	8708	E Bacon

Prepared the engine. Shunted at Lenton south and was relieved at 3.00. I have dropped back into the next link with Charlie Bexon. It is three years since I was with him

Monday 7 October 1957

Time On	Time Off	Job	Engine	Driver
5/10	2.30	223	4812/5636	B Merrit

I went for the Lloyds-Kirkby but I was put on the 6/10 London. We didn't do so well to Kettering where we were relieved at 7/47. We were booked to relieve the Somers Town-Nottingham at 10/19, but owing to a failure in the new colour lighting system at St Pancras all the trains were running 1 to 1 and a half hours late. The new signal box came into operation yesterday.

Wednesday 20 November 1957

Time On	Time Off	Job	Engine	Driver
5.17 at Wellingborough	10.00	617	8225	Bexon

Relieved our booked job at 6.30 and arrived at Wilford Road at 9.30. Waited to see Mr Audinwood until 12.00 and it is fairly certain that I shall get the Clerk's job and I will go straight on top pay as a Class 4. I go to Derby next week for my test.

Thursday 21 November 1957

Time On	Time Off	Job	Engine	Driver
11.47	7/15 at Wellingborough	616	8635	Bexon

Prepared the engine loaded to Wellingborough arriving at the same time as yesterday. I handed my formal application to Mr Jennings for the post of Grade 4 Clerk and I will go for a test on Thursday at the DOS office

Friday 22 November 1957

Time On	Time Off	Job	Engine	Driver
5.17 at Wellingborough	9.50	617	92025	Bexon

We brought 54 empty vans to Nottingham with a Franco-Crosti and we were nearly choked.

Wednesday 27 November 1957

Time On	Time Off	Job	Engine	Driver
8.50		755		S Hardy

First round of the MIC quiz at Leicester. The teams were Nottingham, Burton and Wellingborough. Our team was B Willis, myself, Charlie Hill, Rex Wilcox, Fred and Frank Brunton. We caught the 10.50 to Leicester and the quiz was at 2/15. After we had won 56, 50, 45 respectively we all went to Derby to catch the 5/08 to Nottingham.

Thursday 28 November 1957

Time On	Time Off	Job	Engine	Driver
8.50		755		S Hardy

I went to the office of the DOS and took an education exam for a Grade 4 Clerk. I was there at 9.20 and left at 11.45. I think I may have just passed.

Monday 2 December 1957

Time On	Time Off	Job	Engine	Driver
3.40	11.40	172	6502/2140/3041	Pounder

Prepared the 6.10 Chesterfield and our own, LE to the station to work the 6.26 Derby, we were relieved on arrival at Derby. After walking to the loco we prepared our third engine to work the 9.10 back to Nottingham. Coaches to the sidings and engine to the Shed. Coaled and watered and turned 3041 and left it right for the 1/10 Derby. I haven't had a job as rough as this since I was in the Owl Gang with Fred Cassidy in 1952. I don't yet know the result of the exam.

Thursday 5 December 1957

Time On	Time Off	Job	Engine	Driver
3.40	12.00	172/461	2339/3033	Bexon

Prepared the 6.10 Chesterfield and own to work the 6.26 Derby relieved in station. Prepared 3033 and worked the 9.10 to Nottingham, coaches to the carriage sidings engine to the Shed. Mr Jennings told me that I got 64% in the exam and now I wait for a medical for the superanneration.

Friday 6 December 1957

Time On	Time Off	Job	Engine	Driver
3.40	11.40	172/411	2339/3033	Bexon

Prepared the 6.10 Chesterfield, worked the 6.26 to Derby and the 9.10 Lincoln and back then engine to the Shed. Ken Priestly and fifteen other Firemen have become redundant and they can either go to another depot on LM Region or stay at Nottingham as 'Put Back Fireman'.

Thursday 19 December 1957

Time On	Time Off	Job	Engine	Driver
12/47	8.45	703	3954	Bexon

Prepared the engine loaded to Annesley from Beeston and back to Beeston. I have passed my medical and will soon be starting in the office.

Friday 27 December 1957

Time On	Time Off	Job	Engine	Driver
3.30	11.30	361	4401	Bexon

Prepared the engine LE to Yard West and loaded to Beeston and back to Spike, went across to the loco for relief. I start at 8.30 in the office on Monday.

Monday 30 December 1957

I started my new job in the office. At first I added up all the time cards and also the time check sheets, afterwards I stamped the rate on next week's cards.

Appendix Six

Locomotive survivors with a Nottingham connection

Number	Class	Wheel Arrangement	Present Location (2001)
158A	Kirtley	2-4-0 (1936 to 1947)	MRC, Butterley, (2002)
44027	Fowler 4F (First LMS 4F)	0-6-0 (1935 to 1936)	MRC, Butterley
44806	Stanier Black 5	4-6-0 (1957 to 1964)	Llangollen, Wales
44932		4-6-0 (Annesley)	MRC, Butterley
45407		4-6-0 (1960 to 1962)	Carnforth, Lancs
45699 'Galatea'	Jubilee	4-6-0 (Nov 1946)	BRM, Tyseley
46100 'Royal Scot'	Royal Scot	4-6-0 (1959 to1962)	Bressingham
62660 'Butler Henderson'	Director	4-4-0 (Lincoln)	NRM, York

Note: Where another Shed other than 16A is shown this means that the engine was a regular visitor for valves and piston examination or running repairs.

No1	Bagnall Narrow Gauge	0-4-0 (1956 to 1962)	Huntingdon

This engine was in the drop-pit workshop for repair during 1961 and whilst there the cab side numberplate was stolen.

1089/35	Breakdown Crane (1962 to 1965)	Severn Valley Railway.

Diesels

No10	Ruston Narrow Gauge	0-4-0 (1958 to 1962)	

Northamptonshire Railway Centre, Irthlingborough. This engine had taken the same number as the earlier narrow gauge steam engine 'Batley' which had been withdrawn in 1955.

12052 (Original No 7139)	0-6-0	At Nottingham from July 1957 to Feb 1966.
12098	0-6-0	At Nottingham from Feb 1952 to Nov 1966.
12099	0-6-0	At Nottingham from March 1952 to Nov 1966.
13290 (D3290 then 08220)	0-6-0	At Nottingham from Dec 1956 to Nov 1966. now at Steamtown, Carnforth.
D7585 (25235) Bo-Bo		At Nottingham from Feb 1964 to Oct 1964

Appendix Seven

Office Staff 1960

Chief Clerk - Alf Jennings to be followed by a Mr Wright

Typist - Barbara Dimmock, who became Barbara Greaves when she married Harry Greaves a Passed Fireman and son of Driver Jack 'Loose Coupling Jack' Greaves.

2nd Clerk - Mr Bland followed by Hubert Ward

Paybill Clerk - Herbert Dale

Staff Clerk: - Wilf Sidebottom

Free Pass and Wagon Allocation Clerk - Lillian Attewell

Mileage and Driver Ticket - John Redmund

Repairing Engine Staff Clerk - Ken Waltho

Other Staff - Frank Eite, Ted Brett, Roy Middleton, Dennis Lill, Tom O'Brian, Dolly Thacker, David Greer (these last three transferred from Colwick)

Kathleen Clarke: Additional Typist and daughter of Bill Clerk a Driver known as Piston Bill for his knowledge of steam engines. He was respected by the fitting staff (for a Driver) as he could tell when a piston or valve was faulty.

George Henson
Fred Eite - Brother of Frank who came off the footplate in 1960 eventually going as Running Foreman to Burton-on -Trent.
Cyril Jones - Firing Instructor
Cyril Attenborough - Coal Inspector
Tom Wearing - Locomotive Inspector
David Daft - Firing Instructor
Mr Barber - Locomotive Inspector
Mr Mellors - Locomotive Inspector
Rex Wilcox - Also came off the footplate then went into the Nottingham Control Office and finally became Chief Inspector for Nottingham Division.

Appendix Eight

Royal Scot and Class 8F Experiments

The Royal Scot class engine No 46118 which came to 16A in 1959 had during its lifetime taken part in modification tests concerning the proposal to fit narrow piston valve rings. When first introduced the Royal Scots were very economical, their coal consumption being very close to that recorded by the GWR Castle Class, which were tested on the LMS in 1926. However it was soon found out that as the mileage built up coal consumption increased. There were reports of increases of up to 80% and of running out of coal on the Main Line. In January 1929 four members of the class were tested at various mileages since the last V and P examination and a fifth engine (6118) in March of the same year.

Loco Nos	Miles since V&P exam	No of runs	coal/llb/HP/Hr
No 6115 Scots Guardsman	5800	2	3.75
No 6137 The Prince of Wales Volunteers (South Lancashire)	7240	4	3.90
No 6102 Black Watch	17507	2	4.20
No 6134 The Cheshire Regiment	20000	2	4.52
No 6118 Royal Welch Fusilier	20156	4	4.04

These tests soon established the degree of steam leaks past the piston valves, results, which led to modifications. These modifications consisted of the fitting of multiple rings on each head in place of the single rings fitted as new. GWR engines have single rings but do not suffer from the same problem, this is mainly due to the low degree superheat which does not break down the lubrication as in the high degree superheat of LMS engines. The single brass ring on each head is also pressed up to the valve liner by pressure in the steam chest.

No 6118, was rebuilt in December 1946 and up to 31/12/1963 as No 46118 had run a total of 2,092,730 miles only exceeded by No 46100 (previously No 6152) which accumulated 2,141,229 miles. By co-incidence the two highest mileage Royal Scots were eventually to be based at Nottingham. The original Royal Scot No 6152 (46152) also came to Nottingham for repairs.

This summary shows the basic details about this group of locomotives, which represented only a small part of the total Stanier 8F class. Of the 666 locomotives in service on BR only 50 were modified, representing only 7.5 % of the fleet.

Engines Stored locally before disposal

Number	Location	Dates
48112	Westhouses	11/65-1/66
48198	Toton	8/65-11/65
48361	Colwick	10/66-2/67
48638	Westhouses	1/66-3/66
48644	Westhouses	1/66-3/66
48651	Colwick	11/66-3/67
48662	Colwick	11/66-3/67
48672	Colwick	3/66-6/66

In the 1950s and 60s some of these engines were based at 16A:

No 48024 From July 1959 to Dec 1961 and again in May 1964
No 48117 From Jan 1957 to Dec 1959
No 48638 From Dec 1961 to Dec 1964 (16D)

By this time the manual blowdown experiment had been completed, the special Boilers being fitted to any 8F passing through the works and the blowdown fitting blanked off. The now standard boilers were used as part of the boiler pool. It is therefore remarkable that No 48305 should have been fitted with a boiler from another experimental engine No 48644.

Of the other surviving 8Fs it is not thought that any of them have an ex-Manual Blowdown Boiler boiler.

Surviving 8Fs

Nos	Built		Location
48151	Crewe	12/42	MRC Butterley
48173	Crewe	8/43	Avon Valley Railway
48305	Crewe	11/43	Churnet Valley Railway
48431	Swindon	5/44	Keighley & Worth Valley
48518	Doncaster	3/44	Wales Railway Centre
48624	Ashford	1/44	Peak Rail Matlock
48773	North British	7/40	Severn Valley Railway

No 48773 ran on loan to the LMS between 12/40 and 7/41 as No 8233, built as WD No 307 it saw service in Persia as 41.109. WD No 70307 in 1944 and WD No 500 in 1952. It was then sold to BR in 1957, when its original LMS number was not realised.

45156 North British ex-Turkish Railways

The history of 8Fs is served well by these survivors with both Nos 48151 and 48305 being balanced (star on cab side) and having representatives built by all the pre-BR companies plus private builders. No 48305, with its special boiler, represents the only major experiment with these locomotives.

*A*ppendix Nine

The Documentation of an Incident

The following documents relate to an incident on March 29th 1958 with No 44806 and the subsequent investigation along with an incident with 44776 in January 1959 and that of 41164 in 1958

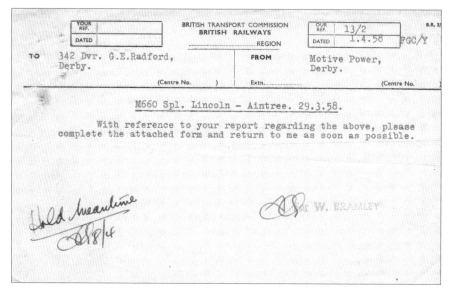

YOUR REF.		BRITISH TRANSPORT COMMISSION		OUR REF.	13/2	B.R. 3/
DATED		BRITISH RAILWAYS		DATED	1.4.58	FGC/Y
		................................REGION				

TO　342 Dvr. G.E.Radford,　　　　　　FROM　　Motive Power,
Derby.　　　　　　　　　　　　　　　　　　Derby.

(Centre No.　)　　Extn..................　　　　　(Centre No.　)

M660 Spl. Lincoln – Aintree. 29.3.58.

With reference to your report regarding the above, please complete the attached form and return to me as soon as possible.

Hold meantime
8/4

W. BRADLEY

44806

44776

```
                                                      Cas.44776
                                                      27.1.59.     LP.

A.R. Madden,Esq., LTO (MP), DERBY.
C.M & E.E., Derby.                                    Derby
D.M.P.S., Nottingham.
D.M.P.S., Saltley.


              Casualty Report Engine 44776. 21.1.59.

              Herewith Derby details in connection with the above:-

Cause of casualty:-      1 burst element at spear end.      0000000
                         6 leaking joints.                  0000000
                                                            0000000
                                                            0000000

Repairs carried out:-    Burst element renewed.
                         Leaking joints refitted.


                              for W. BRAMLEY.
```

41164

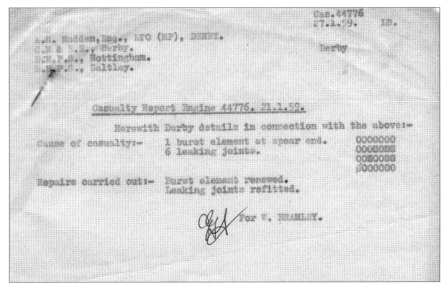

BRITISH RAILWAYS   **DRIVER'S REPORT**   B.R. 32841

Depot _Derby_   M.P. Area _20·1_ 1958

Train from _Manchester_ to _Derby_   _20·1_ 1958

Load (Reg.)   Train Loco. No. _1164_   Asst'g. Loco. No. _3115_

(Act.)   Class   Class

Driver _J. Pigham_   Fireman _G. Bunton_   Guard _S. Bobo_

Depot _Derby_   Depot _Derby_   Station _Dy_

Reg. No. _61_   Reg. No. _494_   Weather _Snow & frost_

SUBJECT   _Weak power of Engine to haul this train_

Driver Reports:- _I have to report that this train lost by the above Engine not steaming & having to close Regulator to observe signals, owing to blowing too much steam at front End of Engine/owing to the valve spindles blowing through leaking, engine not strong enough to haul. G. Boyce up the bank had the have assistance from Chinley to Peak Forest Junction_

Driver's Signature _J. Pigham_

277

41164

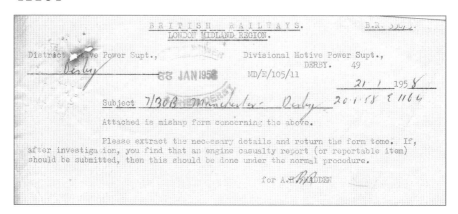

BRITISH RAILWAYS.
LONDON MIDLAND REGION.

B.R. ~~~~

District Motive Power Supt.,

Derby

~~ JAN 1958

Divisional Motive Power Supt.,
DERBY. 49

MD/E/105/11

21 1 1958

Subject 7/30B Manchester - Derby 20.1.58 41164

Attached is mishap form concerning the above.

Please extract the necessary details and return the form to me. If, after investigation, you find that an engine casualty report (or reportable item) should be submitted, then this should be done under the normal procedure.

for A.H. MADDEN

41164

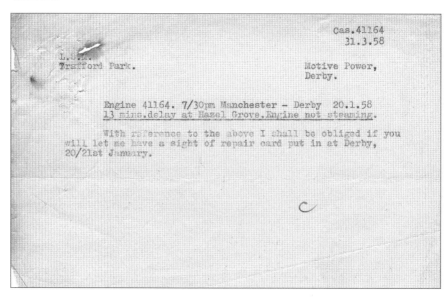

Cas.41164
31.3.58

L.M.R.
Trafford Park.

Motive Power,
Derby.

Engine 41164. 7/30pm Manchester - Derby 20.1.58
13 mins.delay at Hazel Grove. Engine not steaming.

With reference to the above I shall be obliged if you will let me have a sight of repair card put in at Derby, 20/21st January.

41164

B.R. 87315

LOCOMOTIVE CASUALTY REPORT (MECHANICAL)

Locomotive Number

Motive Power Depot	D*y	District	D*y	Date Initiated 24/3

Locomotive No. 41164 Class 4⁶ Allocated to Stock Date of Casualty 20 / 58

Driver Freeland (No.) Fireman Bunting (No.) Stationed at D*y

Working the 1:38 m Class B Train from m/c to D*y

on Mon day, the 20 day of Jan 19 58

Assisting (Locomotive No. 43715 Class ? Allocated to
Assisted by (Driver ? (No.) Fireman ? (No.) Stationed at ?

became a casualty at Hazel Grove causing a delay of 13 mins. Locomotive changed at

No. and Class of Locomotive working forward — Load of train 220 Regulation load 300 for locomotive

NATURE OF CASUALTY Engine not steaming

CAUSE OF CASUALTY (Full description)

High pressure spindle packing blown out

PARTICULARS OF REPAIRS CARRIED OUT NECESSITATED BY CASUALTY

High Pressure Spindle gland repacked

HISTORY OF LOCOMOTIVE NO. 41164 Crawford Coal

Date and classification of last Shop Repair when the part affected received attention ... ... at D State Works

Estimated mileage since

*Date of last " X " Examination at Depot

Working days since

*Date of last Washout Working days since

*Date of last Daily/Weekly Examination at Depot

by (No.) Grade

*Date of last Periodical or Mileage Examination Item No. at Depot

Estimated period/mileage since Extent overdue

ctive part last d or renewed at by (No.) Grade

* If relevant.

41164

BRITISH RAILWAYS
THE RAILWAY EXECUTIVE
_____ REGION

E.R.O. 11

| YOUR REF. | Cas.41164 |
| DATED | 21.3.58 |

| OUR REF. | T.P.Cas. |
| DATE | 2.4.58 |

TO W.Bramley, Esq.,
Derby.   (Centre No.   )

FROM Motive Power Dept.,
Trafford Park.

EXTN _____   (Centre No.   )

Engine 41164. 7/30pm Manchester – Derby, 20.1.58.
15 mins. delay at Hazel Grove. Engine not steaming.

Herewith repair card as requested.

J. A. KNAPMAN
Per

Please return with Thanks

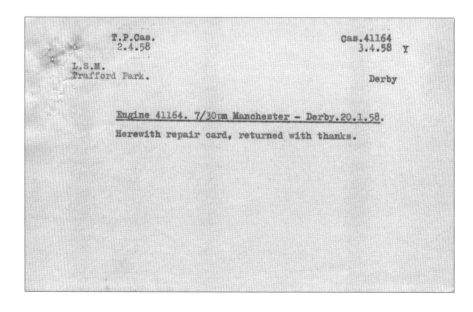

T.P.Cas.
2.4.58

L.S.M.
Trafford Park.

Cas.41164
3.4.58 Y

Derby

Engine 41164. 7/30pm Manchester – Derby.20.1.58.

Herewith repair card, returned with thanks.

41164

BRITISH RAILWAYS   B.R. 87315

LOCOMOTIVE CASUALTY REPORT (MECHANICAL)

		Locomotive Number	41164

Motive Power Depot **Derby**   District **Derby**   Date Initiated **26. 3.58**

Locomotive No. **41164**   Class **4P**   Allocated to **Trafford Pk** Date of Casualty **20.1.58**

Driver **J.Packard** (No.)   Fireman **Bunting** (No.)   Stationed at **Derby**

Working the **7/30** pm Class **B**   Train from **Manchester**   to **Derby**

on **Mon** day, the **20th** day of **Jan** 19**58** .

Assisting { Locomotive No. **43115**   Class **4MT**   Allocated to **Derby**
Assisted by { Driver **?** (No.)   Fireman **?** (No.)   Stationed at **?**

became a casualty at **Hazel Grove** causing a delay of **13** mins. Locomotive changed at

No. and Class of Locomotive working forward _____ Load of train **220**   Regulation load for locomotive **300**

NATURE OF CASUALTY

Engine not steaming.

CAUSE OF CASUALTY (Full description)

High pressure gland xrepacked.spindle packing blown out.

PARTICULARS OF REPAIRS CARRIED OUT NECESSITATED BY CASUALTY

High pressure spindle gland repacked.

HISTORY OF LOCOMOTIVE NO. 41164

Date and classification of last Shop Repair when the part affected received attention ... ... **Trafford Park to stats.**   Works

Estimated mileage since

*Date of last " X " Examination _____ at _____ Depot

Working days since

*Date of last Washout _____ Working days since

*Date of last Daily/Weekly Examination _____ at _____ Depot

by _____ (No.) _____ Grade

*Date of last Periodical or Mileage Examination _____ Item No. _____ at _____ Depot

Estimated period/mileage since _____ Extent overdue

Date defective part last examined or renewed } _____ at _____ by _____ (No.) _____ Grade

* If relevant.

41164

BRITISH RAILWAYS   Concluded. ✓   B.R. 87315

LOCOMOTIVE CASUALTY REPORT (MECHANICAL)

Locomotive Number	41164.

Motive Power Depot ...... Derby ...... District ...... Derby ...... Date Initiated ...... 26.3.58.

Locomotive No. ... 41164 ... Class ... 4P ... Allocated to ... Trafford Pk. ... Date of Casualty ... 20.1.58.

Driver ... J. Parks ... (No.) ... Fireman ... Bunting ... (No.) ... Stationed at ... Derby

Working the ... 7/30 ... in Class ... B ... Train from ... Manchester ... to ... Derby

on ...... day, the ... 20th. ... day of ... Jan. ... 19 ... 58.

Assisting { Locomotive No. ...... 43115 ... Class ... 4MT ... Allocated to ...... Derby

Assisted by { Driver ...... ? ...... (No.) ... Fireman ...... ? ...... (No.) ... Stationed at ...... ?

became a casualty at ... Hazel Grove ... causing a delay of ... 13 ... mins. Locomotive changed at ......

No. and Class of Locomotive working forward ...... Load of train ... 220 ... Regulation load for locomotive ... 300

NATURE OF CASUALTY

Engine not steaming.

CAUSE OF CASUALTY (Full description)

High pressure spindle packing blown out.

PARTICULARS OF REPAIRS CARRIED OUT NECESSITATED BY CASUALTY

High pressure spindle gland repacked.

HISTORY OF LOCOMOTIVE NO. 41164.

Date and classification of last Shop Repair when the part } affected received attention ... 19.11.52 ... at ... Derby ...... Works

Estimated mileage since ... 42,970

*Date of last "X" Examination ... 20.12.57. ... at ... Trafford Park ...... Depot

Working days since ... 1

*Date of last Washout ... 20.12.57. ... Working days since ... 1

*Date of last Daily / Weekly Examination ... 20.1.58. ... at ... Trafford Park ...... Depot

by ... W. Johnson ... (No.) ... 499 ... Grade ... Fitter

*Date of last Periodical or Mileage Examination ... 19.1.58. ... Item No. ... 2 ... at ... Trafford Pk. ... Depot

Estimated period mileage since ... 64 ... Extent overdue ... Nil.

Date defective part last } examined or renewed } ... 19.1.58. ... at ... T/Park ... by ... W. Johnson (No.) 499 ... Grade ... Fitter

*if relevant.

41164

LOCOMOTIVE NO. **41164**

DATE OF CASUALTY **20.1.58**

Particulars of any relevant reports during any of the SIX previous working days, repairs effected, depot, date, names, grades and Staff Nos. of staff carrying out the repairs.

T.Park

Preparation details :—

Prepared by (Name) _____ (No.) _____ Grade _____

Stationed at _____ Oil used _____

RECOMMENDATIONS (Where staff at fault state Name and No., Grade and Depot).

Depot **Derby** _____ (Signed) _____

Date **3.4.58** _____ Grade **Assist. D.M.P.S.**

CONCLUSIONS.

(If Disciplinary action taken give particulars.)

District _____

Date _____

District Motive Power Superintendent.

To **A.H.Madden Esq.,**
Line Traffic Officer(MP)
Derby.

Copies to **Loco Works Manager, Derby**
L.S.M., Trafford Park.

41164

BRITISH RAILWAYS   BR. 358/5.
LONDON MIDLAND REGION
Line Traffic Officer   Motive Power
District Motive Power Supt.,   ~~Divisional Motive Power Superintendent~~
..............*Derby*...........   DERBY. 49.
                              MD/E/105/12.
                                        14 4   195*8*.

Locomotive Casualty Report (Mechanical).

        Referring to   *Your*
Engine No. *41164*   Allocated to *T'Push*   Casualty Report.
Failed On. *20.1.58* With   *1305*
        Please arrange to forward the concluded casualty report as
quickly as possible.

                            for A.H. MADDEN.

In view of the fact that a No 2
mileage exam was carried out
the day previous it would appear
that either the packings were not
renewed or they were not fitted
correctly.

41164

| YOUR REF. | | | OUR REF | T.P.Cas. | E.R.O. II |
| DATED | | | DATE | 16.4.58 | |

TO   A.H.Maiden, Esq., Derby.
     W.Bramley, Esq., Derby.
     Loco Works Manager, Derby.

(Centre No.

FROM   Motive Power Dept.,
       Trafford Park.

Extn..........   (Centre No.   )

Casualty Engine 41164. 20.1.58.

Trafford Park details:-

Last Shop Rep. 19.11.52 at Derby. Miles Since 43,970.
Last X Exam. 20.12.57 at Trafford Park. Days Since 1.
Last W.O. 20.12.57. Days Since 1.
Last Daily Exam. 20.1.58 at Trafford Park, W.Johnson, 499, Fitter.
Last Period.Exam. 19.1.58, No.2. at Trafford Park. Miles Since 64.
Overdue Nil.
Defective Part Last Exam. 19.1.58 by W.Johnson, 499, Fitter.
Previous Reports Nil.

Mr Mitchell
Any special reason for
packing blowing out -
note only 1 day from wo.?   J.A. KNAPMAN
                              17/4

Cas.41164.
23.4.58.   FGC/LB.

J.A. Knapman, Esq.,   Derby.
D.M.P.S.,
GORTON. (For Trafford Park).

Casualty Report Engine 41164. 20.1.58.

        With reference to your details under reference TP.Cas.
dated 16.4.58., concerning the above; as this engine failed on
the first trip after mileage examination, please say what action
has been taken with Fitter W. Johnson, to enable me to conclude
the report.

                        For W. BRAMLEY.

41164

B R I T I S H   R A I L W A Y S   BR. 358/5.
LONDON MIDLAND REGION LINE TRAFFIC OFFICER (MOTIVE POWER)
                              MIDLAND LINES, DERBY.

District Motive Power Supt.,   Divisional Motive Power Superintendent,
..............*Derby*..............   DERBY. 49.
                                      MD/E/105/12.
                                                    28. 4.   1958.

Locomotive Casualty Report (Mechanical).

          Referring to   *Your*
Engine No. *41164*   Allocated to *T'Park*   Casualty Report
Failed On. *20·1·58* With   *SOS*
     Please arrange to forward the concluded casualty report as
quickly as possible.

                         for A.H. MADDEN.

B R I T I S H   R A I L W A Y S.   BR. 358/5.
LONDON MIDLAND REGION.

District Motive Power Supt.,   8   Divisional Motive Power Superintendent,
............*Derby*...........   DERBY. 49.
                     MD/E/105/12.
                                      7. 5.   1958

Locomotive Casualty Report (Mechanical).

          Referring to   *Your*
Engine No. *41164*   Allocated to *T'Park*   Casualty Report
Failed on   *20·1·58* With   *SOS*

     Please arrange to forward the concluded casualty report as quickly
as possible.

                         for A.H. MADDEN.

41164

Cas.41164.
9.5.58.　　LB.

J.A. Knapman, Esq.,　　　　　　　　　　　　　Derby.
D.M.P.S.,
GORTON. (For Trafford Park.

Casualty Report Engine 41164. 20.1.58.

　　　　Will you please advise me if you are now in a position
to reply to my letter of the 23rd. April, as my Line Traffic
Officer (Motive Power), is pressing for a concluded report.

For W. BRAMLEY.

MD/E/105/12.　　　　　　　　　　　　　Cas.41164.
7.5.58.　　　　　　　　　　　　　　　　8.5.58.　　LB.

A.H. Madden, Esq.,
Line Traffic Officer (M.P.),　　　　　　　Derby.
DERBY.

Casualty Report Engine 41164. 20.1.58.

　　　　In reply to your BR.358/5, I am awaiting a reply from
the D.M.P.S. for Trafford Park.

　　　　I have written him today, and my concluded report will
follow upon receipt of his letter.

For W. BRAMLEY.

41164

Cas.41164.
28.5.58.   LB.

J.A. Knapman, Esq.,   Derby.
D.M.P.S.,
GORTON.(For Trafford
            Park).

<u>Casualty Report Engine 41164. 20.1.58.</u>

Will you please advise me if you are now in a position
to reply to my letter of the 9th. instant.

for W. BRAMLEY.

B R I T I S H   R A I L W A Y S.   BR.358/5.
LONDON MIDLAND REGION. LINE TRAFFIC OFFICER (MOTIVE POWER)
                                                              MIDLAND LINES, DERBY.

District Motive Power Supt.,   Divisional Motive Power Superintendent,
..Derby...............................   DERBY. 43.
                                        MD/E/105/12.
                                                            10'June   1958

Locomotive Casualty Report (Mechanical).

Referring to your
Engine No. 41164   Allocated to Trafford Park   Casualty Report
Failed on 20 Jan   With 401.

Please arrange to forward the concluded casualty report as quickly
as possible.

for A.H. HAMMEN.

41164

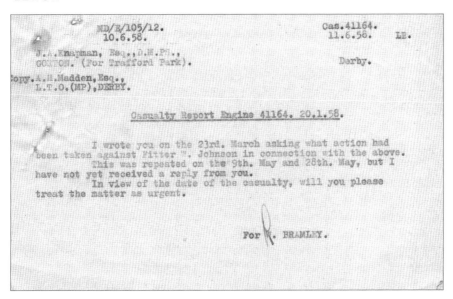

MD/E/105/12.   Cas.41164.
10.6.58.   11.6.58.   LE.

J.A.Knapman, Esq.,D.M.PS.,
GORTON. (For Trafford Park).   Derby.

Copy.A.H.Madden,Esq.,
L.T.O.(MP),DERBY.

Casualty Report Engine 41164. 20.1.58.

      I wrote you on the 23rd. March asking what action had
been taken against Fitter W. Johnson in connection with the above.
      This was repeated on the 9th. May and 28th. May, but I
have not yet received a reply from you.
      In view of the date of the casualty, will you please
treat the matter as urgent.

                       For W. BRAMLEY.

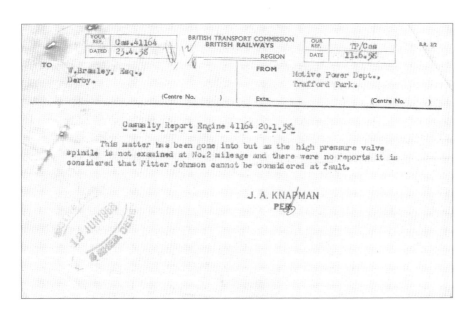

| YOUR REF. | Cas.41164 | BRITISH TRANSPORT COMMISSION
BRITISH RAILWAYS | OUR REF. | TP/Cas | B.R. 3/2 |
| DATED | 23.4.58 | ——————— REGION | DATE | 11.6.58 | |

TO   W.Bramley, Esq.,   FROM
      Derby.   Motive Power Dept.,
                              Trafford Park.

      (Centre No.   )   Extn._____   (Centre No.   )

Casualty Report Engine 41164 20.1.58.

    This matter has been gone into but as the high pressure valve
spindle is not examined at No.2 mileage and there were no reports it is
considered that Fitter Johnson cannot be considered at fault.

                    J. A. KNAPMAN
                      PER

41164

LOCOMOTIVE No. 41164

CASUALTY REPORT (MECHANICAL)

DATE OF CASUALTY.

Particulars of any relevant reports during any of the SIX previous working days, repairs effected, depot, date, names, grades and Staff Nos. of staff carrying out the repairs.

Nil.

Preparation details:—

Prepared by (Name) .... (No.) .... Grade ....

Stationed at .... Oil used ....

RECOMMENDATIONS (Where staff at fault state Name and No., Grade and Depot).

Depot .... Derby .... (Signed) .... P.J. Clarke ....

Date .... 3.4.58. .... Grade .... Asst. D.M.P.S.

CONCLUSIONS.

(If Disciplinary action taken give particulars.)

Cause of failure due to high pressure piston valve packing fused.

No recommendations.

District .... Derby. ....

Date .... 16.6.58. .... District Motive Power Superintendent.

To .... A.E.Madden, Esq., ... Copies to:- .... C.M. & E.E., Derby.

.... Line Traffic Officer (MP), ... D.M.P.S., Trafford Park.

.... Derby.

Appendix Ten

Miscellaneous

44776

BRITISH RAILWAYS   BR. B7315/1

LOCOMOTIVE CASUALTY REPORT (MECHANICAL)

Initiated 23.1.59

Nottingham   Depot Nottingham   District   Engine No 44776   Class 5MT

Allocated to Saltley   Depot. Driver Naylor   (No 16A) Fireman Crowder   (No 16A)

working the 1.56 m. (class)   A   train from Sheffield   to Derby

on Wed day, the 1st day of Jan 59   Assisting / Assisted by   Engine No. —   Class —

Allocated to —   Depot. Driver —   (No.) Fireman —   (No.)

became a casualty at En route   causing a delay of 10 mins. Engine changed at Derby

No. and Class of engine working forward   Derby to state   Load of train 303T   Regulation load — for engine

NATURE OF CASUALTY   Driver states – On relieving Driver at Sheffield he told me engine did not steam and suspected elements. However on reaching Dore and Totley, I had to stop under signal protection to obtain steam. Fresh engine supplied at Derby.

CAUSE OF CASUALTY (Full description)
1 Burst Element at Spec. End
6 Leaking Joints
        Derby to state.

FOR MOTIVE POWER DEPT
24 JAN 1959

PARTICULARS OF REPAIRS CARRIED OUT NECESSITATED BY CASUALTY
Burst Element renewed
Leaking Joints refitted
        Derby to state.

HISTORY OF ENGINE No. 44776 Saltley to state.

Date of last Shop Repair .... at .... Works

Estimated Mileage since Shop Repair ....

Date of last Routine Examination .... at .... Depot

by .... (No.)   Grade ....

Date of last Periodical (time or mileage) Examination .... at .... Depot

Estimated mileage since Periodical Examination .... Extent overdue ....

Date defective part last examined .... by .... (No.) Grade ....

                                                  P.T.O.

Casualty Report on 44776 showing which tubes had failed

Jim Perkins

E.R.O. 23354
O.P. 2

L M S 4 Shed M.P.TA DEPOT, April 2nd 1958

DRIVER'S REPORT OF TRAIN BREAKING LOOSE.

Date March 29th 1958 Time of occurrence 9.27a.m. Place Ambergate Stat. Delay none Hrs. mts

TRAIN : Time 98a.m. Description Class AM660 From Lincoln To Aintree

Stationed at

No. of Engine 4806 Class 5 Driver Towle Fireman — Notts 16A

No. of Assisting Engine 4818 Class 5 Driver G. Radford Fireman H Jones Derby 17A

Loading } Number of vehicles : Regulation _____ Actual 11 No. of vehicles } 11
of Train } Tonnage _____ : Regulation 390 Actual 336 on which the continuous brake was used.

Portion of Draw Gear broken Hook End Leading Coach

Whether defective Not Known How disposed of _____

Position in train of vehicle on which breakage occurred Leading Coach Front or rear of vehicle Front

Number of vehicle 27942 Owner B. Railways Whether detached No

Cause of Break-loose Unknown

Whether Break-loose occurred when starting, stopping or running Stopping

Was Rule 142 (d) observed? Yes Weather Clear

How far ran before discovering Breakage No distance was covered before breakage was found

Distance between two portions when brought to a stand No more than 6 inches

If wrong line working necessary state whether} Wrong Line orders not used as train was
appropriate order received and from whom} not actually parted.

General remarks :—
After train becoming stationary, almost at once I felt slight jolt on
engine, while looking back I noticed Inspector Gardner who travelling
on train appear to shout something, train driver and I went to
ascertain what he wanted and noticed half of coupling hook on train
had broken, After examining coupling on coach we transfered it to
Engine hook and left station on time, Both flexible train pipe and
warming pipe were intact in proper manner, Guard unaware of any
breakage untill notified by Station Staff.

To District Locomotive Superintendent.

(Signed) Passed Foreman
G E Radford

Incident at Ambergate Station

Jim Perkins

Plate 187
Nottingham Carriage Sidings with the ex-GNR Low level station on the left

Bill Reed

Plate 188
Nottingham Carriage Sidings with Engineer Shed in the middle insert view

Bill Reed

Dimensions of Buffer faces ....

Type of Buffer (spring or dead) ....

Is engine fitted with ash-pan ? ....

Whether contour and thickness of tyres and the distance between the backs of tyres is

satisfactory ....

Does the minimum clearance above rail level come within the dimensions permitted, as shown

on the diagram below ? .... If not, indicate on this diagram

the position of the part concerned, together with the clearance above rail level and the distance

from the centre of rail.

Rail clearance on LOFTUS &
WHITBY LINE (NER) are marked
thus ⊕.

Rail clearance on Electrified Portion of
MANCHESTER & BURY LINE & TOTTINGTON
BRANCH are marked thus ✳.

MINIMUM DIMENSIONS

The following are the minimum dimensions permitted :—

Rigid wheelbase—5ft. if to run in freight trains, 4ft. 9ins. if to run light in steam or to be hauled
by special engine.

Coupled wheels—2ft. 6in. diameter.   Bogie wheels 2ft. diameter.

Thickness of tyres for engines with the following axle loads :—

Under 15 tons—1¼in. on tread.   15 tons and under 18 tons—1⅜in. on tread.

18 tons and above—1½in. on tread.

In the case of an engine having axle loads under 10 tons, and the tyres formed solid with the
rims of the wheels, the minimum thickness on the tread may be 1 inch.

*Height of centre of Buffers—3ft. 4in. above rail level unless the buffer faces are sufficiently
large to prevent locking.

*Height of centre of Drawgear—3ft. 2in. above rail level.

*The maximum height not to exceed 3ft. 6in.

REPORT OF EXAMINATION

I have examined the Engine referred to hereon, and certify that, apart from loading gauge

requirements, it is — fit / unfit — to travel — dead / in steam — on its own wheels.

The examination does not extend to the boiler, boiler fittings, or firebox.

Examiner .... Grade ....

Note.—The cost incurred by this depot in connection with this engine given below.

....

District Motive Power Superintendent.

TO ....

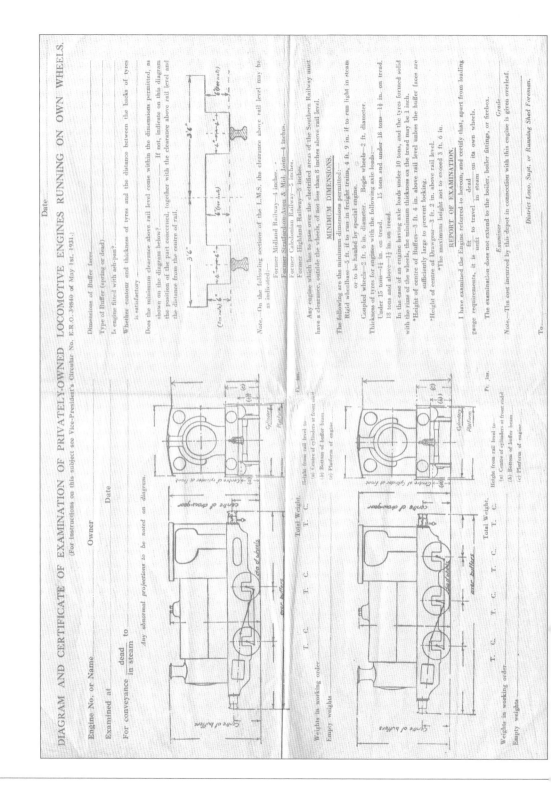

Part of Fig 10 continued

Jim Perkins

References and Bibliography

Authors/Sources	Source Titles
Nottingham Local Studies Library	Nottingham Review
Baxter and Baxter	British Locomotive Catalogue 2A
Notts CC Archives	Maps and Lithographs
Various Sources	Locomotive Allocations
Rowledge J W P	Heavy Goods Engines of the WD Vol 2
Radford J B	Derby Works and Midland Locomotives
Redfern C	Memoirs (unpublished)
Bolger P	BR Steam Motive Power Depots LMR
Reed W	Memoirs (unpublished)
Wilson L	Stephenson Loco Soc
	Journals Nos22/23 1946/1947
Railway Magazine	Various
Goode, C.T	Midland Railway, Derby-Lincoln Line
Essery R J & Jenkinson D	An Illustrated Preview of Midland Locos
Higginson M	MCR 1839-1989, Pictorial Survey
Hawkins C and Reeve G	LMS Engine Sheds
Kondratiev N D	Major Economic Cycles (Russia 1925)
Duffy M C	Technomorphology and the Stephenson
	Traction System (Newcomen Soc)
Hewitson C H	Locomotive Boiler Explosions
Atkin P	NRM, York
HMSO	Railway Accident Reports
Hill S	Memoirs (unpublished)
Vanns M	Rail centres, Nottingham
Petchey Tim	British Railway Companies
Cater Peter	Railway Collectors Journal No 61 July 1996
Best Stephen	NIA Journal No 11 Autumn 1996

Erratum and
Additional Information

Volume I
List of Factual and other errors

Page	Location	Item
23	Para 2	Rathbone is 'Theodore Rathbone' see p46.
43	Para 2	Should read 'the' District.
44	Para 1 Line 5	This should read 10' diameter not 8'.
56	Fig	The view of the Hicks and Co engine is Fig 16
57	Para 2	Should read 'seen in fig 17 above' not 18.

Volume II

Page	Location	Item
2		Address is 1 Chapel Mews not 16.
18	Plate 5	Should read 'rear of' not repair.
28	Para 1	Second minute should read 27998.
	Para 2	Should Read 'Kapitan Herrman Kraushaar'.

Further information on World War One casualties

33	First Entry	Private W H Atkins No 15960. Died 08 Oct 1916 Age 28 of 13 Garfield Terrace, Deering St, The Meadows. He was killed in the almost continual Battle of the Somme (1 July to 18 November 1916). He has no known grave and is remembered amongst the 13,000 names on the Thiepval Memorial. His name also appears on the Loggerheads' memorial inside the 'Loggerheads Inn, Cliffe Road, Broadmarsh, Nottingham.
33	Second Entry	Should read: M. Beales No 48649. Died 27th August 1916 Age 27. Son of Annie Beales, 106 Union Road, Nottingham. Buried at Gordon Dump Cemetery, Oviller-La Boiseille, Somme.
	Fourth Entry	Private Lewis Clarke 11th Bn, Northumberland Fusiliers, Killed in action 4th October 1916. He has no known grave and is commemorated on the Thiepval Memorial.
	Fifth Entry	Private Albert William Cooper, 1st/5th Battalion, Sherwood Foresters. Died 7th October 1918. Buried Vis-en-Artois British Cemetery, Pas de Calais. One of 9000 men who died between 8th August and 11th November 1918 in the Picardy area during the 'Advance to Victory'.

Also Private Charles Mason 2nd/6th Battallion Sherwood Foresters. Arras Memorial, Pas de Calais. Died 21st March 1918.

Rifleman John Wilson, 2nd Battalion, Kings Royal Rifle Corps died 25th September 1915 and has no known grave. One of the 20,000 remembered on the Loos Memorial.

Able Seaman, Albert Arthur Johnson, HMS 'Good Hope' died at the Battle of Coronel 1st November 1918.

Boy 1st Class, Moses Weston, HMS 'Black Prince' died Battle of Jutland 31st May 1916 Aged 18.

36	Second Entry	Should read GW Hurry: Died 25 Feb 1917 and is buried in the Amara War Cemetery, Iraq.
37	Photograph	Percy Croydon is on the Right.
40	Plate 21	Should read Mansfield Junction.
41	Plate 22	Should read 2-4-0.
44	Plate 25	Should read 1923.
49	First Line	Should read September 1925 not 1926.
53	Plate 31	Should read R Hoggard.
72	Plate 53	Photograph by Norman Hudson who had come to Nottingham from Grimesthorpe (d1986) Photograph is courtesy of Dave East and shows 5552 with Frank Thompson (d in Feb 1972) leaning out of cab.
100	Plate 81	Further information on the accident to one of these engines: It was Driver Charlie Rugge and Fireman Charlie Mee who were preparing to move forward. In error it was in reverse gear and then shot out of control backwards out of No 3 Shed towards Wilford Road Signalbox. Both jumped off and the loco crashed head on into a Class 2P coming onto the Shed killing Driver Duffy of Peterborough.
111	Plate 88	Photographs shows Driver Wilfred Mosley, of Mansfield.
121	Plate 93	View of Colwick LNWR locoshed .

Acknowledgments

'X' Experiment data by Andrew Biwandi
'Whatever Happened to Steam?' by PB Hands
'Heavy Goods Engines of the WD Part 2, 2-8-0 8Fs' by J W P Rowledge